Augsburg College
George Sverdrup Library
Minneapolis, MN 55454

The Palestine Liberation Organization

The Palestine Liberation Organization

FROM ARMED STRUGGLE
TO THE DECLARATION
OF INDEPENDENCE

Jamal R. Nassar

PRAEGER

New York
Westport, Connecticut
London

Library of Congress Cataloging-in-Publication Data

Nassar, Jamal R. (Jamal Raji)
  The Palestine Liberation Organization : from armed struggle to
the declaration of independence / Jamal R. Nassar.
    p.   cm.
  Includes bibliographical references and index.
  ISBN 0-275-93779-8 (alk. paper)
  1. Palestine—International status. 2. Munaẓẓamat al-Taḥrīr al-
Filasṭīnīyah. I. Title.
JX4084.I8N37 1991
322.4'2'095694—dc20   90-44335

British Library Cataloguing in Publication Data is available.

Copyright © 1991 by Jamal R. Nassar

All rights reserved. No portion of this book may be
reproduced, by any process or technique, without the
express written consent of the publisher.

Library of Congress Catalog Card Number: 90-44335
ISBN: 0-275-93779-8

First published in 1991

Praeger Publishers, One Madison Avenue, New York, NY 10010
An imprint of Greenwood Publishing Group, Inc.

Printed in the United States of America

The paper used in this book complies with the
Permanent Paper Standard issued by the National
Information Standards Organization (Z39.48-1984).

10 9 8 7 6 5 4 3 2 1

To Hanan

Contents

Preface		ix
1.	Contemporary Palestinian Arab Nationalism: Historical Roots	1
2.	The Problem of Legitimacy	25
3.	Internal Organization	49
4.	Strategy and Tactics	79
5.	The PLO and the Arab States	115
6.	The PLO and the International Community	149
7.	The Palestinians and Israel	179
8.	Conclusion: Problems and Prospects	207
Appendix 1: The Balfour Declaration		217
Appendix 2: The Palestine National Covenant		219
Appendix 3: The Palestinian Declaration of Independence		223
Selected Bibliography		227
Index		235

Preface

If the nation-state is the primary actor in today's international system, it is not the sole actor. In fact, the state has not always been the predominant element in global politics and has never been the only element. After all, the state-centric model of international politics dates back only to the Peace of Westphalia of 1648. The significance of non-state actors in global behavior has been recognized by many scholars in the field.

The past few decades have witnessed an increase in the number and significance of non-state actors. Multinational corporations have so grown in power as to draw the attention of many observers. Hijackings, kidnappings, assassinations, and street demonstrations illustrate the role of nongovernmental groups at a global level. In today's global system, independent groups such as Islamic revolutionaries, the Palestine Liberation Organization (PLO), the Irish Republican Army, or people demonstrating in the streets of the Soviet Union have a marked effect on international political behavior.

In the Middle East, the Palestinian guerrilla groups have a dramatic, if not sustained, impact on regional politics. While there are many other non-state actors in the Middle East, their impact on world politics has not attracted as much attention as that of the Palestinians. Ranging from oil corporations to regional organizations such as the League of Arab States, the non-state actors of this region have generally coordinated their actions with those of selected states in the area. Only the Palestinians have often acted independently of states. Only the Palestinian groups have a popular base of support among a population that generally holds no loyalty to any existing state and that is scattered throughout the region.

The Palestinian movement consists of several major groups and a number of splinter ones. Some of them are organized mainly within one Arab country, others are transnational. However, all unite around the single objective of liberating Palestinian territory from Israel and restoring the national rights of the Palestinian people. While differing in ideology and tactics, Palestinian groups agree that the PLO is their sole legitimate representative and at one point or another have participated or currently participate in its decision making.

This book is an attempt to explicate the PLO in terms of its origin, legal status, goals, strategies, achievements, and failures, and to investigate the organization's role in regional and international politics. In it I have tried to show the dynamics of the power relationships responsible for the PLO's successes and failures, and to reveal not only major patterns and trends in the organization's functioning but also the conditions under which these patterns and trends have developed. Furthermore, it provides the reader with some insights concerning the legitimacy of the PLO and the prospects for its participation in a peaceful resolution of the Arab-Israeli conflict.

The first chapter of this study outlines the historical background of the Palestinian experiences that have contributed to the rise of the PLO. Palestinian nationalism is portrayed in an Arab context and as such is shown to have taken root in the struggle against Zionism and British colonialism.

Chapter 2 reaches two major but tentative conclusions: (1) The PLO is a legitimate movement of self-determination, and (2) There is legal substance to the argument that the PLO is the sole legitimate representative of the Palestinian people. Arguments opposing both conclusions exist as well.

The third chapter reviews the PLO's structural development. In this chapter, it is made clear that the PLO is quasi-governmental in its hierarchical structure and its multifaceted activities. It is also concluded here that, in spite of the charges of autocracy leveled against the PLO, there is substantial evidence of a democratic spirit existing within the organization. In fact, given the constraints normally affecting a liberation movement, the PLO has operated as democratically as one could expect.

Guerrilla warfare and its ideological, psychological, and historical roots are reviewed in Chapter 4. Contradictions and similarities between the various Palestinian guerrilla groups are also studied here. While this chapter concentrates on ideological differences, it also concludes that unity of action is possible. It is argued that the use of violence takes root mainly in the Palestinian perception of Israel as a colonial-settler state.

The political ramifications and the dynamics of PLO activities as a regional actor are discussed in Chapter 5. Inherent tensions between the PLO as a revolutionary force and the Arab countries as independent and sovereign states have led to a number of serious clashes and civil wars. It is concluded that the majority of the PLO-Arab alliances, whenever they exist, are no more than tactical arrangements subject to breakdowns. Even though the PLO is not a government, its significance goes beyond that of some existing regional governments. The PLO role in regional politics has a mixed record of achievements and setbacks. That it has a role, however, is beyond doubt and cannot be disregarded by Middle Eastern scholars.

This discussion is carried further in Chapter 6, which investigates PLO relations with the international community. At this point, it becomes clear that the PLO has achieved many successes. In fact, the greatest achievements of the PLO may be seen to have been at this international level. The PLO has offices, quasi-embassies actually, in more than a hundred nations. The PLO also continues to gain support in the United Nations. On July 22, 1977, for example, the U.N. Economic and Social Council voted overwhelmingly to give the PLO full membership in the Economic Commission for West Asia. This was the first time a non-state was ever granted full membership in any U.N. body. Even the United States is beginning to recognize the role of the PLO. Zbigniew Brzezinski, who was President Carter's advisor on national security affairs, indicated this recognition when he wrote in *Foreign Policy* that a peaceful agreement in the Middle East cannot take place without the participation of the PLO. The U.S. position, however, has fluctuated. It shifted with the signing of the Camp David Accords and the subsequent Reagan Peace Plan, only to shift back with the start and continuation of the Palestinian uprising in the Occupied Territories.

Palestinian interaction with Israel is the subject of Chapter 7. In the final analysis, it is not international recognition or relations with foreign powers that will bring about "lasting peace," but mutual understanding and recognition between the Palestinians and the Israelis. Perhaps this mutual understanding will come about, but the events of the day offer little hope for peace and provide many indications of more conflict in the future. At every level of interaction, relations between the Palestinians and Israel are still extremely problematic. Fear, resentment, and outright hatred exist between the two peoples. Negotiations on the future of the Palestinians are dependent, in the final analysis, on Palestinian consent. This consent has clearly been issued with the Declaration of Independence. The Palestinians have clearly come to grips with the reality of Israel's existence. Israel, however, has yet to come to grips with the Palestinian national existence.

The PLO may not be a classic case of guerrilla insurgency, but its activities have significant implications for the countries of the region as well as for international relations. During the past two decades, it has proven to be a major actor in the Middle East, and one no less significant than a number of the area's sovereign states. Its power, however, is negative. It cannot hope to achieve its objectives independently of other regional powers, but it can prevent these powers from resolving the Arab-Israeli dispute on terms that it strongly opposes. In fact, a number of peace initiatives have been foiled by the PLO. Today, it is indisputable that peace negotiations must have the consent of the Palestinians, which seems to mean, in practice, the PLO. But so long as Israel refuses to talk to the PLO and so long as it continues to attempt to stop the Palestinian uprising by force, the conflict is likely to continue. If, on the other hand, Israel decides to negotiate with the PLO, as did the Americans with the Vietnamese guerrillas and the French with the Algerian resistance movement, then the PLO might be transformed into a tool for peace and a responsible sponsor of an emergent Palestinian entity.

Many people have extended their aid to this study over the years. Those who must be singled out include Professors W. F. Abboushi and Leila Meo. Hamdi Shaqqura worked very hard as my graduate assistant on the production of the final draft. Illinois State University provided resources and support services. But no one worked as hard or had to put up with as much as my wife, Hanan. She was my editor, typist, monitor, and critic.

1

Contemporary Palestinian Arab Nationalism: Historical Roots

John Foster Dulles, the late U.S. Secretary of State, believed that the Palestine problem would be solved only with time. His contention was that the new Palestinian generation would be totally unassociated with Palestine and lose memory of the land of their forefathers and of their past. Hisham Sharabi, a professor of Middle Eastern studies at Georgetown University, disagrees with Dulles and contends that "far from proving Dulles right, the new generation has produced a guerrilla movement dedicated to the principle that national liberation can only be achieved by armed struggle."[1]

This chapter intends to examine the validity of Sharabi's contention by looking at the historical roots of Palestinian Arab nationalism and the rise of the Palestinian guerrilla movement. A basic assumption of this part of the research is that Palestinian Arab nationalism does exist.[2] Its existence lies not only in a unique Palestinian setting, but also in a larger Arab context.

It is accepted that national movements are not spontaneous; they generally develop as a result of certain conditions that may be internal or external to a specific society. The Palestinian Arab national movement is no exception. It is embedded in the rise of Arab nationalism in the nineteenth and twentieth centuries.

THE RISE OF THE ARAB NATIONAL MOVEMENT

The rise of the modern Arab national movement is rooted in the rise of Islam in the seventh century A.D. Islam, the third great monotheistic faith to develop in the Middle East, inspired the people of the Arabian

Peninsula to break out from their desert homeland and to establish a remarkable empire. At the time when Europe was in its Dark Ages, the Arab-Islamic Empire, stretching from India to Spain, played a leading role in the advancement of world civilization.

Islam was instrumental in reshaping Arab history. Moreover, this religion, advocated by the Messenger of God, Mohammad, was able to weld the Arabs and those who were Arabized through conquest and assimilation into a new dynamic community, unified through the Muslim faith and the Arabic language. The process of Arabization was made possible by Islam's known tolerance towards other monotheistic religions. This Arab-Muslim community and empire attained significant spiritual, social, and economic achievements. Even though it collapsed centuries ago, Islam has remained influential in the lives of its adherents and as a political force in the region.

In the course of 400 years, the Arab-Islamic Empire began to disintegrate. By 1517, most of its domain had fallen under Ottoman rule. Under the Ottoman Turks, the Arabs experienced cultural stagnation and political decay. They lost their political independence and became isolated from major currents of thought in the world.[3]

In 1798, Napoleon invaded Egypt. This invasion is viewed by some historians as the spark that gave birth to Arab nationalism.[4] During the short French rule in Egypt, Arabs came, for the first time since the fall of their empire, into direct contact with Europe. To foster support for his occupation of Egypt and to separate Arabs from the Ottoman Turks who were regarded locally as Muslim brothers, Napoleon stressed Arab national identity.

Napoleon introduced an Arabic press, printed statements that discussed past Arab glories, and attempted to revive the Arabic language. However, Napoleon's efforts were doomed to failure. The Egyptian population resisted his occupation and considered the Christian French, rather than the Muslim Turks, to be the enemy.

Mehemed Ali, soon to become master of Egypt, took Napoleon's appeal to heart and attempted to build his own Arab empire. Ali was an Albanian officer who was commissioned by the Ottoman Sultan "to put an end to Bonaparte's invasion."[5] By 1805, Ali was in control of Egypt and started his own expeditions to build an Arab empire under his rule.

As did Napoleon before him, Ali challenged the Turks and attempted to mobilize the Arabs for his cause. He emphasized the Arabic language, taught Arab history, and stressed the heritage of the Arabs. By 1833, his power had spread into Syria. His dream of an empire, however, "was never realized: it crashed on the rock of Palmerston's opposition."[6] Nevertheless, his rule over Syria, through his son Ibrahim, was tolerant, and emphasized the Arab character of the people within his domain. It also fostered contacts with Western civilization, permitted Western missionary activities, and promoted education.

George Antonius, a noted scholar on the Arab national movement, contends that the countries of the Western world, especially France and the United States, were "the foster-parents of the Arab resurrection."[7] These powers came to Syria through their missionary activities and began competing for influence and supremacy. In so doing, they sparked a revival of the Arabic language and introduced a movement of literary awakening which in time was integrated into all aspects of Arab life, including that of politics. Most experts agree with Antonius on the primary role of American and French missionaries in sparking real, long-lasting Arab nationalism. In fact, early Arab nationalists were mainly the Christian Arabs of the Levant area (today's Lebanon).

By 1875, an infant Arab nationalist movement had been born. This movement was organized secretly in Beirut to avoid Turkish reprisals. Its placards were revolutionary; they contained attacks on the corrupt Turkish rulers and urged the Arab people to rebel and overthrow them. While Antonius concludes that their objective was to achieve Arab independence from the Turks, Professor Zeine Zeine, another prominent scholar on Arab nationalism, contends that the drive for independence did not take place until after the emergence of the Young Turks, a nationalist Turkish movement, which seized power in 1908 and embarked on a program of Turkification. Both contentions may be correct. The Christian Arab minority in Lebanon in the 1870's was eager for independence, but the Muslim Arab leadership at the time sought only autonomy.

Whatever the ultimate political objective, this infant Arab nationalist movement advocated recognition of Arabic as the official language, removal of censorship and all restrictions on freedoms, and the formation of an Arab army. By the turn of the century, it became clear that this movement was influenced by the Young Turks' Turkification program and was advocating an Arabization program for the Arab parts of the Ottoman Empire.

This infant Arab movement was met with suppression, but its aspirations soon spread among the people of Syria, Egypt, Arabia, and Iraq. By 1914, the Arab nationalist movement found a leader in the Sharif of Mecca, Hussein Ibn Ali. His position of leadership in Mecca and his descent from the family of the Messenger of Islam made him attractive to the nationalists.

On June 5, 1916, Hussein initiated the "Arab Revolt" against the Turks. The "Arab Revolt" was partly due to the influence of Levant Arab nationalists on Hussein. In doing so, Hussein was aspiring to create an independent Arab kingdom under his rule. The British had contacted

Hussein and pledged independence for the Arabs in return for their participation in World War I on the side of the Allies. This pledge was made by Sir Henry McMahon, then British High Commissioner in Egypt, and later reiterated by other British and Allied officials in their declarations. Among them were the Anglo-French Declaration of 1918 and the Hogarth Message. The Anglo-French Declaration consists of a statement printed in various Arab newspapers on November 7, 1918. In this statement, France and Britain identified their war-aims in the region in terms of complete liberation of populations living under the Turks. The Hogarth Message, on the other hand, refers to a meeting between Hussein and Dr. David George Hogarth, head of the Arab Bureau in Cairo, in January, 1918. At that meeting, Dr. Hogarth relayed an oral message to Hussein in which Britain assured the Arabs of British intentions to safeguard Arab sovereignty in Syria (including Palestine).[8]

While the British were making promises of independence to the Arabs, they were at the same time making commitments to other Allied powers to share colonization of the area. The Sykes-Picot Agreement of 1916, for example, divided the Arab inhabited Middle East "in such a manner as to place artificial obstacles in the way of unity."[9] It placed Syria and Lebanon under direct French administration, and Iraq and Egypt under a British one. Palestine was to be placed under an international administration. Moreover, the British soon after issued the Balfour Declaration promising a "Jewish Home" in Palestine. This declaration was in response to the program of the World Zionist Organization established in 1897. This organization advocated the establishment of a Jewish state in Palestine, as will be discussed later in this chapter. Thus, the "European powers decided the future of the Arab Middle East without consulting the Arabs."[10]

These developments angered the Arab nationalists, who felt betrayed by the Western powers. The betrayal was instrumental in mobilizing the Arab populace on the side of the nationalists, who advocated independence and Arab unity.

Today, independence has been formally achieved by most Arabs, but unity remains the top priority for Arab nationalists.

ARAB NATIONALISM IN PALESTINE

The Arab Revolt of 1916 had a great impact on the Arab nationalist movement, particularly in Palestine. With the defeat of the Ottoman Empire at the hands of the Allied forces in 1918, Arab expectations of independence and unity were high. After the 1918 armistice, the Arabs came to be aware of the conflicting Allied promises and felt a deep sense of betrayal.

Until then, Palestine was considered part of Ottoman-dominated

Syria.[11] The area known as Syria under the Ottomans was now divided into four distinct territories: Syria and Lebanon, which came to be dominated by France, and Palestine and Trans-Jordan, which were dominated by Great Britain.

Under the Ottomans, the Arab people living in what came to be known as Palestine became "poor and neglected," but the area "was still their country, their home, the land in which their people for centuries past had lived and left their graves."[12] Their Arab identity was evident in their language, culture, religion, and way of life.

When the Arab Revolt was declared, Palestinian Arabs joined other Arabs and Allied powers in the fight against the Ottoman Turks. The British raised recruits by telling them "that they were fighting in a national cause to liberate their country from the Turks."[13] Many Palestinians serving in the Ottoman army deserted to join the Allies, and many others left their farms, businesses, and families to fight their Ottoman masters in order to liberate their lands. The Palestinian recruits, along with other Arab volunteers, made a significant contribution to the Allied cause. The Arab volunteers were responsible for pinning down "something like 65,000 Turkish troops, thus freeing a number of British divisions for other tasks."[14] Moreover, they put the Turks in the awkward position of having to fight in hostile territory. When finally the British troops entered Jerusalem, they were welcomed as liberators.

Like other Arabs, the Palestinians had aspired to independence. Their aspirations were reinforced in November of 1918 by a joint French-British communiqué. That communiqué was read to the press and posted on bulletin boards in the towns and villages of Palestine. The communiqué included the following statement:

> The goal envisaged by France and Great Britain... is the complete and final liberation of the peoples who have for so long been oppressed by the Turks, and the setting up of national governments and administrations that shall derive their authority from the free exercise of the initiative and choice of the indigenous populations.[15]

On the basis of this statement and other previous promises made to the Arabs, "the real impression left upon the Arabs generally was that the British were going to set up an independent Arab state which would include Palestine."[16] But the Arabs in general and the Palestinians in particular were to be disappointed. Their lands were placed under mandatory Allied rule, and it became evident that contradictory promises concerning Palestine had been made to the Arabs and the Zionists.

Arab protests prompted the Paris Peace Conference to recommend in 1919 that an Allied fact-finding commission be sent to the area. However, only the United States delegation was truly interested in recording how the Arabs felt and, therefore, Dr. Henry C. King and Charles Crane of the United States traveled to the Middle East and reported to the conference "that an overwhelming number of Palestinian Arabs wanted Palestine to remain part of Syria with Feisal (Sharif Hussein's son) as the head of state."[17] It was also evident to the commission that the Palestinians were aware of Zionist programs for Palestine and warned that the "Zionist proposals as a whole would be unfair to the Arab majority."[18] The commission's report included an analysis of the situation in Syria with special emphasis on Palestine. It also included this warning:

The Peace Conference should not shut its eyes to the fact that the anti-Zionist feeling in Palestine and Syria is intense and not lightly to be flouted. No British officer, consulted by the Commission, believed that the Zionist programme could be carried out except by force of arms. The officers generally thought that a force of not less than 50,000 soldiers would be required even to initiate the programme. That of itself is evidence of a strong sense of the injustice of the Zionist programme on the part of the non-Jewish populations of Palestine and Syria. Decisions requiring armies to carry [them] out are sometimes necessary, but they are surely not gratuitously to be taken in the interests of serious injustice. For the initial claim, often submitted by Zionist representatives, that they have a "right" to Palestine, based on an occupation of 2,000 years ago, can hardly be seriously considered.[19]

It is clear, then, that Arab nationalism in Palestine was no different from that of Syria except for the fact that their territory was the target of a Zionist program. In addition to sharing aspirations with the Syrians and other Arabs for independence and unity, the Palestinians had to contend with the dangers of Zionism.

THE ZIONIST MOVEMENT

Zionism is a nationalist political movement organized in a visible manner in the latter part of the nineteenth century. Contrary to popular views, "Zionism is not rooted in the history and culture of the Jews."[20] In fact, while the Jewish prayers and rituals were built around the theme of returning to Jerusalem, the founder of Zionism, Theodor Herzl, did not insist on a return to Palestine. His objective was the creation of a state for the Jews as a remedy for anti-Semitism in Europe. In addressing himself to the issue of territorial location of the advocated state he wrote: "We shall take what is given us, and what is selected by Jewish public opinion."[21] Therefore, while Herzl might have preferred Palestine, his objective was not the territorial occupation of Palestine as much as it was bringing about an end to Jewish persecution.

The rise of political Zionism is rooted in the national, socialist, populist and utopian ideas that swept Europe in the latter part of the nineteenth century. As nationalists, however, the Jews had a special impetus because of anti-Semitic persecutions. Especially in eastern Europe where the Russian Czars ruled, Jews were regarded as subversive aliens bringing in dangerous ideas from the West (especially after the French Revolution). Restrictions on them were becoming increasingly severe. Socially, they were ostracized. This background, coupled with many centuries of exile, led to the development of many movements with a concern for alleviating the Jewish conditions. Ironically, the most practical response came from a West European Jew, Theodor Herzl, who called for the creation of a Jewish state. His life in the Austro-Hungarian Empire, and his experiences in France as a newspaper correspondent at the time of the Dreyfus trial, convinced him that anti-Semitism was endemic even in liberal countries. In 1896, he published a book entitled *The Jewish State*, which caught the imagination of the Jews in Europe.

In response to Herzl's call, the First Zionist Congress met at Basel on August 29, 1897. In his opening address, Herzl stated the objective of the meeting in the following words: "We are here to lay the foundation stone of the house which is to shelter the Jewish nation."[22] The congress then enthusiastically proceeded to found the Zionist Organization. By the time they were ready to adjourn three days later, the conferees agreed on Palestine as the geographic location of the proposed state and issued a statement that came to be known as the Basel Program. The program stated that "the aim of Zionism is to create for the Jewish people a home in Palestine secured by public law" and formulated the following means to obtain this objective:

1. The systematic promotion of the settlement of Palestine with Jewish agriculturalists, artisans, and craftsmen.
2. The organization and federation of all Jewry by means of local and general institutions in conformity with the local laws.
3. The strengthening of Jewish sentiment and national consciousness.
4. Preparatory steps for the procuring of such government assents as are necessary for achieving the object of Zionism.[23]

The Basel Program was well received in the European press. However, it also found many critics among the Jews. After attending the Basel Congress, Ahad Ha'am, a spiritual Zionist, declared that "the salvation of Israel will be achieved by prophets, not by diplomats."[24] Ahad Ha'am, among many others, was a spiritual Zionist who felt that, in accordance with the Torah, Jews were to wait for the Messiah to lead them back to the "Promised Land." Yehuda Laib Mnuchim, a Jewish critic of Zionism, explained his feelings after the congress: "In Basel, yesterday, I sat lonely among my brothers, like a mourner at a wedding...."[25] Many Jewish leaders rejected Zionism as it emerged out of Basel. But one conclusion stands out as significant; this was reported by yet another Jewish critic of Zionism, Judah L. Magnes, who said: "We seem to have thought of everything except the Arabs."[26]

In fact, there are indications that many of the founders of Zionism, including Herzl himself, were not aware that Palestine was an inhabited country. It is reported that "when Herzl's colleague Max Nordau heard for the first time that there was an Arab population in Palestine, he ran to Herzl crying: 'I did not know that; but then, we are committing an unjustice!' Herzl gave him the silent treatment."[27]

After the congress, Herzl, who was selected as the first president of the Zionist Organization, began using his diplomatic contacts to obtain legal authority and official support for the Zionist enterprise. In 1898, he met with Kaiser Wilhelm II, but his plea was rejected.[28] He then met with the Sultan of Turkey in 1901, only to experience a similar rejection.[29] In 1902, Herzl initiated negotiations with the British, who in the following year offered the Zionists the right to colonize a portion of East Africa (Kenya).[30] Feeling an urgency to alleviate Jewish conditions in Europe, Herzl favored the Kenya offer, but many of his colleagues, including Dr. Chaim Weizmann, opposed it vehemently.[31] This offer, which was dropped after the death of Herzl in 1904, was significant. "Its serious consideration by the Zionists as a substitute for Palestine provided indication of the secular character of the movement. It was also revealing in demonstrating British imperial sympathy and support for the territorial objectives of Zionist nationalism."[32]

In 1904, Dr. Weizmann became the president of the Zionist Organization and moved to London because of his conviction that, of all the European nations, Great Britain would be the most likely source of effective outside support for Zionism.[33] His efforts in London bore fruit in 1917 when, on November 2nd, British Foreign Minister Arthur Balfour issued his famous declaration. The Balfour Declaration was essentially an official letter to a private British subject, Lord Lionel Walter Rothschild, indicating the British government's support for "the establishment in Palestine of a national home for the Jewish people."[34] The declaration also included provisos safeguarding the rights of indigenous Palestinians and Jews abroad—which, in effect, put limitations on the "national home" promise. In fact, the Balfour Declaration was a masterpiece of doubletalk in the sense that British promises to both the Zionists and Palestinian Arabs were couched in ambiguous terms. The intention of the ambiguity was that Britain itself could interpret the declaration at a later date in accordance with its own perceived interests. Although some scholars view the declaration—and its incorporation in the mandate document—as a British commitment to the creation of a Jewish state, other scholars support the Arab claim of their right to majority rule. No matter how the British intended to cloud the issue, and regardless of whatever promises they made to Jews and Arabs, Britain intended to hold onto Palestine. World War I highlighted the strategic importance of Palestine for the protection of the Suez Canal. Britain's primary reason for producing the Balfour Declaration was, perhaps, not to provide a Jewish state, but to obtain Zionist support in France to win French consent to put Palestine under British, rather than international, control—as provided for in the Sykes-Picot Agreement.

PALESTINE UNDER BRITISH MANDATE

The year 1917 marked a major turning point in the history of Palestine. It witnessed the issuance of the Balfour Declaration and the beginning of the British presence in the area. In December 1917, General Allenby's forces entered Jerusalem and set up a British military administration in Palestine. The Arabs in the country welcomed Allenby as a liberator, hoping that they would soon attain independence within a larger Arab state. These hopes were soon dashed, as the British began working on a program to place Palestine under their mandate. Moreover, the Balfour Declaration was incorporated under the terms of the mandate, which was formally approved by the League of Nations in 1922, and became effective in 1923.

Arab nationalism in Palestine was now rapidly taking shape in response to British rule and Zionist plans for their homeland. Evidence of the nationalist reponse is found in newspaper articles as early as 1919. On November 2nd of that year, an editorial in the Jerusalem daily *Al-Quds* stated:

The British policies will not break the national spirit—the heart of the Arab people. We [the Arab people of Palestine] regard the rejection of our demands on the part of the powers as an affront to our rights. Our demand has been for self-rule, for unity of territory, for a rejection of a Zionist immigration—from these demands we shall not move. And we shall not permit our land to become home for the Jews.[35]

Under the mandate, Britain assumed two obligations that were proven contradictory. Article II of the mandate lists these obligations in the following terms:

The Mandatory shall be responsible for placing the country under such political, administrative, and economic conditions as will secure (1) the establishment of the Jewish National Home . . . and (2) the development of self-governing institutions, and also for safeguarding the civil and religious rights of all inhabitants of Palestine, irrespective of race and religion.[36]

The first obligation was viewed by the Zionists as well as some British officials as an obligation to create a Jewish state. Dr. Chaim Weizmann, then president of the Zionist Organization, was clear in his interpretation of the terms "Jewish National Home":

It means, as I say, at that time, and speaking in political parlance, a Jewish State; and when I was asked at the Peace Conference quite impromptu by Mr. Lansing, "What do you mean by a Jewish National Home?" I gave this answer: *"To build up something in Palestine which will be as Jewish as England is English."*[37]

Being a clear majority of 92 percent, the Arabs of Palestine interpreted the second obligation of the Mandate agreement as an obligation to implement a British pledge for Arab independence. However, their efforts to hold Britain responsible for the implementation of this pledge were unsuccessful. In time the Arabs came to feel that when the two obligations came in conflict, in most cases the one committed to the creation of a Jewish National Home took precedence over the other.

The Arabs felt that their failure was a result of Zionist influence in London. Knowing that they had neither the means nor the capacity to combat this influence, they turned to other means of making their views known. Thus, there were demonstrations and outbursts of violence. Such incidents were clearly anti-Zionist and, increasingly, anti-British. They occurred in April 1920, May 1921, August 1929, and October 1933. After each outbreak of violence, the British government appointed a commission of highly qualified experts to travel to the country and to "ascertain the underlying causes of the disturbances" and "to make recommendations for their removal and for the prevention of their recurrence."[38]

One after the other, without exception, each of these commissions came to the conclusion after its investigative tour that the "underlying causes" of the disturbances were:

1. The desire of the Arabs for national independence.
2. Their hatred and fear of the establishment of the Jewish National Home.[39]

Since the "underlying causes" were well known, the commissions' conclusions could just as well have been written in London in advance of the outbursts. However, that is not to say that the reports were insignificant because they included some important details and recorded a well-documented history of Palestine during that very important period. Without the reports, this history could have been lost or at least distorted.

Several attempts were made to establish a form of self-rule in Palestine. But these attempts were frustrated because at times the Zionists and

Palestinian Arabs saw them as moves by Britain to deviate from her specific mandatory obligations to them. However, the Jewish Agency, the main Zionist organ in Palestine, succeeded in achieving a form of self-rule for the Jewish settlers, but the Palestinians remained without effective representation. As a result, by 1947, the British Government reported to a United Nations Special Commission on Palestine that "from 1922 until the present day, the High Commissioner... governed Palestine with the aid of Councils consisting exclusively of British officials."[40]

Perhaps the failure of the British themselves in bringing about limited self-rule in Palestine was handicapped by their conflicting policies during the mandate period, which sometimes appeared to favor the Zionists and at other times the Arabs. Consequently, both groups complained. Admittedly, the British task was difficult. When their attempts at instituting self-rule for the Arab communities failed, the Zionists took advantage of the situation and formed the Jewish Agency. The Arabs, for their part, refused British suggestions to form a similar Arab Agency. The nationalists argued that creating such an agency would mean recognizing the mandate and its terms. Traditional leaders feared that such an agency would only serve to further split an Arab society already broken up by the millet system, which, inherited from the Ottomans, subdivided civil authority into religious communities.

Arab nationalism in Palestine manifested itself in organized political and para-political activities during the 1930s. During this decade, Palestinian Arabs witnessed the emergence of their earliest guerrilla groups. Also, a number of political parties were formed. These parties included the *Istiqlal* (Independence) Party (1932), the *Difa'* (National Defense) Party (1934), and three others formed in 1935: the Palestine Arab, Arab Reform, and National Bloc parties. All these parties—with the exception of the Independence Party—were organized and controlled by heads of influential families. Though each party was loyal to the particular notable who headed it and the family he represented, all parties, without exception, advocated national independence and opposed political Zionism.

In addition to bypassing family and class loyalties, the Independence Party had a well-defined political program. Yet, the Independence Party refused to cooperate with the other parties because of their traditional (family-based) structure. This lack of cooperation can be viewed as a tactical error, but one that is often repeated by radical Palestinian groups even today. The Independence Party advocated the immediate termination of the mandate, independence of Palestine, and the unity of the country with Syria, Jordan, and Lebanon (all known as Syria under the Ottomans). For the most part, the party attracted the young, educated, and nationalist elements of the population. However, it failed to mobilize and attract the rural population, which constituted more than 70 percent of the total Arab population, and thus it was no more effective than the rest of the parties.[41]

During this period also, the notion of popular armed struggle emerged in Palestine. Generally, the guerrillas opposed the political parties and represented a challenge to their leadership. One of the earliest of these was the movement of Shaykh Izz el-Din al-Qassam. The leading guerrilla movement today, Fateh, often points to this groups as its forerunner. Qassam was able to mobilize a peasant following and train them in the use of arms. These guerrillas advocated unity and independence, and vowed to take up arms against the British and the Zionists. Qassam and some of his guerrillas were surrounded and killed by the British in November of 1935. He was mourned in Palestine as a hero and a martyr. His movement inspired many young Palestinians, and soon after his death they began forming their own guerrilla units.

The climax of Palestinian resistance during the mandate came in 1936, when the famous 1936–39 revolt began. To coordinate the uprising, the factions and political parties joined in a central command then known as the Arab Higher Committee. Hajj Amin al-Hussaini, the High Mufti of Palestine, presided over the committee and became the spokesman of the Palestinian people.

The committee called for a boycott of the British authority and a general labor and business strike. Briefly, the aim of the boycott was to paralyze the entire country in order to bring attention to Arab grievances and force the British to fulfill Arab demands.

Once again, the British appointed a commission to go to Palestine and ascertain the "underlying causes" of the boycott. Known as the Peel Commission, it summarized Arab demands as follows:

1. The need for self-governing institutions.
2. The prohibition of land purchases by the Jews.
3. To put an end to Jewish immigration.
4. The use of Arabic as the major official language.
5. Increased funds for education.[42]

The Peel Commission's report concluded that no common ground existed between the two communities and proposed the partition of Palestine into a Jewish and an Arab state, with Jerusalem under an international administration. This recommendation, however, came at the wrong time in the aftermath of the Arab boycott. The boycott strike was total. It lasted for six months and was accompanied by individual acts of sabotage and violence. It ceased only when the surrounding Arab governments urged their fellow Arabs in Palestine to end it. The Arab governments were themselves pressured by Britain into calling for the cessation of the strike.

The violence, however, did not stop with the end of the strike. It continued until 1939, when the British government initiated negotiations with the Arab Higher Committee at a London round table conference. The conference culminated in a British statement of policy known to the Arabs and the British as the 1939 White Paper.

The White Paper restricted Jewish immigration and the transfer of Arab lands to the Jews, and made known the British objective of "the establishment within ten years of an independent Palestine State ... in which Arabs and Jews share in government in such a way as to insure that the essential interests of each community are safeguarded."[43] Some Palestinians welcomed this new policy. The Arab Higher Committee, however, rejected it and insisted on immediate independence. The Zionists not only rejected it but some reacted to the announcement by waging a campaign of violent activities against the Palestinian Arabs and the British administration. These activities reached their peak after the end of World War II. But during the war, Hitler's atrocities further solidified the Zionist enterprise with more Jewish refugees and greater international support.

The violence continued unabated during 1945, 1946, and 1947. Throughout these years, Palestine was in a state of turmoil and unrest. As Arab violence had proved effective in bringing about a change in British policy in 1939, Zionist violence was eventually successful in ousting the British from Palestine. In 1947, the British Government announced, after many attempts at a solution, that "the Mandate has proved to be unworkable in practice, and that the obligations undertaken to the two communities have been shown to be irreconcilable."[44] One of those British attempts at a solution involved the United States, when the two countries established a joint Anglo-American Committee in 1946. The committee visited the region and recommended in its report the establishment of a trusteeship over Palestine, the termination of the 1939 White Paper policy, and the admission of 100,000 refugees from the European displaced persons camp. By this time, however, Palestine's Jewish population numbered about 30 percent of the total population, and the Jewish community had become a formidable force in the country.

PALESTINE AND THE UNITED NATIONS

It was at this juncture that the United Nations began to play an important part in the affairs of Palestine. The General Assembly of the United Nations delegated a special committee to travel to Palestine and investigate the situation. The report submitted by the special committee (U.N. Special Commission on Palestine, UNSCOP) incorporated two plans: A *majority plan* of partition and economic cooperation, and a *minority plan* of a federal state.[45] To insure the passage of the majority plan, Zionist pressures were applied inside and outside the United Nations. As President Truman of the United States stated at the time, "So much lobbying and outside interference has been going on in this question [the partition plan] that it is almost impossible to get a fair-minded approach to the subject."[46] In 1956, Truman wrote in his *Memoirs*:

As the pressure mounted, I found it necessary to give instructions that I did not want to be approached by any more spokesmen for the extreme Zionist cause. I was even so disturbed that I put off seeing Dr. Chaim Weizmann, who had returned to the U.S. and asked for an interview with me.[47]

The Arabs of Palestine did not have the means to counteract the Zionist lobbying activities in the United States or other countries. In the United States, politicians found it expedient to capitalize on Jewish concern about the Nazi victims. The Arabs had no such appeal. The Zionists had the necessary organizational infrastructures in the United States, while the Arabs had none. Moreover, to many Americans, the idea of a Jewish state in Palestine seemed appropriate in that it coincided with religious prophecies. Thus, on November 29, 1947, the General Assembly adopted by a two-thirds majority the majority plan of partition. The vote was 33 for the partition, 13 against, and 10 abstentions.[48]

The partition plan divided Palestine into six parts—three of which (56 percent of the total area) were to become a Jewish state, and the other three (43 percent) were to become an Arab state. Jerusalem and environs (0.65 percent) was reserved for an international administration by the United Nations.[49] This resolution meant that the Jewish state would include 498,000 Jews and 497,000 Arabs (not including the Beduins of the Negev), and the Arab state would include 725,000 Arabs and 10,000 Jews.

It has been argued that the Arab governments mishandled the partition debates and, thereby, helped to bring about its passage. Instead of debating Palestinian rights, the Arab delegations insisted on denying the legal or the moral right of the United Nations to partition Palestine. In fact, the Arab delegations, having an advantage of six member-states in the United Nations, introduced a resolution requesting an advisory opinion of the World Court of Justice on the legality of such a U.N. action, thus placing their argument in opposition to the United Nations itself rather than on the merits of the Palestinian case. Even prior to approval of the majority report, it was clear that it had a better chance of adoption mainly because the majority of UNSCOP was behind it. Moreover, the major powers, including the Soviet Union, supported the majority plan. Thus, the partition resolution was adopted.

The Arabs rejected the partition. They claimed that it violated the provisions of the U.N. Charter on the people's right of self-determination. The Arab rejection also was based on the notion that, while the population of the Jewish state was half Arab and while the Jews owned less than 10 percent of the total land area, the Jews were to rule that state.[50] On the other hand, the Zionists accepted the partition, even though, according to Mrs. Golda Meir, it was "not what we wanted."[51]

THE ESTABLISHMENT OF ISRAEL

The United Nations' resolution to partition Palestine was followed by a wave of protests, demonstrations, and disturbances in the country. As soon as the resolution was adopted, British authorities started to withdraw from specific areas, and both Arabs and Zionists attempted to gain control of them. This situation resulted in immediate attacks on the local inhabitants. Edgar O'Ballance wrote "it was the Jewish policy to encourage the Arabs to quit their homes," and "they ejected those who clung to their villages."[52] Other Arabs, according to Sir John Bagot Glubb, were "encouraged to move by blows or by indecent acts."[53] Many Jews, as well, were attacked, and some were forced to flee the Arab dominated areas. But the Zionists were more successful in their efforts, and many middle-class Palestinians began to flee, leaving their communities without effective leadership.

Confronted with the tragic situation in Palestine, the leading champion of partition, the United States, began to have second thoughts. On March 19, 1948, it formally submitted to the U.N. Security Council an alternative proposal. The U.S. government proposed the formation of a temporary United Nations trusteeship over a united Palestine.[54]

While the United Nations was reexamining the Palestinian question, Zionists were establishing their authority over their allotted parts of the land. Chaim Weizmann reminisced: "Our only chance now . . . was to create facts, to confront the world with these facts, and to build on their foundation." Later, he was able to proclaim that "while the United Nations was debating trusteeship, the Jewish State was coming into being."[55]

The manner in which the Jewish State "was coming into being" was not peaceful, "but rather [characterized by] violence and bloodshed," as U.N. mediator Count Folke Bernadotte put it.[56] The most frequently mentioned incident among those behind the panic flight of the Arabs was the massacre of Deir Yassin. On April 9, 1948, 254 men, women and children in the village of Deir Yassin were massacred by Jewish attackers. Menachem Begin, who was leader of the attack and later became the Prime Minister of Israel, stated: "The massacre was not only justified, but there would not have been a state of Israel without the victory at Deir Yassin."[57] Similar, but less effective, incidents took place against Jewish communities as well. Hatred between the two communities reached its climax in 1948, but the mutual resentment and fear generated in 1948 still remain strong today.

On May 14, 1948, the U.S. abandoned its trusteeship proposal. At midnight on May 14, 1948, the State of Israel was proclaimed. President Truman gave full diplomatic recognition to Israel sixteen minutes later.[58] The newly born state incorporated not only the area specified to it in the partition resolution, but an enlarged area it had just occupied.

THE FIRST ARAB-ISRAELI WAR

It was at this time that the full Arabization of the Palestine conflict occurred. Prior to mid-May, 1948, volunteers and donations were arriving from the Arab countries in aid of the Palestinian Arabs.[59] However, it was only after the withdrawal of the last British soldier from Palestine on May 15, 1948, that the Arab armies entered the country. This move, even though it failed to drive out the Israelis, had the effect of strengthening Arab nationalism in Palestine.

The Arab offensive included military units from Jordan, Syria, Egypt, Lebanon, Iraq, Yemen, and Saudi Arabia. However, "they lacked common leadership and a coherent plan of action."[60] The Arab armies were also ill-equipped and lacked training in modern warfare. Moreover, as did the Palestinians before them, they had underestimated the strength of the Israelis.

The Israelis, on the other hand, were better prepared in terms of leadership, unity, organization, and sophistication. Even their numbers exceeded those of the Arab armies. They soon were on the offensive and were able to hold back the Arab armies. By the time Dr. Ralph Bunche, the U.N. mediator, was able to arrange for armistice agreements in 1949, Israel had gained more territory (2,500 square miles). Jordan took control of the remaining part of Palestine including the old city of Jerusalem but excluding the Gaza district (2,200 square miles), and Egypt controlled the Gaza strip.

Thus, a Jewish state was established in Palestine. The Arabs of the country were left without a state of their own. They became not only a stateless people but the majority of them a homeless people as well.

THE REFUGEE PROBLEM

The six months preceding the establishment of Israel witnessed an Arab exodus from Palestine. By the end of 1948, most of the Palestinian Arabs were displaced.

As to the method of displacement, there are conflicting opinions. Zionists claim that the Arab inhabitants fled the country at the instigation of the leaders of the Arab states. Arabs, on the other hand, often claim that the refugees were driven out of their homes by the Israelis. There is much evidence supporting the Arab argument. For example, Nathan Chofshi, an Israeli Jew, wrote in 1959:

We old Jewish settlers in Palestine who witnessed the flight could tell . . . in what manner we, Jews, forced the Arabs to leave cities and villages. . . . Some of them were driven out by force of arms; others were made to leave by deceit, lying, and false promises.[61]

One can go on quoting Israelis and Arabs on this issue; however, the problem cannot be resolved by debating the merits of these arguments. Professor Erich Fromm, a noted Jewish writer and thinker, summed it up very well when he wrote:

It is often said that the Arabs fled, that they left the country voluntarily, and that they therefore bear the responsibility for losing their property and their land. . . . But in general international law, the principle holds true that no citizen loses his property or his rights of citizenship; and the citizenship right is *de facto* a right to which the Arabs in Israel have much more legitimacy than the Jews. Just because the Arabs fled? Since when it is punishable by confiscation of property and by being barred from returning to the land on which a people's forefathers have lived for generations? Thus, the claim of the Jews to the land of Israel cannot be a realistic political claim. If all nations would suddenly claim territories in which their forefathers had lived two thousand years ago, this world would be a madhouse.[62]

The U.N. General Assembly discussed the refugee problem and on December 11, 1948 adopted a resolution asserting "that the refugees wishing to return to their homes and live in peace with their neighbors should be permitted to do so." It also established "that compensation should be paid for the property of those choosing not to return."[63] Many similar resolutions have been adopted by the United Nations since that time; however, none has been implemented. The number of refugees today is far larger than it was in 1948, and the political effects of their plight are undoubtedly far greater today, as indicated by the rise of the Palestinian guerrilla movement.

THE PALESTINIANS IN THE DIASPORA

By the end of 1948, most of the Palestinian Arabs were homeless, demoralized, and living in a perpetual state of shock. Their country was occupied and their leaders discredited. Most of them, however, continued to hope that the world would come to realize that an injustice had been committed against them and somehow undo it.

The most interesting feature of this period was the Palestinians' belief that the remedy for their plight lay in Arab unity. This phenomenon indicates that the Palestinian problem strengthened, rather than weakened, the sense of Arab nationalism among the Palestinians. Palestinian intellectuals discussed modernization as a prerequisite to unity.[64] As one author puts it, the Arabs "showed naivete in politics" and "weakness in diplomacy."[65]

To bring about modernization and unity, the Palestinians felt that the first step would be to change the traditional leadership, whom they felt had betrayed their cause. In July, 1951, a Palestinian Arab assassinated King Abdullah of Jordan in Jerusalem. The assassination was in reaction to his reported secret negotiations with the Israelis and the general feeling among the Palestinians that he betrayed the Palestinian cause. Also, it was not surprising that most Palestinians hailed the overthrow of King Farouk of Egypt in 1952. The Palestinians were among the most enthusiastic supporters of the Egyptian revolution and its spokesman, Gamal Abdel Nasser.

Some Palestinians, however, were to be disillusioned with Nasser's rhetoric after the 1956 Suez crisis. They had come to realize that the Arab states were unable to liberate Palestine and that the superpowers were unwilling to see Israel dissolved. As we shall see later, these younger Palestinians began organizing for a war of national liberation by mean of popular and armed struggle.

To symbolize Palestinian-Arab solidarity, the League of Arab States allowed for Palestinian representation in its meetings. This issue of Palestinian representation was first formally delineated in the appendix of the League's charter: "Considering Palestine's particular position and until Palestine attains its independence, the Arab League Council is commissioned to select a Palestinian Arab delegate to participate in its proceedings."[66] Thereafter, the Arab League Council adopted a resolution granting the Palestinian delegation the right to vote "on issues pertaining to the Palestine problem as well as on matters that Palestine could implement."[67]

At the United Nations, a united Arab effort was able to convince the various organs of this body to regularly adopt resolutions demanding repatriation of the Palestinian refugees. In fact, Israel's admission into the United Nations on May 11, 1949 was conditional upon its implementation of such resolutions. Of all members admitted to membership since the establishment of the United Nations, Israel was the only state the admission of which was predicated on the understanding that it implement specific resolutions of the General Assembly.

THE ESTABLISHMENT OF THE PLO

In spite of the concerted Arab effort at the United Nations with regard to the Palestine issue, deep rivalries existed among the Arab countries. These inter-Arab rivalries may have played a part in bringing about the creation of the PLO.

Inter-Arab rivalries crystallized almost immediately after the creation of Israel in 1948. They were intensified in 1956-1957 between Egypt and Iraq over the Baghdad Pact issue. The Arab leaders' mistrust and suspicion of each other peaked in 1961, when Syria seceded from the union with Egypt. The war in Yemen further divided the Arabs into "progressive" and "conservative" camps and the conflicting Ba'th political rivalries of Syria and Iraq led to a further deterioration of the situation.[68]

While the Arabs were busy with their feuds, Israel was implementing a plan to divert the waters of the Jordan River for its own use. This plan was at the completion stage by 1964 and, to counteract it, President Nasser of Egypt called for an urgent meeting of Arab heads of state to discuss the prospects for the execution of an Arab counterplan.

Accordingly, a conference was held on January 13-16, 1964 in Cairo. Realizing that the Arab armies were no match for Israel's military capabilities, the Arab leaders reverted to rhetoric and denunciations, and put forth an alternative plan to war, which was to divert the headwaters of the Jordan River before Israel could divert the river further downstream. However, this alternative was doomed to failure because of Arab incapabilities in defense. The water diversion project in Syria, for example, was destroyed in its initial stages by Israeli air attacks. The head of the Palestinian delegation to the meeting, Ahmad al-Shukairy, wrote:

The Arab kings and heads of state had nothing to discuss during this session. ... The Iraqi President, Abdul Salam Aref [who acted as the chairman of the conference] then asked the delegates: "Let us then discuss [the role of] the Palestinian delegate."[69]

It was at this point that President Nasser proposed the formation of a "Palestinian entity." Nasser's intentions for this proposal may have been to divert his people's attention from his (as well as other Arab leaders') inability to stop Israel's Jordan River scheme, or it may have been to solicit greater support for his leadership among the Palestinians.

Regardless of intentions, however, it soon became apparent that "the opinions of the Arab leaders regarding the nature and the goal of the proposed Palestinian entity were not in accord."[70] King Hussein, for example, feared the phrase, "Palestinian entity," because more than half of the population of his kingdom were Palestinians. The West Bank of

Jordan was Palestinian land, and if "entity" meant an eventual state, he stood to loose a major chunk of his kingdom. Amin al-Hafez, President of Syria, actually suggested making the West Bank and the Gaza Strip the territorial domain of a Palestinian state. King Saud called for the establishment of a Palestinian government in exile, while Bourguiba of Tunisia and Ben Bella of Algeria advocated the formation of a national liberation front. Egypt's Nasser was content with the symbolic creation of a limited official institution with propaganda functions only.[71]

As a result of this diversity of opinions, the summit conference recommended that:

> Mr. Ahmad al-Shukairy, Palestine's representative at the Arab League, should resume contacts with the member states and with the Palestinian people for the purpose of establishing a sound basis for organizing the Palestinian people in order to enable them to assume their duties in liberating their homeland and determining their destiny.[72]

This mandate did not mention a "Palestinian entity" nor did it "entrust [Shukairy] with the task of establishing [one] at all."[73] However, al-Shukairy took the initiative and formulated in broad outline a scheme for establishing a Palestinian entity. Then, he embarked on a tour of the Arab countries and consulted with many sectors of the Palestinian population. On the 24th of February, 1964, Shukairy proclaimed in Jerusalem that a draft constitution of twenty-nine articles had been promulgated. Its contents included the basic principles for "the liberation of Palestine."[74]

On May 28, 1964, a Palestine Council of 422 Palestinians, representing various sectors of the Palestinian population, met in Jerusalem to discuss the draft constitution. Representatives to the council were selected by preparatory committees composed of Palestinians residing in the Arab countries. The final list of representatives included 242 Palestinians from Jordan, and 146 from Syria, Lebanon, Gaza, Iraq, and the Arab gulf countries.[75]

On Monday, June 1, 1964, the council, by resolution:

1. Proclaimed the existence of the Palestine Liberation Organization.
2. Elected Mr. Ahmad al-Shukairy as chairman of the Executive Committee.
3. Elected Mr. Abdul Majeed Shuman as chairman of the Palestine National Fund.
4. Transformed itself (the council) into the First National Congress of the PLO.
5. Adopted a National Covenant for the organization and a fundamental law to govern it (see Appendix 3).
6. Authorized the chairman to select an executive committee of fifteen Palestinian representatives.[76]

It was anticipated that the National Covenant would emphasize the Arab character of the Palestine problem. Article 1 defined Palestine in these terms: "Palestine is the homeland of the Palestinian people. It is an inseparable part of the bigger Arab nation, and its people are an integral part of the Arab people." In spite of substantial growth in the national Palestinian sentiment among today's Palestinians, the Arab character remains very strong. In an interview on "60 Minutes" in April 1977, Yasser Arafat, now chairman of the Executive Committee, responded to a question about Palestinian-Arab relations as follows:

We are one nation but we have been divided. Actually, we were one nation and we look for the future to be one nation again. So, you have to look at this relationship from this point of view . . . that we are one nation.[77]

CONTEMPORARY PALESTINIAN NATIONALISM

While "Palestinians have always had to adjust their ways to the demands and political needs of outside powers,"[78] their nationalism has, in time, evolved to the point where some Palestinians perceive themselves as members of a Palestinian rather than Arab "umma" or nation. In the process, they have come to be seen as a potential threat to Arab regimes. Palestinian nationalism has become so strong that Palestinian loyalty to the PLO often far exceeds their loyalty to the states in which they live or even to the Arab umma. While some of the reasons contributing to this growth are discussed later in this book, it is clear that bitter experiences at the hands of Arab regimes have contributed substantially to this phenomenon.

Undoubtedly, however, the single most significant contributor to the rise of Palestinian nationalism has been their diaspora. Soon after their diaspora began, Palestinians "developed a whole mystique of The Return."[79] The dream of a return to their homes became a Palestinian obsession. More than a bit ironic, then, was the fact that just as Zionism was achieving its zenith, a "Palestinian Zionism" was being born. Just as early Zionists looked for outside powers to help them bring about their version of The Return, Palestinians at this early stage looked for help from the Arab governments. In time, especially after 1967, the Palestinians lost hope in being able to achieve their goals through the Arab states, and felt that their only recourse was guerrilla warfare. This change put the Palestinians at a collision course with Arab regimes. As Palestinian power grew, so did Arab fears. In some cases, the Palestinians became a state within a state, which led to military confrontations with some Arab regimes. Perhaps, Palestinian obsession with The Return contributed to their insensitivities towards the needs and interests of their hosts. Confrontations with Arab states strengthened Palestinian nationalism as a distinct force in the region. Today, Palestinian nationalism is a reality.

NOTES

1. Hisham Sharabi, *Palestine Guerrillas: Their Credibility and Effectiveness* (Washington D.C.: Georgetown University Press, 1970), p. xi.

*2. Many authors have addressed themselves to the issue of Palestinian Arab nationalism; among those are: W. F. Abboushi, Naseer Aruri, Michael Hudson, Fuad A. Jabber, Ann Lesch, William B. Quandt, and Hisham Sharabi. See the bibliography for their specific contributions.

3. Zeine Zeine, *Arab-Turkish Relations and the Emergence of Arab Nationalism* (Beirut: Khayyat Press, 1958), p. 50.

4. Najla Izzedin, *The Arab World* (Chicago: Henry Regnery, 1953), p. 65.

5. George Antonius, *The Arab Awakening: The Story of the Arab National Movement* (Philadelphia: Lippencott, 1965), p. 21.

6. Ibid., p. 23.

7. Ibid., p. 35.

8. League of Nations, *Mandates: Report of the Palestine Royal Commission* (London: H. M. Stationery Office, 1937), p. 11.

9. Antonius, *Arab Awakening*, p. 248.

10. W. F. Abboushi, *The Angry Arabs* (Philadelphia: Westminster Press, 1974), p. 138.

11. Great Britain, Foreign Office, *Palestine Royal Commission Report*, Command Paper (Cmd.) 5479 (London: H. M. Stationery Office, 1936), p. 6.

12. League of Nations, *Mandates*, p. 6.

13. Great Britain, Foreign Office, *Palestine Royal Commission Report*, Cmd. 3530 (London: H. M. Stationery Office, 1930), p. 127.

14. E. A. Speiser, *The United States and the Near East* (Cambridge, Ma.: Harvard University Press, 1947), p. 51.

15. Quoted in Fred J. Khouri, *The Arab-Israeli Dilemma* (Syracuse: Syracuse University Press, 1976), p. 10.

16. Great Britain, Cmd. 3530, p. 127.

17. Khouri, *Arab-Israeli Dilemma*, p. 13.

18. Ibid.

19. Recommendations of the King-Crane Commission with regard to Syria-Palestine and Iraq, August 28, 1919, in Antonius, *The Arab Awakening*, p. 449.

20. Alan R. Taylor, "Vision and Intent in Zionist Thought," in Ibrahim Abu-Lughod, ed., *The Transformation of Palestine* (Evanston, Ill.: Northwestern University Press, 1971), p. 101.

21. Theodor Herzl, *The Jewish State* (New York: Scopus, 1943), p. 42.

22. Quoted in Arthur Hertzberg, ed., *The Zionist Idea: A Historical Analysis and Reader* (New York: Python Press, 1959), p. 50.

23. John Norton Moore, ed., *The Arab-Israeli Conflict: Documents* (Princeton, N.J.: Princeton University Press, 1974), Vol. 3, p. 4.

24. Ahad Ha'am, *Selected Essays*, trans. Leon Simon (Philadelphia: Jewish Publication Society, 1936), p. 31.

25. Moshe Menuhim, *Jewish Critics of Zionism* (Detroit: Association of Arab-American University Graduates, 1976), p. 22.
26. Quoted in ibid., p. 22.
27. Ibid., p. 11.
28. Esco Foundation for Palestine, *Palestine: A Study of Jewish, Arab and British Policies* (New Haven, Conn.: Yale University Press, 1947), Vol. 1, p. 43.
29. Ibid., p. 44.
30. Ibid., p. 48.
31. Chaim Weizmann, *Trial and Error: The Autobiography of Chaim Weizmann* (New York: Harper, 1949), pp. 110–117.
32. W. T. Mallison, Jr., *The Balfour Declaration: An Appraisal in International Law* (North Dartmouth, Mass.: Association of Arab-American University Graduates, 1971), p. 64.
33. Leonard Stein, *Weizmann and England* (London: W. H. Allen, 1964), p. 64.
34. For a full text of the declaration, see Appendix 1: *The Balfour Declaration*.
35. *Al-Quds*, November 2, 1919, cited in Esco, *Palestine*, p. 260.
36. Great Britain, Foreign Office, *Mandate for Palestine*, Command Paper 1785 (London: H. M. Stationery Office, 1922), p. 1.
37. Chaim Weizmann, *The Jewish People and Palestine* (Jerusalem: Palestine Publishing, 1936), p. 19. Emphasis in original.
38. Great Britain, Cmd. 5479, p. ix.
39. Ibid., p. 110.
40. Great Britain, Foreign Office, *The Political History of Palestine under British Administration: Memorandum to UNSCOP* (Jerusalem: Government Printing Office, 1947).
41. For a detailed study on Palestinian political parties during this period, see Taiseer Nashef, "Al-Nukhbah al-Siyasiyah fil-Mujtama' al-Arabi fi Filastin" (The Political Elites of the Arab Society in Palestine), *Shu'un Filastiniyah* 48 (August 1975), pp. 131–167. Translation here and throughout this study is that of the author unless otherwise specified.
42. Great Britain, Cmd. 5479, p. 365.
43. Great Britain, Foreign Office, *Statement of Policy*, Com. 6019 (London: H. M. Stationery Office, 1939).
44. Great Britain, *The Political History*, p. 27.
45. United Nations, General Assembly, *Official Records*, Second Session, UN Special Committee on Palestine, Annex 19 (A/364), 1947.
46. Quoted in John Snetsinger, *Truman, the Jewish Vote and the Creation of Israel* (Stanford: Hoover Institution Press, 1974), p. 75.
47. Harry S. Truman, *Memoirs: Trial and Hope* (Garden City, N.Y.: Doubleday, 1956), p. 160.
48. U.N. General Assembly Resolution 191 (II), 29 November 1947.
49. Sami Hadawi, *The Arab-Israeli Conflict* (Beirut: Institute for Palestine Studies, 1969), p. 16.
50. Ibid., p. 17.
51. Golda Meir, *My Life* (New York: Putnam's, 1975), p. 211.
52. Edgar O'Ballance, *The Arab-Israeli War, 1948* (New York: Praeger, 1957), p. 64.

53. Sir John Bagot Glubb, *A Soldier with the Arabs* (New York: Harper and Row, 1957), p. 251.

54. Official Records of Security Council, 271st meeting, 19 March 1958, 29 ff.

55. Quoted in Fayez A. Sayegh, *A Palestinian View* (Amman: General Union of Palestine Students, 1970), p. 4.

56. UN Document A/648, p. 5.

57. Menachem Begin, *The Revolt: Story of the Irgun* (New York: Henry Schuman, 1951), p. 164.

58. Khouri, *The Arab-Israeli Dilemma*, p. 63.

59. Odeh P. Odeh, *Masra' Falastine* (The Death of Palestine) (Jerusalem: Sandukah Brothers, 1950), p. 30.

60. W. F. Abboushi, *Political Systems of the Middle East in the 20th Century* (New York: Dodd, Mead, 1970), p. 224.

61. *Jewish Newsletter*, 9 February 1959, quoted in Erskine B. Childers, "The Worldless Wish: From Citizens to Refugees," in Abu-Lughod, ed., *Transformation of Palesrine*, p. 184.

62. Ibid.

63. UN General Assembly Resolution 194 (III), 11 December 1948, par. 11.

64. Qustantin Zurayq, *The Meaning of the Disaster* (Beirut: Khayyat Press, 1956).

65. Odeh, *Masra' Falastin*, pp. 12–13.

66. The League of Arab States, *Charter* (Cairo: League of Arab States' Printing Office, 1946), Appendix.

67. Adli Hashshad, *The Palestinian People and Their Repatriation* (Cairo: n.p., 1964), p. 103.

68. For a full account of these rivalries, see Malcolm H. Kerr, *The Arab Cold War: Gamal Abdel Nasser and His Rivals* (New York: Oxford University Press, 1970).

69. Ahmad al-Shukairy, *From Summit to Defeat* (Beirut: PLO Research Center, 1971), p. 44.

70. Isam Sakhnini, *P.L.O.: The Representative of the Palestinians* (Beirut: Palestine Research Center, 1974), p. 13.

71. Leila Kadi, *Arab Summit Conferences and the Palestine Problem* (Beirut: PLO Research Center, 1966), p. 99.

72. Shukairy, *From Summit*, p. 50.

73. Ibid., pp. 61–62.

74. PLO, *Al-Yawmiyat al-Filastiniyah li-Am 1964* (Palestine Yearbook 1964) (Beirut: Institute for Palestine Studies, 1965), p. 73.

75. Shukairy, *From Summit*, p. 104.

76. For details of these resolutions see PLO, *Al-Yawniyat al Filastiniyah*, 1964.

77. "60 Minutes," CBS Telecast, 27 March 1977.

78. Donna Robinson Divine, "The Dialectics of Palestinian Politics," in Joel S. Migdal, ed., *Palestinian Society and Politics* (Princeton, N.J.: Princeton University Press, 1980), p. 214.

79. David Hirst, *The Gun and the Olive Branch* (New York: Harcourt Brace Jovanovich, 1977), p. 266.

2

The Problem of Legitimacy

In his book *The Rebel*, Albert Camus said that "rebellion cannot exist without the feeling that, somewhere and somehow, one is right."[1] The Palestinian revolution is no exception. The Palestinians feel that their dispersal was unjust and that they have the right to organize and struggle for what they consider to be their rights of return and self-determination.

It is the task of this chapter to attempt to answer two crucial questions: (1) Does the PLO's claim that Palestinians have the right of self-determination have a basis in international law? and (2) Is there legal substance to the argument made by the PLO that it represents the Palestinian people?

SELF-DETERMINATION

In 1924, Charles G. Fenwick, a well-known international law expert, concluded that "the so-called 'right of self-determination' on the part of subject nationalities has not attained the validity of a legal rule."[2] However, by 1963, Rosalyn Higgins, another international law scholar, was able to state that a number of UN resolutions

> clearly indicate that the great majority of states in the United Nations believe that a legal right of self-determination exists and that neither Article 2 (7), nor, indeed, domestic constitutional issues in general, can impede the implementation of that right and United Nations jurisdiction for that purpose.... It therefore seems inescapable that self-determination has developed into an international right....[3]

In fact, post-World War II scholars have come to accept the right of self-determination as a legal right. An indication of this general acceptance of the concept was its incorporation into the Charter of the United Nations (Article 1, paragraph 2).

The Charter of the United Nations defines the concept of self-determination as the right of all peoples "to determine their political, economic, social, and cultural status."[4] This definition is generally accepted by most scholars. For example, Alfred Cobban explains self-determination as the right of each nationality group "to constitute an independent state and determine its own government."[5] Rupert Emerson defines it as the right of nations "to determine their own destiny and maintain their identity."[6]

Logically, therefore, in order to determine the applicability of the right of self-determination to the Palestinian people, one should begin with an attempt to define the nation. The next task will be to relate the concept to the Palestinians and see if they constitute a nationality group.

Cobban provides us with a definition of nationality group that seems fairly well accepted by the scholarly community. He considers it to be as "any territorial community, the members of which are conscious of themselves as members of a community, and wish to maintain the identity of their community."[7] This definition, however, is by no means unanimously agreed upon by all scholars and philosophers. Charles Maurras, for example, disputes the definition's basic premise that nationality depends on one's wishes, and argues that the decisive characteristic is one's parents' nationality. Maurras writes: "It is not our will that has made us French. . . . We no more choose our *patrie*—the land of our fathers—than we choose our father and mother."[8] Cobban responds to this argument by pointing out that children of immigrant parentage would be denationalized if we were to accept the argument.

Regardless of which definition one adheres to, the Palestinians of mandated Palestine could argue their right to nationhood. They had their territorial community and were conscious of themselves as Palestinian Arabs just as the Iraqis and Egyptians considered themselves Iraqi or Egyptian Arabs. This consciousness was evident as early as 1919, as pointed out in the previous chapter.

Parenthood and the fact of birth can also be argued by the Palestinians. Their ancestors had lived in Palestine for centuries.

It is possible to conclude that mandated Palestine had its nationality group. However, since 1948, the Palestinians have been dispersed. Do they remain a nationality group? This question has not been answered definitively. Some argue that they do, others remain unconvinced.[9] History provides us with many examples of nationalities that have disappeared by assimilating into other communities. History also has examples of nations reborn, i.e., the Israeli-Jews themselves.[10] One thing is certain, the Palestinians claim that they are a people with specific cultural, political, and ethnic ties to all other Arabs. They see themselves to be as much a part of a nationality as the people of Egypt, Syria, Iraq, Lebanon, and Jordan.

Today, very few dispute the presence of a Palestinian people. Many U.N. resolutions have referred to the Palestinians as a people with inalienable rights (GA Resolution No. 3210, for example), and the United States has come to accept the Palestinians as a people with limited rights. Former President Carter has on more than one occasion referred to the Palestinians as a people with a right to a homeland. Even some Israelis have come to accept the existence of a Palestinian people as a fact of life. Matti Peled, retired Israeli army major general and director of the Arab Studies Department at Tel-Aviv University, has, for example, said "that this land (Palestine) is the homeland of two peoples—the peoples of Israel and the Palestinian Arab people," and proposed a two-state solution to the conflict.[11]

If one accepts the argument that a Palestinian nationality exists, then one is in agreement with the Palestinians on their right of self-determination. In fact, the Mandate Agreement for Palestine made the mandatory "responsible for placing the country under such political administrative and economic conditions as will secure ... the development of self-governing institutions. ..."[12] The British government had reiterated, in the White Paper of 1939, its willingness to grant Palestine independence within ten years. Actually, it was Britain's responsibility to do so. Article 22 (4) of the Covenant of the League of Nations specifically mentions the areas previously governed by Turkey and declares them provisionally independent. The task of the mandatory is to render "administrative advice" after taking into consideration the wishes of the communities.

The previous chapter discussed the failure of Britain to carry out its responsibility as the mandatory power in Palestine. Nevertheless, the point remains clear that Britain, as well as the League's covenant, did recognize a right of independence and self-determination for the people of Palestine provided that a Jewish National Home is founded there as well.

Today, the Palestinian right to self-determination is recognized by many nations. At the United Nations, the General Assembly has adopted a number of resolutions recognizing this right. General Assembly Resolution 2535 of 10 December, 1969, for example, "reaffirms the inalienable rights of the people of Palestine."[13] In 1970, two similar resolutions were adopted. One "condemns those governments that deny the right to self-determination of peoples recognized as being entitled to it, especially of the peoples of Southern Africa and Palestine."[14] The other resolution "recognized that the people of Palestine are entitled to equal rights and self-determination, in accordance with the Charter of the

United Nations."[15] A similar resolution was adopted again in 1971. This resolution "recognizes that the people of Palestine are entitled to equal rights and self-determination, in accordance with the Charter..." and "expresses its grave concern that the people of Palestine have not been permitted to enjoy their inalienable rights and to exercise their right to self-determination."[16] Resolution 2963 (XXVII) of December 13, 1972, reaffirms the previous resolution and expresses "once more its grave concern" that the Palestinians have not been permitted to exercise "their right to self-determination."[17] In 1973, 97 countries voted in favor of a resolution condemning "all Governments which do not recognize the right to self-determination and independence of peoples, notably the peoples of Africa still under colonial domination and the Palestinian people."[18] Resolution 2792 of 1971 was also readopted in 1973.[19] Since then, dozens of similar resolutions have been adopted.

This international support at the General Assembly was highlighted in 1974 by the invitation of PLO leader Yasser Arafat to address the Assembly. This invitation received 105 votes in favor and only 4 against.[20] Soon after Arafat's address, the Asembly adopted Resolution 3236, which to date is the most comprehensive U.N. recognition of Palestinian national and individual rights. The resolution confirmed the legitimacy of the PLO and called upon "the Secretary-General to establish contacts with the Palestine Liberation Organization on all matters concerning the question of Palestine."[21]

The Palestinian right to self-determination has also been affirmed by the nonaligned countries, the Islamic countries, members of the Organization of African Unity, Warsaw Treaty members, the European Parliament, the World Peace Council, and many independent nations.

In their conference of Heads of State or Government of Non-Aligned Countries in 1964, leaders of third-world countries adopted a resolution that endorses "the full restoration of all the rights of the Arab people of Palestine to their homeland and their inalienable right to self-determination."[22] This resolution was reaffirmed in later conferences held in 1970, 1973, 1976, 1980, and 1984.

Similarly, conferences of Islamic countries have adopted resolutions that "give support to the Palestinian people in their... right to self-determination."[23]

The Organization of African Unity has adopted a number of resolutions that affirm "the exercise by the Palestinian people of their right to self-determination and to recognition of their national rights."[24] Similar resolutions have also been adopted by Warsaw Treaty members regarding "the legitimate rights of the Arab people of Palestine."[25]

Many other international entities and groups have issued similar statements. In the World Peace Council session, held in Sofia, Bulgaria, in February 1974, for example, a strong declaration reaffirmed Palestinian national rights. Even the Vatican has often voiced its support for the rights of the Palestinian people and has not yet recognized the State of Israel.[26] A list of joint communiqués and speeches of various independent countries supporting this right would be too long and an unnecessary task. But the fact remains that a Palestinian right of self-determination is well recognized in the international arena.

PROBLEMS OF PALESTINIAN SELF-DETERMINATION

If the concept "self-determination" is ambiguous, its ambiguity increases when applied to the Palestinians. As mentioned earlier, there is no uniformity of definition with regard to this concept. It is not unusual that the right of self-determination is interpreted in such a manner as to suit the interests of those who seek to use it.

The problems associated with the concept and its implementation have bogged down so many scholars that Rupert Emerson concluded that "all peoples do not have the right of self-determination: they have never had it, and they will never have it."[27] One problem stems out of the necessity of establishing what the "self" is to which the right applies. The obvious answer is that the "self" is the "nation," but even that concept is bitterly disputed. Even if one reaches an acceptable definition of "nation," the question remains: With whom does the authority to speak for it rest?

Another basic problem relates to the actual conditions of the application of the right of self-determination. Under what conditions can this right be transferred into an operative one? Is this right a manifestation of a right of revolution, or does it apply within an established system? Moreover, does the right continue to exist once it has been exercised by a community, or does it cease to exist after independence?

Even if one finds acceptable answers to all these questions, the concept remains problematic when applied to present-day Palestine. It is recognized that the Palestinian Arabs have a right to self-determination. However, Israel is a recognized state and a member of the international community. Thus, international law gives protection to Israel's right of existence and to the Israeli Jews' right of self-determination. Which right then takes precedence and when? Or, can one people's right ever be applied at the expense of another's?

It can be argued that international declarations recognizing the Palestinian right of self-determination are not contradictory to Israel's rights. This argument would explain that Palestinian self-determination applies only to the Occupied Territories of the West Bank and Gaza Strip. These territories are not part of Israel (from a legal perspective) and are inhabited by Palestinians. However, the PLO claims to be the only representative of the Palestinians and the guardian of their rights.

If the PLO's claim is justified, then the Palestinian right to self-determination implies a PLO right to self-determination.

THE PLO AND PALESTINIAN REPRESENTATION

Two factors ascertain the legitimacy of a movement's representation of its people. The first is the amount of support of the organization by the people themselves. The second is official, international recognition of the movement. So far in this chapter we have dealt with international recognition of the PLO as a movement of national liberation and self-determination. In the following section, we will attempt to find out if that recognition is accompanied by a corresponding Palestinian acknowledgment of the PLO.

Palestinian Support for the PLO

International recognition of the PLO as the legal representative of the Palestinians would be inconsequential if it were not fully supported by the Palestinians themselves. Plebiscites and other normal channels of public opinion measurement are less than reliable among the Palestinians, whose population is dispersed and lives under various conditions that may, to say the least, not allow for democratic procedures. Therefore, any attempt to determine the opinion of the Palestinian people must rely heavily on structural setups that exist among them. Another means is to tap the views of opinion makers to be found in editorials in Palestinian newspapers and the pronouncements of community leaders. A third method would be to study the finances of the PLO to determine the extent of Palestinian financial support. It is also possible, in certain cases, to look at elections and analyze the voting behavior of the Palestinians. Demonstrations in support of or against the PLO and its policies could also give an indication of the Palestinian will.

Existing institutions among the Palestinian people include labor and student unions, women's groups, underground political parties, resistance organizations, various professional and popular conferences, and some community groups.

Palestinian labor unions were among the first groups to proclaim their support of the PLO. As early as April 14, 1964, the General Union for Palestine Workers (GUPW), held in Gaza, confirmed in a major resolution that the PLO is the only representative of the Palestinian people. The conference also proclaimed that the union is an integral part of the PLO. The GUPW incorporates 27,000 Palestinian workers in eight divisions in Lebanon, Syria, Iraq, Egypt (including Gaza), Kuwait, Jordan, West Germany, and Sweden.[28] Workers' conferences since have not failed to reaffirm the legitimacy of the PLO as the representative of all the Palestinian people. In fact, the GUPW conferences have always included top PLO officials, including Yasser Arafat, at the opening sessions and have concluded with resolutions supporting the PLO.

There is evidence to indicate that the most outspoken supporters of the PLO have been the Palestinian students. In its first conference after the establishment of the PLO held in Gaza on November 16, 1964, the General Union for Palestinian Students proclaimed its full support of the PLO. The conference also stated that it regarded itself to be a component part of the PLO. The resolutions adopted at this union's fifth conference, held in Amman in 1969, supported the PLO as a representative of all Palestinian fighters and institutions. At their sixth conference, held in Algiers in 1971, the students condemned the Jordanian regime for its attack on the Palestinian revolution and reaffirmed their support of the PLO.[29]

Students have also led demonstrations supporting the PLO in occupied Palestine and other parts of the world. Students studying abroad have formed their unions and proclaimed their support of the PLO. The General Union of Palestinian Students in East Germany, for example, has declared that "the PLO is the sole legitimate representative of our [Palestinian] people."[30] In Czechoslovakia, Palestinian students wrote Arafat declaring their support for the PLO and reaffirming their stand on its legitimacy.[31] Palestinians studying in Yugoslavia, Romania, Spain, France, Pakistan, West Germany, England, the United States, and many other countries have issued resolutions supporting the PLO.[32]

Palestinian women have also stood in support of the PLO. Those residing in the Occupied Territories have organized and led many demonstrations supporting the PLO. The General Union of Palestinian Women has since its inception in 1965 supported the PLO. Its charter proclaims the union an integral part of the PLO.[33]

In addition, Palestinian workers' groups, students, women, professionals, camps, and communities are represented in the PLO National Council, as will be seen in Chapter 3. Even Palestinians residing abroad are represented on this top policymaking body of the PLO. Palestinians living in the United States are represented at that body. Even those Palestinians carrying foreign citizenship do not hesitate to proclaim their support for the PLO by sending observer delegates to the National Council.[34]

It should be mentioned here, however, that usually it is the active members of a community who tend to join various political and advocate groups. Therefore, one can assume that such Palestinian groups as those mentioned above are not as representative of the Palestinian population as it might appear. Thus, a question must be asked: Is there a silent Palestinian majority? Clearly, this question is easier asked than answered. John Edwin Mroz studied private perceptions among Arabs and

Israelis, and concluded that "emerging private opinions often contradicted public policies and official pronouncements."[35] Mr. Mroz, however, did not deal with the question of PLO representation, but his conclusion stands as a reminder that public pronouncements of official and organized entities might not reflect popular attitudes. Perhaps, public opinion surveys and elections can answer Mr. Mroz's concern.

Similarly, political parties and guerrilla groups support the PLO as the legitimate representative of the people of Palestine. The guerrilla groups have been active in the PLO since its inception in 1964. A memorandum sent by Fateh, the largest guerrilla group, to the Third Conference of Arab Leaders held in Casablanca in September 1965 states: "From the outset, we have been cooperating with the PLO, and we have participated in its activities with other Palestinian citizens."[36] However, in an official capacity, this participation goes back only to 1968. In that year, at the Fourth Palestine National Council, guerrilla groups were invited to send delegates and participate in the decision-making process of the PLO. By 1971, all resistance groups were active members in the PLO. The executive committee that emerged in 1971 represented all principal factions of the guerrilla movement.

The involvement and participation of all major Palestinian guerrilla groups in the PLO's legislative and executive bodies implies their approval of its charter and endows the PLO with a representational power greater than at any time before. The program adopted at the Ninth Congress in July of 1971 states the following:

The PLO is the sole representative of the Palestinian people and of their military and political organizations, and all other organizations regardless of their trend, provided that they abide by the decisions of the legislative and executive bodies of the PLO as well as by their military and political programs and their organizational setup.[37]

Today, however, minor commando groups are split. This, of course, is not the first time these groups have differed. But today these splinter groups are outside the PLO. Consequently, seven commando groups and splinter-groups met in Damascus, Syria, and founded the Palestinian Salvation Front, which advocates changing the leadership of the PLO. At no point, however, did this front challenge the legitimacy of the PLO's representative character. On the contrary, the Salvation Front was careful to remind people everywhere that the PLO is the sole legitimate representative of the Palestinian people.

Palestinian political parties have also endorsed the PLO's right to represent the people of Palestine. In spite of the fact that these parties are underground, they have openly supported the PLO since 1964. The Arab Nationalist Movement, which was predominantly a Palestinian party and is the parent organization of the PFLP, was represented at the National Councils held before 1967. Its spokesman, Saleh Shibl, declared on May 21, 1965 that "the positive initiative taken by the Palestinian branch of the Arab Nationalist Movement to join the PLO is no longer a secret."[38]

The Jordanian Communist Party, another predominantly Palestinian underground party, had continuously supported the PLO. When the Arab leaders decided at their Rabat summit meeting to recognize the PLO as the sole legitimate representative of the Palestinians, this party hailed the decision as the "beginning of the road for Palestinian continuation of their struggle for the liberation of their homeland."[39] The West Bank branch of this party, known now as the Palestinian Communist Party, has also endorsed the PLO. In cooperation with the PLO, this party, in 1973, established an indigenous underground coordinating committee in the West Bank and the Gaza Strip known as the Palestine National Front. The front issued a declaration upon its founding that incorporated this call:

We call upon our people in the West Bank and Gaza Strip to stress its unity behind the Palestine Liberation Organization; and to reject all the efforts by the other sides to pose as the representatives of the Palestinians and to segregate and disperse the Palestinians who are united behind the PLO.[40]

The Palestinian Communist Party later officially joined the PLO and since 1987 has been represented on its Executive Committee. Other Palestinians have joined various Arab parties such as the Ba'th Party, the Syrian Nationalist Party, the Moslem Brotherhood, and a number of other less significant groups. Without exception, these and all other Arab political parties have endorsed the PLO as the sole legitimate representative of the Palestinian people.

Further support of the PLO was expressed at the Popular Palestine Conference of 1972. This conference was held in Cairo for representatives of all Palestinian organizations, unions, and groups in sixteen Arab and eight non-Arab countries. The conferees passed the following:

The PLO is the supreme political organization of the Palestinians and their only spokesman on all fateful matters. The PLO alone shoulders the responsibility of directing all activities pertaining to the Palestinians' right of self-determination. It is the sole legitimate representative of Palestinians voicing their will and their aspirations. No one else can make any decisions or pronouncements relating to the future of Palestinians except for what is decided by the Palestinians as expressed through the PLO in accordance with its Charter and its avowal of liberating the entirety of Palestine. Accordingly, any arrangement or agreement emanating from another source is illegitimate and will remain as such.[41]

Support for the PLO's claim to representation of the Palestinians comes also from the Palestinian press. In spite of the fact that Palestinian newspapers are censored by various governments, their support of the PLO remains strong. Even in Israel itself, the Nazareth Arab newspaper *Al-Ittihad* (The Union) often calls upon Israel to recognize the PLO and favors the establishment of a Palestinian state in the West Bank and Gaza under the PLO. In Gaza, the daily *Gaza* newspaper writes boldly: "No one represents the Palestinians but the PLO."[42]

In the occupied West Bank, a number of Palestinian newspapers are published. All have advocated Israeli recognition of the PLO and proclaimed the PLO as the legitimate representative of the Palestinians. The (Jerusalem) newspaper *Al-Quds* took an independent line until the Rabat Summit of 1974. In 1970, *Al-Quds* announced, "the Palestinians need neither Jordan, nor Israel, nor the PLO."[43] However, after the Arab Summit Meeting of 1974, *Al-Quds* hailed the Arab leaders' resolution recognizing the PLO as the sole legitimate representative of the Palestinians. In an editorial regarding the Geneva peace talks, the newspaper's editor called upon the "inhabitants of the occupied land (to) join their brothers abroad... [in] going to Geneva with a delegation including the PLO..."[44] *As-Sha'b* (People), another Jerusalem newspaper, is more forward in its support of the PLO. Its editors do not hesitate to clearly write that "the Palestine Liberation Organization is the sole legitimate representative for us and all the Palestinian people."[45] Another very outspoken supporter of the Palestinian revolution and the PLO is the *Al-Fajr* (Dawn) newspaper. This newspaper advocates the establishment of a Palestinian state in the West Bank and Gaza and openly supports the PLO and its struggle against Israel—a reason for the occasional suspension of its activities by political authorities.

This Palestinian support of the PLO has even caught on in Israeli newspapers. Lea Ben Dor, a former editor of the *Jerusalem Post*—Israel's English daily newspaper—wrote in the *Post* advocating negotiations with the PLO: "There are two ways to end a conflict: fighting and talking. For goodness sake, let us talk. And go straight to the worst enemy, the only one who matters (the PLO)."[46]

In the Arab countries, newspaper editorials can always be cited in support of the PLO's claim of representation. Even in Jordan, where King Hussein had denied the PLO claim, the press has played a conciliatory role and since the 1974 summit resolution has moved into supporting the PLO. Both major Jordanian newspapers, *Al-Dostour* (The Constitution) and *Al-Ra'y* (The Opinion), now insist on PLO's inclusion at any peace talks, as representative of the interests of the Palestinians.

PLO support has come from almost all sectors of Palestinian society. Community leaders have reflected this support in their pronouncements. Even the Arabs of Israel have indicated this support. Mr. Tawfiq

Zayyad, the Mayor of the City of Nazareth, has declared his "full support of the PLO as the sole legitimate representative of the Palestinian people" and its strategy of armed struggle. He said: "We find no substitute for armed struggle."[47]

In the West Bank and Gaza, Arabs have been more outspoken on the issue. In a memorandum to the Arab summit conference in Cairo, the late Ramallah Mayor, Karim Khalaf, wrote defending his Palestinian brothers in Lebanon:

This presence of the Palestinian people in its diaspora in the neighboring Arab countries and also the presence of the Palestine Liberation Organization, the sole legitimate representative for us and all the Palestinian peoples—this temporary presence is not a privilege or a gift or a donation from anyone, but is a natural right that stems out of the unity of the Arab land and the oneness of Arab history and the oneness of Arab thinking and language, and the oneness of suffering, hope, and Arab destiny.[48]

A *Jerusalem Post* reporter who interviewed the West Bank municipal leadership after the 1976 elections concluded: "The elections may have backfired if the original aim [was] to create a new West Bank political leadership with which Israel could discuss a future political settlement." The reporter went on to say that the West Bank mayors had met and agreed collectively to "foil any attempt by the Israeli authorities to involve us (the mayors) in political deliberations." The mayors added that the West Bank people are part of the Palestinian people "whose political representative is the PLO and not us." "These sentiments," the reporter wrote, "were echoed by even the most moderate of the West Bank mayors, Bethlehem's Elias Freij, who said that the Israeli authorities should confine their dealings with the West Bank leadership to purely municipal matters.[49]

Even the Israeli-deposed pro-Jordanian mayor of Gaza, the late Rashad Shawa, never denied the representative character of the PLO, and continuously demanded the release of the pro-PLO detainees in Israeli jails.[50] However, the people of Gaza themselves had provided the PLO continuous support. Israeli analysts Zeev Schiff and Raphael Rothstein report in their book, *Fedayeen: Guerrillas Against Israel*, that "in Gaza the fedayeen were more successful, Israeli authorities found that as many as 80 percent of those youths (of Gaza) approached by the fedayeen responded affirmatively."[51]

Palestinians in the diaspora are more open in their support of the PLO. This may be due to the fact that they do not live under military occupation as do other Palestinians in the West Bank and Gaza. Their leaders speak of the PLO as "the Revolution." Nabeel A. Shaath, formerly a professor at the American University of Beirut and currently a

PLO organizer, says: "The... happiest moment of my life was definitely the day of Karameh, March 21, 1968, when the Palestinian revolution was truly born."[52] When Raja Farraj, a Palestinian businessman living in Jordan, was asked a similar question, he echoed Shaath: "I think the happiest moment was the birth of the resistance movement."[53]

Another way to determine the relationship between the Palestinian masses and the PLO is to look at the financial aspects of the latter. Isam Sakhnini writes that the seventh fiscal report of the Palestine National Fund, presented to the Palestine National Council in July 1971, stated that the income of the PLO was 1,226,577 Jordanian dinars during the period between July 7, 1970 and February 28, 1971. Of this amount, 940,672 came from liberation taxes (which range between 3 percent and 6 percent of a Palestinian citizen's income payable to the PLO). In addition, 4,903 JD were deducted from the salaries of the PLO employees as contributions. Moreover, another significant source of income has been the Joint Palestine Appeal in Jordan and Kuwait, which has accumulated 88,487 J.D. A large share of this sum was donated by Palestinians residing in these countries. Therefore, Mr. Sakhnini concludes that approximately 80 percent of the PLO's income has originated from the Palestinian people.[54]

A later article in *Time* magazine did not dispute Sakhnini's conclusion and added that "Palestinians living outside the Middle East, including at least 150 multi-millionaires in Europe and the Western Hemisphere, make regular and generous contributions to the cause."[55] But, clearly, the PLO's finances are more dependent upon Arab than upon Palestinian contributions.

Public opinion analysts usually investigate voting behavior and analyze election outcomes to determine popular sentiments. This method of opinion measurement may be superior to the indicators that were tapped in this study. Since the Palestinians are dispersed and live under various Arab governments, they do not have their independent elections for political office. However, municipal elections were held in the West Bank. Since West Bank electors are all Palestinians, analyzing these elections could be beneficial.

The first municipal elections since 1966 in the West Bank were held in 1972, almost five years after the Israeli occupation. The PLO opposed the elections and called upon the people not to vote. The PLO feared the elections might be an Israeli move to find substitute representatives of the Palestinian people.[56] This opposition took its toll on the election process. In Nablus, for example, the nomination deadline expired without having a sufficient number of candidates to fill available city council seats. This forced the Israeli authorities to extend the deadline and, according to a Palestinian source, to "coerce personalities to nominate themselves."[57] Two cities, Hebron and Salfit, did not need to vote because the nominees won by acclamation since there were no others in the running. Ten municipalities held their election on March 28, 1972, at which time 13,000 people voted. Thirteen others held elections on May 2, 1972, and 10,000 voters showed up at the ballot boxes. The percentage of participants amounted to only 3 percent of the total population of the West Bank. Four observations can be made about these elections:

1. The majority of the winners were members of the old councils and won reelection. Thus, no new significant leadership emerged.
2. Most of the elected members were nonpolitical and represented the working and business community. They demonstrated their lack of political ambition through their pronouncements and refusal to negotiate with Israeli authorities on behalf of their people. The mayors of Nablus and Tulkarm, for example, stated this refusal.[58]
3. The election process was not peaceful. Antielection demonstrations took place in many cities. In Nablus, for example, Israeli security forces had to be brought in to break up the demonstrations leading to violent clashes.
4. There is evidence to indicate that many Palestinian voters participated in the election out of fear. Personal identification cards, which must be carried by West Bankers at all times, were stamped at the voting places. Rumors immediately began spreading about the possibility of Israel taking vengeance against those not participating.[59]

If there were any doubts about the sentiments of the West Bank Palestinians, the 1976 municipal elections should have dispelled them. In these elections, held in April, 1976, a new leadership emerged. Of the 191 contested seats, 143 were won by newcomers. These newcomers, *The New York Times* speculated, represent a "younger, more outspoken leadership that is likely to stress Palestinian issues and be less cooperative with the Israeli occupation authorities."[60] *The Washington Post* reported that not only were the newcomers supporters of the PLO, but even "two incumbent mayors who endorsed the PLO during the campaign were easily reelected."[61]

The PLO, in fact, was a campaign issue. The National Bloc candidates openly proclaimed their support of the PLO as the only legitimate representative of all the Palestinians. They won most of the council seats in the major cities of the West Bank, including Hebron, Nablus, Ramallah, Tulkarm, Jericho, Beit Jala, and Beit Sahur. One exception was Bethlehem, where the traditional leadership won seven of the eleven contested seats. However, in Bethlehem, Mayor Elias Freij, who was reelected, did not reject the PLO in the campaign; he simply did not make it an issue. However, after the election, Freij proclaimed, "the PLO is us." The most radical change occurred in Hebron, which had been ruled by traditionalist Sheikh Jabari. In Hebron, all contested seats were swept by PLO sympathizers.

Following his victory, the new mayor of Hebron, the late Fahd Kawasme, said: "Why shouldn't the people of the West Bank accept the PLO as our representative? The rest of the Arab world does. Most of the nations of the world do. Why should we be different?"[62]

Israeli officials were surprised and dismayed by the extent of the pro-PLO victory. Defense Minister Shimon Perez saw the results as "a national challenge with which we will now have to grapple."[63] Zevulen Hammer, Minister of Social Welfare, concluded that the election results should be a reason for not returning the West Bank to Jordan because "it will pass immediately—in a matter of hours—into the hands of the PLO."[64] The Mafdal secretary general, Zvi Bernstein, felt that Israel had made a grave mistake by not cancelling the elections. "In the opinion of the Mafdal secretary general, the election results legalize the PLO claim that it represents the Arabs in the West Bank."[65] Josef Goell, of the *Jerusalem Post*, agreed with Mr. Bernstein when he wrote: "One clear result of last month's municipal elections on the West Bank is the demonstration of unified support by the area's leaders and population for the PLO . . . "[66]

In spite of Palestinian claims and Israeli fears, it must be noted here that the elections were municipal elections and did not include the villages and rural areas in the West Bank. Urban population in the West Bank is known to be less than 40 percent of the total West Bank population.[67] Therefore, while the election results might have indicated Palestinian sentiments, they were limited to a minority of West Bank Palestinians.

By far, other than military and guerrilla operations, the most violent manifestation of popular Palestinian sentiments in the Occupied Territories had been the demonstrations. Since the Israeli occupation of the West Bank and the Gaza Strip in 1967, the area had witnessed many demonstrations and strikes. In fact, public schools in the area proclaimed a general strike only weeks after the advent of the occupation. One of the early mass demonstrations took place in December, 1968, when massive demonstrations took place in all major West Bank and Gaza Strip cities. These uprisings, which were started by students, lasted until March 1969. Demonstrators shouted revolutionary slogans and carried pro-PLO placards.

Another major uprising began on the morning of November 13, 1974, the day Yasser Arafat addressed the United Nations General Assembly. This time the demonstrations were highly organized and coordinated between the various cities of the West Bank. The political nature of these demonstrations was rather obvious. The demonstrators distributed pamphlets supporting the PLO and carried pictures of Arafat. They continuously chanted the slogan "Yes to the PLO. No to occupation. No to Hashemite rule."[68] These demonstrations did not subside for two weeks, during which there were many clashes between the demonstrators and Israeli forces. Curfews had to be imposed throughout the West Bank in order to control the demonstrators.

A third major outbreak of violent demonstrations took place in early 1976. In fact, 1976 witnessed continuous demonstrations throughout the Occupied Territories and the Arab towns of Israel. In February, the West Bank was the scene of violent demonstrations and general strikes, which protested a ruling by an Israeli court allowing Jews to pray at the Aqsa Mosque, one of Islam's holiest shrines and the site of the Wailing Wall. In spite of their religious background, the demonstrations soon became political when the Christian towns of Ramallah and Bethlehem rose up demonstrating against Israeli occupation. These demonstrations went on for seven weeks and inspired demonstrations by the Arabs of Israel on March 30. Israel's Arabs declared a "land day" and marched in support of their fellow Arabs in the Occupied Territories and in objection to Israeli confiscation of Arab land in Galilee. The demonstrators here, as on earlier occasions, chanted pro-PLO slogans and carried Palestinian flags. In July, more violent demonstrations took place in the Occupied Territories to protest the sales tax, which had been increased to 8 percent. Again, the political character of the demonstrations was evident in the organization and the slogans of the demonstrators. In August, demonstrators marched the streets in support of Palestinians fighting in Lebanon. On December 5th, a general strike was proclaimed in support of the struggling PLO in Lebanon and was followed by major demonstrations throughout the West Bank and Gaza. In all, 1976 witnessed the most violent demonstrations of all the years of Israeli occupation up to 1987. Twenty-eight Arabs died as a result of the demonstrations, and a number of Israeli soldiers were wounded. Since then, political demonstrations have become commonplace in the West Bank and the Gaza Strip.

If nothing else, the slogans carried by the demonstrators are an indication of the political line supported by those marching. Examples of these slogans are: "Yes to the PLO ... No to Occupation No to Hashemite Rule." "We are all Fedayeen ... Revolution ... Revolution until Victory." "Palestine is Arab ... we swear to continue the struggle."[69]

By far the clearest and the most obvious form of political expression has been the uprising (*intifada*) which began in December 1987. The intifada, as will be discussed in Chapter 7, spread rapidly to every corner of the Occupied Territories to encompass all geographic regions and all sectors of Palestinian society. The message of the intifada is simple and clear: the end of the occupation and the creation of an independent Palestinian state through negotiations with the PLO. Within days of the start of the intifada, the political forces formed a joint command known as the Unified National Leadership of the Uprising (UNLU). The UNLU began to issue directives in the form of a biweekly communiqué. The communiqués, signed UNLU/PLO, became the most powerful form of written political expression of the Palestinians under occupation. To those Palestinians, the communiqué was transformed into a sort of a biweekly constitution that was obeyed at all costs. Thus, to the Palestinians there, the PLO is already their ruling body.

From the preceding review, it is evident that there is widespread support for the PLO among the Palestinian masses. It is, however, possible to cite the pronouncements of some Palestinians who believed otherwise. A few Palestinians may have supported Jordan's claim to the West Bank. Others see the PLO as too rigid or too soft in its position on negotiations. Mayor Elias Freij of Bethlehem, for example, warned in 1982 that the proliferation of Israeli settlements on the West Bank could mean "in the next ten years we (the Palestinians) will be witnessing a Jewish West Bank" and urged the PLO to recognize Israel and negotiate with it.[70] Since then, the PLO has in fact moved in that direction. Similarly, Rashad Shawa, the deposed mayor of Gaza advocated PLO recognition of Israel and stated that the PLO is only a part of the Palestinian people.[71] This could be interpreted to mean that the PLO is not the "sole legitimate representative" of the Palestinians. Nevertheless, there is unquestionably a great amount of support among the Palestinians for the PLO.

International Recognition of the PLO

Palestinian support for the PLO and their acknowledgement of its representational character is further reinforced by a fairly large degree of regional and international recognition. At the regional level, the PLO is recognized by all Arab and Islamic countries of the entire Middle East/North Africa region.

The official Arab recognition of the PLO was extended at the Arab League meeting of June 17, 1964. This recognition entailed PLO participation in all activities of the League and is equivalent to that of any Arab state. This resolution has been occasionally reaffirmed by the League, individual Arab states, and even Arab summit conferences. At their summit conference of 1973 in Algiers, the Arab leaders spelled out clearly the meaning of PLO recognition when they reiterated that "the Palestine Liberation Organization is the sole legitimate representative of the Palestinian people."[72] The Arab summit meeting in Rabat in late October 1974 again endorsed the PLO and went on to declare that the PLO should head an "independent national authority" to be set up on any "Palestinian land that is liberated" from Israeli occupation.[73] This resolution was accepted by all Arab leaders, including Jordan's King Hussein. This may explain why Arafat said: "This summit conference has been like a wedding feast for the Palestinians."[74]

The official Arab recognition was coupled with formal international recognition. As early as October 1964, the conference of Heads of State or Government of Non-Aligned Countries held in Cairo decided to invite the PLO to participate as an observer at one of the conference's meetings.[75] At their Fourth Conference, held at Algiers in September 1973, the non-aligned countries' leaders adopted a resolution which stated, "The Conference ... declares its recognition of the Palestine Liberation Organization as the legitimate representative of the Palestinian people and of their just struggle."[76]

The Islamic countries have also recognized the representative character of the PLO. At the Conference of Foreign Ministers of the Islamic Countries, held in Libya in March 1973, the conferees decided to "reaffirm that the Palestine Liberation Organization is the sole legitimate representative of the Palestine people."[77] The kings and presidents of these countries reaffirmed this resolution in their second nonaligned countries summit conference, held at Lahore, Pakistan in February 1974, and at their later meetings.[78]

The Organization of African Unity has adopted similar resolutions. In June 1974, the OAU declared "its full support for the PLO as the sole legitimate representative of the Palestinian people in their heroic struggle against Zionism and racism."[79]

The Afro-Asian Peoples' Solidarity Organization declared in 1972 that "... The PLO with its national council and executive committee is the sole representative of the Palestine people, ... (and it) expresses (the) people's will and aspirations, and it has the right to speak in their name."[80]

These resolutions were reinforced by a large number of joint communiqués between the PLO and many countries and between the Arab states and other countries. A joint communiqué issued by the PLO and East Germany in August 1974 stated "The Democratic Republic of Germany affirms that it considers the PLO the sole legitimate representative of the Palestinian Arab people..."[81] Another example of such communiqués was the one issued by presidents of Syria and Yugoslavia in August 1974. In that one as well, both parties affirmed that they considered the PLO "the sole legitimate representative of the Palestinian people."[82]

At the United Nations, the PLO plays a significant role testifying to its representational character. The PLO participates in the workings of many U.N. organs and their conferences. At the General Assembly, it has observer status. In July 1977, the Southwest Asia Section of the Social Council admitted the PLO to membership, the first membership ever to be granted a nongovernmental entity by any U.N. Agency.[83]

In 1974 alone, the PLO had participated in the following U.N. conferences:

1. The Diplomatic Conference on the Reaffirmation and Development of International Humanitarian Law Applicable in Armed Conflicts, Geneva, Switzerland, February 20–March 29, 1974.
2. The World Food Conference, Rome, Italy, November 5–16, 1974.
3. The Third Conference on the Law of the Sea, Caracas, Venezuela, June 22–August 29, 1974.
4. The World Population Conference, Bucharest, Rumania, August 19–30, 1974.
5. Meeting of the Assembly of the International Civil Aviation Organization, Montreal, Canada, September 24–October 15, 1974.
6. The UNESCO General Conference, Paris, France, October 17, 1974.

The General Assembly has also endorsed the representational character of the PLO. In a resolution adopted on October 14, 1974, the General Assembly invited "the Palestine Liberation Organization, the representative of the Palestinian people, to participate in the deliberations of the General Assembly on the question of Palestine in plenary meetings."[84] This resolution was adopted by 105 votes to 4, with 20 abstentions. The opposing countries were Israel, the United States, Bolivia, and the Dominican Republic. As a result of this resolution, Yasser Arafat, chairman of the PLO, addressed the General Assembly on November 13, 1974.

In less than a month, the General Assembly adopted another resolution inviting "the Palestine Liberation Organization to participate in the sessions and the work of the General Assembly in the capacity of observer" and in the work of "all international conferences convened under the auspices of the General Assembly...."[85] While the status of an observer does not mean full diplomatic recognition, it implies a form of recognition. This form, however, is the highest possible for any nongovernmental group.

Another form of international recognition of the status of the PLO can be the large number of countries permitting the PLO to open a political office in their major cities. The PLO today has offices in more than a hundred Western European, Latin American, Socialist, and third-world countries.

It is evident, then, that the PLO has acquired a level of international support for its claim that it represents the Palestinian people. There is also evidence that the Jordanian option (Jordan's claim that it represents the Palestinians) was weakened, if not totally eliminated, after King Hussein severed administrative ties to Palestine in July of 1988. King

Hussein himself has conceded the PLO claim and has reiterated often that the Palestinians, as represented by the PLO, should participate in peace negotiations. His position, however, has been changeable, depending on the pressure of politics. Although Jordan accepted the Rabat summit decision in 1974, it is possible that King Hussein might accept a peace plan that would give him a meaningful role in the West Bank. However, even Israeli leaders have come to realize the end of the Jordanian option. Yigal Allon, then Israel's foreign minister, has "come out against negotiations solely with Jordan on the Palestinian problem."[86] Since the end of 1988, however, no Israeli official has come out in favor of a "Jordanian option."

If the PLO has acquired this level of recognition, why then did it not form a government-in-exile? In fact, a number of Arab countries, including Egypt, have proposed the transformation of the PLO into a government-in-exile. Moreover, the PLO, as will be discussed in Chapter 3, performs many governmental functions; however, the burdens of a government-in-exile are more complicated than mere governmental functions. While the formation of a government-in-exile could enhance the PLO's diplomatic image, it could also hinder its growth and limit its policy options. In 1988, the PLO issued a Palestinian Declaration of Independence. Independent states have governments. Thus, there is every expectation that the PLO will soon form such a government.

On the other hand, Israel has claimed that the PLO does not represent the Palestinians and, consequently, it refuses to negotiate with it. Thus, another dimension is added to the question of representation: Is it necessary that the PLO be legally certified as a representative of the Palestinian people for Israel to negotiate with it? In other words, is representation a prerequisite to negotiations in a conflict situation?

There seems to be more helpful evidence in historical experience to argue that recognition and negotiations are two different processes. During the British Mandate in Palestine, the Jewish Agency officially spoke on behalf of the Jewish communities before the Palestine Government. Did the Jewish Agency represent all the Jews of the country? This question has not been answered. It is known that there were some Jews who did not feel that the agency represented them. Dr. Judah Magnes of the *Ihud* (Union) party was an outspoken critic of the agency and its policies. The Communist party did not agree with the agency on all matters. Menachem Begin, Israel's former prime minister, did not always agree with the Jewish Agency, and his group, the Igrun, often defied its instructions.

The PLO was invited in 1974 to discuss the Palestine question before the United Nations just as the Jewish Agency was in 1947. In that year, David Ben Gurion and six other representatives of the agency testified in support of the partition plan in front of UN committees. Even Dr.

Chaim Weizmann, president of the Zionist Organization, appeared before a U.N. committee to testify in favor of partitioning Palestine.

There are examples from other areas of the world. In a conflict situation like Vietnam, the legal questions of representation were sidetracked to allow a resolution of the conflict. The United States and the Viet Cong were both at the Paris Peace Conference prior to the end of the Vietnamese War. Similar examples can be drawn from Algeria, Korea, China, South Yemen, Zimbabwe/Rhodesia, and Namibia.

In fact, analogies can be drawn from the practice of the states that did not recognize (and were unfriendly to) each other. The United States and China as well as the United States and Cuba negotiated directly without answering the legal questions. Even some Arab states and Israel have negotiated on borders—at Geneva, Jerusalem, Cairo, and Camp David—prior to recognition.

Another Israeli argument for refusing to negotiate with the PLO was "reiterated in emotional terms" by Prime Minister Begin "on the ground that it (the PLO) is committed to the destruction of Israel."[87] In fact, this may have been Israel's strongest argument. However, even here historical analogies can be helpful. The Viet Cong, for example, were committed to the destruction of the South Vietnamese state. In spite of this, negotiations were held in Paris. Furthermore, the PLO itself has moved away from that objective and has now put forth a program aimed at establishing an independent Palestinian state in the Occupied Territories.

It seems to this writer that legal questions should be eliminated altogether if peaceful negotiations are intended. To clear up all the legal questions before peaceful negotiations may not be feasible or possible. Recognition, while important in law, is secondary in practice. Neither the PLO nor Israel should demand recognition prior to negotiations. Negotiations should aim at culminating in mutual recognition and recognition should not constitute a precondition to negotiations.

NOTES

1. Albert Camus, *The Rebel* (New York: Vintage Books, 1956), p. 13.
2. Charles G. Fenwick, *International Law* (New York: Century, 1924), pp. 106–107.
3. Rosalyn Higgins, *The Development of International Law Through the Political Organs of the United Nations* (London: Oxford University Press, 1963), p. 103.
4. Louis B. Sohn, *Cases on United Nations Law* (Brooklyn: Foundation Press, 1956), p. 808.
5. Alfred Cobban, *National Self-Determination* (London: Oxford University Press, 1945), p. 4.
6. Rupert Emerson, *Self-Determination Revisited in the Era of Decolonization*

(New Haven, Conn.: Houvert University Center for International Affairs, 1964), p. 31.

7. Cobban, *National Self-Determination*, p. 48.

8. See *Nationalism*, a report by a study group of members of the Royal Institute of International Affairs, 1939.

9. Golda Meir, a former Israeli prime minister, for example, argued that Palestinian nationalism does not exist. The Israeli government maintains that line. Palestinian leaders, on the other hand, insist that their people have a right to nationhood.

10. While the Zionists argue that Jews constitute a nation, many Jewish thinkers disagree. They agree that Judaism is merely a religion and disagree with Israel's claim that it reconstituted the old Jewish nation. However, it is clear today that Israeli Jews constitute a nation under international law.

11. Matti Peled, "Peled's Two-State Peace Proposal," *Journal of Palestine Studies* 6, no. 2 (Winter 1977), p. 160.

12. Great Britain, Foreign Office, Cmd. 1785, *Mandate for Palestine*, London: H. M. Stationery Office, 1922).

13. General Assembly Res. 2535 (XXIV), 10 December 1969, Part B.

14. General Assembly Res. 2649 (XXV), 30 November 1970.

15. General Assembly Res. 2792 (XXV), 8 December 1970.

16. General Assembly Res. 2792 (XXVI), 6 December 1971, Part D.

17. General Assembly Res. 2963 (XXVII), 13 December 1972, Part E.

18. General Assembly Res. 3070 (XXVIII), 7 December 1973, Part D.

19. General Assembly Res. 3089 (XXVIII), 7 December 1973, Part D.

20. General Assembly Res. 3210 (XXIX), 14 October 1974.

21. General Assembly Res. 3236 (XXIX), 22 November 1974.

22. Conference of Heads of State or Government of Non-Aligned Countries, Cairo, Egypt, October, 1964, quoted in *International Declarations on the Rights of the Palestinians* (Washington, D.C.: Free Palestine, 1975), p. 5.

23. Ibid., p. 5.

24. Adopted by the Council of Ministers at the 23rd Ordinary Session held in Mogadishe, Somalia, in June 1974, quoted in *Watha'eq Filastiniyah*, 1975 (Documents on Palestine) (Beirut: The Institute of Palestine Studies, 1975).

25. Statement by the Political Consultative Committee of the States Parties to the Warsaw Treaty, Warsaw, Poland, April 1974, quoted in *Watha'eq Filastiniyah*, 1975.

26. Golda Meir, *My Life* (New York: Putnam's, 1975), p. 406. See also Joseph L. Ryan, S. J., *Rome and Jerusalem: The Roman Catholic Church and the Middle East Crisis* (Beirut: NEEBII, no date).

27. Emerson, *Self-determination*, p. 64.

28. "Al-Mu'tamar al-Rabi' lil-Ittihad il-'Am lil-Ummal al-Filastiniyin" (Fourth Conference of the General Union of Palestine Workers), *Shu'un Filastiniyah* 5 (Nov. 1971), pp. 304–306.

29. "Al-Mu'tamar al-Sades lil-Ittihad il-'Am lil-'Talabah al-Filastiniyin" (Sixth National Conference of the General Union for Palestine Students), *Shu'un Filastiniyah* 5 (Nov. 1971), pp. 307–310.

30. *Falastin al-Thawra* (Revolutionary Palestine) (Beirut) 3, no. 135 (March 23, 1975), p. 1.

31. Ibid.
32. For text of these resolutions, see *Falastin al-Thawra*, various issues.
33. Isam Sakhnini, *P.L.O.: The Representative of the Palestinians* (Beirut: Palestine Research Center, 1974), p. 26.
34. See Ibrahim Abu-Lughod, *The Thirteenth Session of the Palestine National Council* (Detroit: Association of Arab-American University Graduates, 1978).
35. John Edwin Mroz, *Beyond Security* (New York: The International Peace Academy, 1980), p. 22.
36. Naji Aloush, *Debates on the Palestinian Revolution* (Beirut: n.p., 1970), p. 23.
37. Published by Fateh at the conclusion of the Ninth Palestine National Council, July, 1971.
38. Sakhnini, *P.L.O.*, p. 27.
39. *Falastin al-Thawra* 3, no. 123 (22 December 1974), p. 19.
40. *Al-Hadaf* (Beirut) 5, no. 231 (12 December 1973), p. 5.
41. Sakhnini, *P.L.O.*, p. 28.
42. *Gaza Daily* (Gaza) 17 September 1970, cited in *Al-Ahram* (Cairo) 5 May 1971.
43. *Al-Quds* (Jerusalem), 10 September 1970, cited in Ibid.
44. Ibid., 12 December 1976.
45. *Al-Sha'b* (Jerusalem), 26 October 1976.
46. Lea Ben Dor, "Talking for the PLO," *Jerusalem Post*, 19 November 1976.
47. *Washington Star*, January, 1977, cited in *Palestine* 3, no. 2 (1 February 1977), p. 5.
48. *As-Sha'b* (Jerusalem), 26 October 1976.
49. *Jerusalem Post*, 16 April 1976, p. 1.
50. Ibid., 2 May 1976, p. 1.
51. Zeev Schiff and Raphael Rothstein, *Fedayeen: Guerillas Against Israel* (New York: David McKay, 1972), pp. 203–204.
52. Cited in Frank H. Epp, *The Palestinians: Portrait of a People in Conflict* (Scottsdale, Pa.: Herald Press, 1976), p. 144.
53. Ibid.
54. Sakhnini, *P.L.O.*, p. 25.
55. *Time* Magazine, 19 July 1977, p. 34.
56. Taiseer Nabulsi, "Intikhabat al-Diffah al-Gharbiyah" (West Bank Elections), *Shu'un Filastiniyah* 11 (July 1972), p. 38.
57. Ibid., p. 39.
58. Ibid., p. 40.
59. Ibid., p. 47.
60. *The New York Times*, 14 April 1976, p. 1.
61. *The Washington Post*, 14 April 1976, p. 1.
62. *The New York Times*, 15 April 1976, p. 3.
63. Ibid., 14 April 1976, p. 1.
64. Ibid.
65. British Broadcasting Company, 15 April 1976, cited in *Swasia* 3, no. 16 (April 23, 1976), p. 3.
66. Josef Goell, "A Different Breed," *Jerusalem Post*, 7 May 1976.
67. Gholam H. Razi, "The Hashemite Kingdom of Jordan," in *The Middle East:*

Its Government and Politics, Abid A. Al-Marayati, ed. (Belmont, Mass.: Duxbury Press, 1972), p. 236.

68. Ghazi Khalili, "Durus al-Intifadah" (Lessons of the Uprising), *Shu'un Filastiniyah* 57 (May 1976), p. 23.

69. *Falastin al-Thawra* (Special Issue) January 1977, p. 50.

70. *Christian Science Monitor*, 19 February 1982, p. 13.

71. Ibid.

72. Sakhnini, *P.L.O.*, p. 18.

73. Quoted in *Watha'eq Filastiniyah*, 1974 (Documents on Palestine) (Beirut: The Institute of Palestine Studies, 1974), pp. 144–145.

74. *Newsweek*, 11 November 1974, p. 51.

75. PLO, *Al-Kitab al-Sanawi al-Filastini, 1964* (Palestine Yearbook, 1964) (Beirut: PLO Research Center, 1965), p. 87.

76. *International Declarations on the Rights of the Palestinians* (Washington, D.C.: Free Palestine Press, 1975), p. 12.

77. PLO, *Al-Kitab al-Sanawi al-Filastini, 1973* (Palestine Yearbook, 1973) (Beirut: PLO Research Center, 1973), p. 58.

78. PLO, *Al-Kitab al-Sanawi al Filastini, 1974* (Palestine Yearbook, 1974) (Beirut: PLO Research Center, 1974), p. 73.

79. Ibid., p. 139.

80. Fuad A. Jabber, ed., *International Documents on Palestine* (Beirut: The Institute of Palestine Studies, 1972), p. 234.

81. Ibid., 1974, p. 231.

82. Ibid., p. 252.

83. Sardar Muhammed, "Restoration of Human Rights of the Palestinian People: The Role of the United Nations and the Superpowers," paper presented at the Third United Nations Seminar on the Question of Palestine, 10–14 August 1981, Columbo, Sri Lanka, p. 102.

84. U.N. General Assembly Resolution No. 3210 (XXIX), 14 October, 1974.

85. U.N. General Assembly Resolution No. 3237 (XXIX), 22 November, 1974.

86. *Jerusalem Post*, 21 May 1976, p. 1.

87. *U.S. News and World Report*, 1 August 1977, p. 23.

3

Internal Organization

"The starting point in the liberation of Occupied Territories," the Palestinian leadership believes, "is the dependence upon the masses as a revolutionary power capable of eliminating occupation and direct colonization."[1] The Palestine Liberation Organization (PLO) has taken many steps to mobilize the masses. However, in spite of some successes, there have been some failures as well. The PLO itself, is perhaps not fully capable of total mobilization in that is is no more than a loose umbrella organization with limited control over the Palestinians and their organizations.

The current configuration of forces forming the PLO is the result of a gradual process of organizational and regional developments. As mentioned in Chapter 1, the Arab summit conference of January 1964 recommended that a Palestinian organization be formed. In pursuance of this recommendation, Ahmad al-Shukairy called for a Palestinian conference, which was held in Jerusalem on May 28, 1964. It was at that conference that the PLO was created.

THE FUNDAMENTAL LAW

The conference, known as the First Palestine National Council, drew up the Palestine National Covenant (see Appendix 2) and a proposed constitution for the PLO. The covenant laid down the national rights and obligations of the Palestinians.[2] It stressed the Arab character of Palestine (Article 1) and adopted three principles: National Unity, National Mobilization, and Liberation (Article 10). The proposed constitution, known as the Fundamental Law, constitutes the bylaws of the

PLO. The organization of the PLO, which will be discussed in this chapter, is set forth in the Fundamental Law.

It becomes clear after one looks at the Fundamental Law that the structure of the PLO is modelled after governmental institutions. Its organization is elaborate and its activities go far beyond the military needs of a guerrilla movement. In fact, structurally and functionally the PLO is a quasi-government.

Similar to the constitution of a country, the Fundamental Law prescribes that all Palestinians are natural members of the PLO (Article 4). This law subordinates organizational relations to the national struggle and its needs under a system of collective leadership (Article 3).

THE MAJOR POLICYMAKING BODIES OF THE PLO

The Fundamental Law established the two major policymaking organs of the PLO, which are based on governmental legislative-executive models: the Palestine National Council and the Executive Committee.

The National Council

Similar to a parliament, the Palestine National Council (PNC) is the supreme authority of the PLO. It draws up the policies, plans, and programs for the organization (Article 7).

Members of the National Council are supposed to be elected directly by the people of Palestine (Article 5). However, the law prescribes that in case it is not possible to hold such elections, the present (1964) council will continue to function until favorable conditions prevail (Article 6). So far it has not been possible to hold direct elections. Nevertheless, the council membership has been revised, as will be discussed later in this chapter.

Normally, the council serves for a three-year period (Article 8). It has a presidency office composed of a president, two vice-presidents, and a secretary general elected at the first session of each council (Article 9). During its session, the council considers the following policy matters (Article 10):

1. The annual report of the Executive Committee. This report details the achievements of the PLO and its organs.
2. The budget known as the National Fund. The fund must be approved annually by the council.
3. Suggestions and plans of the various committees.
4. Any other issue submitted for its consideration including amendments to the covenant and the Fundamental Law as well as all major policy matters.

The Executive Committee

The Fundamental Law of 1964 prescribes that an executive committee of fifteen members (Article 14) shall be the highest executive authority in the PLO (Article 15). It seems that, like other colonized people, the Palestinians' political future has been influenced by the colonial power. A modified version of the British cabinet system seems to be the backbone of the executive branch of the PLO.

Originally, it was the chairman, not the committee, who was named by the National Council. In turn, the chairman (prime minister) selected the members of the Executive Committee (Article 13). However, later changes resulted in the election of all fifteen members of the committee. Duties of the committee were set as follows (Article 16):

1. Representation of the Palestinian people.

2. Supervision of the different institutions of the organization.

3. Issuing periodic directions and adopting the necessary decisions to organize the functions of the PLO.

4. Executing the policies of the PLO, including financial matters.

The Fundamental Law also gives the Executive Committee the right to establish the necessary departments (Article 18). Departments established in 1964 by the Executive Committee included a Liberation Department, a Department of the Budget (Palestine National Fund), a Department of Public Affairs and National Guidance, and a number of others. These, however, have since gone through a process of reorganization, as indicated in the organizational Chart of the PLO.

Article 22 provides for the establishment of Palestinian military units. Such units were formed with the agreement and approval of the Arab states. They became a conventional Palestinian army known as the Palestine Liberation Army (PLA). Recruitment for the PLA came from the Palestinian population.

It is evident then that the birth of the PLO was contemplated by Arab governments and highly influenced by Arab thinking. Conventional warfare, rather than a guerrilla war of national liberation, was the underlying philosophy of the founders of the PLO. In a matter of two years, the PLO had built up an elaborate if not very dynamic bureaucratic structure.[3] At this stage of the organization's development, therefore, the PLO was merely a political movement that "raised the hopes of the Palestinian people," but was contained within the Arab framework.[4]

Figure 1

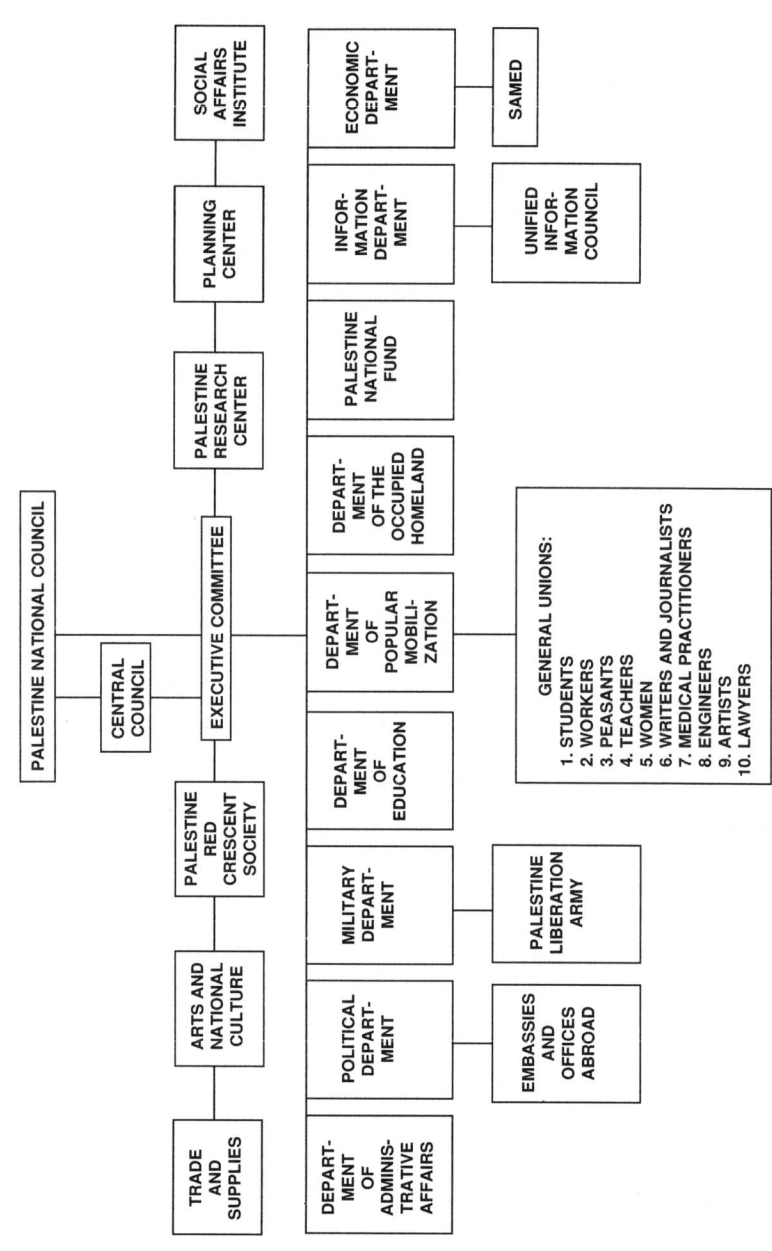

INTERNAL CONFLICTS

Many Palestinians supported the new organization. They felt that it set the stage for their involvement in the struggle for the liberation of their country. Most of the Arab governments, also, supported the PLO, and none expressed opposition. However, a significant number of Palestinian intellectuals had misgivings.[5] They reasoned that, since the PLO was the creation of the Arab states, it had been formed partly to contain the growing power and influence of the Palestinians. To support their argument, they cited Shukairy's subordination of the PLO to the policies of the Arab states.[6] In fact, Shukairy had no alternative, since he was the appointee of the Arab League.

This subordination, coupled with Shukairy's reputation as an autocratic and irresponsible propagandist, is cited by Quandt, Jabber, and Lesch as the reason for the internal leadership crisis of 1966–67.[7] Shukairy's opposition to commando activities against Israel, however, may have been the major factor behind the opposition he faced. Prior to 1967, the PLO stressed the notion of conventional warfare rather than guerrilla warfare. PLO leaders actually believed that the Arab states and armies would ultimately be strong enough to defeat Israel and return all of Palestine to the Palestinians. This position led the PLO to reject the notion of guerrilla warfare culminating in the opposition of those who supported the guerrillas. This opposition came from many rank and file members of the PLO. Prominent among them were Shafiq al-Hut, director of the Beirut PLO bureau and General Wajih al-Madani, commander-in-chief of the PLA.

The opposition eventually became so intense that Shukairy dissolved the Executive Committee in an attempt to dislodge the dissidents. This move, however, backfired and "by mid-February 1967 there were reports of a widespread movement in Palestinian circles designed to reassert the principle of collective leadership within the PLO and in support of fedayeen action."[8] A week later, Shukairy bowed to the pressure and formed a new Executive Committee, which included some opposition members. It was in this atmosphere of crisis that Shafiq al-Hut described the PLO as a "house without walls or roof."[9]

The overwhelming Arab defeat in the June 1967 war took the Arab people by surprise. This defeat was seen as proof that to rely on the Arab governments and regular armies to liberate Palestine would lead nowhere.[10] It strengthened opposition to Shukairy within the PLO and gave the Palestinian guerrilla movement, operating separately and semi-clandestinely, new opportunities. (Chapter 4 details the rise of the guerrilla movement.)

In fact, the Palestinian guerrilla movement predates the PLO by scores of years. Palestinian guerrillas had been on the Middle Eastern scene as early as 1931, when Shaykh Izz el-Din al-Qassam organized his anti-Zionist, anti-British campaign. However, with their defeat in 1948, the Palestinians became dependent upon the Arab states. By 1958, they began organizing for a new guerrilla movement. On January 1, 1965, the guerrillas became a military reality with Fateh's first commando operation in Israel. After the 1967 Arab defeat, the Palestinian guerrilla movement became the symbol of the Arab masses and a new and major force in Mid-Eastern politics as will be discussed in Chapter 4. Prior to the war of 1967, the commando groups were very small, with only limited backing by the Palestinians. Only Syria, of all the Arab states, gave them support. After the war, however, Palestinians lost hope in being able to achieve their goal by means of Arab states and their armies and felt that the only recourse left was guerrilla warfare.

Faced with a major defeat, a strengthened opposition, and a growing mass support for the guerrilla movement, Shukairy resigned his PLO leadership position on December 4, 1967—prior to the Fourth Palestine National Council session held on July 10, 1968. This council meeting was attended by representatives of the different guerrilla organizations.[11] The council elected Yahya Hammuda, a noncontroversial lawyer, in place of Shukairy.

The Guerrillas Take Over

Among the most decisive and far-reaching consequences of the June 1967 war were the growth of Palestinian nationalism and the emergence of the new militant guerrilla groups as a significant force in Arab politics. These developments forced new realities upon those concerned with the Arab-Israeli conflict. For many years after the establishment of Israel, the Arab-Israeli conflict was considered by most Western, Arab, and Israeli observers as one involving Israel and the neighboring Arab states. The Palestinians were seen merely as refugees and their plight as a humanitarian concern.

Even after the 1967 war, Israel, the Western powers, the Soviet Union, and most Arab states continued to consider the problem as one between Israel and the Arab states (as evidenced by Security Council Resolution 242). As late as June 15, 1969, Golda Meir, then Israel's prime minister, was reported in *The Times* of London to say: "There was no such thing as Palestinians. It was not as though there was a Palestinian people and we came and threw them out and took their country away from them. They did not exist."[12]

Today, not only the major powers but also many Israelis recognize that the Palestinians are at the core of the Arab-Israeli conflict. Now, the world realizes that "any decision concerning Palestine would be impossible without the Palestinians."[13] This development was largely due to the growth and prominence of the Palestinian commando organizations.

The popularity of the commandos, coupled with their intention to join—and perhaps even take over—the PLO rather than just remain as an alternative to it, led to their eventual control of that organization. This control was facilitated by the already existing power struggle within the ranks of the PLO. By 1968, the majority of the PLO rank and file had come to support the concept of armed struggle, and thus, the strategy of the commando groups. The Karameh battle on March 31, 1968 increased support for the commandos. That battle, which will be discussed in Chapter 4, gave the Palestinians a sense of achievement through guerrilla warfare only a few months after the disaster faced by regular Arab armies in June of 1967. Dependence on the Arab regimes had by now become discredited just as the Arab regimes themselves were discredited after their defeat in the 1967 war. Moreover, the popularity of the guerrilla groups and their style of warfare among the Palestinian and Arab masses made it difficult, if not impossible, for the PLO officials to oppose the guerrilla leadership. The first act to be taken by the guerrillas regarding the PLO was to amend the National Covenant. The Fourth National Council, convened in Cairo on July 10–17, 1968, voted in favor of the proposed amendments. The membership of that council had undergone drastic changes. The number of delegates was reduced to only 100, and the traditional faces disappeared. The guerrillas argued that the PLO should consist of armed fighters, not "arm-chair revolutionaries."[14] Fateh's style "is recognizable in the new Covenant."[15]

Perhaps the most significant amendment in the covenant was the insertion of the revolutionary doctrine that "armed struggle is the only way to liberate Palestine; it is therefore a strategy and not a tactic" (Article 9). Article 10, also amended by the Fourth Council, states that "commando action is the nucleus of the Palestinian popular liberation war."

By February, 1969, the commandos were in control. The National Council meeting in February, 1969, was numerically dominated by the commando groups. This numerical advantage was turned into a political victory leading to the election of Fateh's official spokesman, Yasser Arafat, as chairman of the PLO Executive Committee. Fateh, as will be seen in the next chapter, was and remains the largest guerrilla organization. With its position enhanced, Fateh set out to achieve what its predecessors could not, namely integration of the military efforts of all the Palestinian army and commando organizations.

Problems of Integration

While most Palestinian commando groups agree on objectives, serious differences developed among them over ideology and tactics. Initially, the commando organizations accepted each other as competitors. It was generally believed that armed struggle should precede mobilization of the masses.

Professor Hisham Sharabi explains the multiplicity of guerrilla organizations in a historical context. He argues that "all liberation movements in the twentieth century have experienced two fundamental transformations before emerging as united fronts.... The first stage of revolutionary activity always saw the almost simultaneous rise of several groups, which, though different from one another in organization and ideology, strove toward the same goals." In the second stage, tension is resolved "either by unification within a broad framework or by fragmentation and eventual collapse."[16]

By controlling the PLO in February, 1969, Fateh was in a position to attempt unification. The first move in this direction was the formation of the Palestine Armed Struggle Command (PASC) in April 1969. All Palestinian military and commando groups became members of the PASC, except for the Popular Front for the Liberation of Palestine (PFLP), which differed with Fateh on ideological grounds. In February 1970, the PFLP joined as well, and the PASC was renamed the "Unified Command." Therefore, for the first time since their inception, the Palestine guerrilla forces and military units joined hands within the formal structure of the PLO. This unity, as will be noted later, may have been influenced by the common perception of a threat to their existence from the Jordanian regime. In May 1970, this paper unity was turned into a more meaningful framework when all members of the Unified Command signed an agreement which "articulated ... a common programme, and which served as an instrument of mutual recognition."[17]

The agreement stated that, "All resistance movement groups regard the Palestine Liberation Organization as the broad framework for national unity." It further emphasized the belief of all groups in "popular revolutionary war" as "the main path to the liberation of Palestine." The most significant clause, perhaps, was that which committed all groups on matters agreed upon by the Unified Command and those "related to the security of the revolution...."[18]

All commando groups attended the seventh Palestine National Council held in late May and early June 1970. There they agreed to form a Central Committee of the PLO. The Central Committee is composed of twenty-seven members including all members of the Executive Committee, a representative from each commando group, three independent members and the chairman of the Council. Following a confrontation with the Jordanian army, a general secretariat of the Central Committee was established. The general secretariat was formed of six members representing the larger Palestinian organizations. "Although the executive committee continued to exist, for all practical purposes its authority had been transferred to the more representative central committee and the general secretariat."[19]

Unity of the commando groups, therefore, has been an objective of the PLO since its domination by these groups. Indeed, some commando organizations such as the PFLP have constantly rejected unity if it meant their domination by Fateh. These groups differ with Fateh on ideology. While Fateh is basically nationalist, these groups have persistently emphasized the importance of ideology for the promotion of the objectives of the PLO. Therefore, these groups, in spite of introducing the element of disunity within Palestinian ranks, have been a modernizing factor in Palestinian politics as they introduced the ideas of Marx, Lenin, Mao, and Trotsky into Palestinian political thought. Their cooperation with the PLO, however, has been forthcoming so long as it did not contradict their ideological tenets.

In fact, the issue of disunity among the Palestinians may have been overemphasized by the observers. As Abu Omar, a Fateh leader, put it: "What unites these commando movements is much greater than that which divides us—if we look not at our rhetoric but at our action."[20] The May 1970 agreement, the ensuing struggle with the Jordanian regime, and the Lebanese crisis (discussed in Chapter 5) may have proven Abu Omar right. However, in spite of all the factors that unite the Palestinian commando groups, there remain some sources of disunity. The friction and lack of cohesiveness do not derive from differences over objectives, but rather from tactical problems. Personalities and style are also a source of friction. Loyalty to certain Arab regimes may be another. But the most important cause of friction stems from disagreement about the role the PLO should play in achieving a peaceful settlement.

All of the above conflicts could have a negative influence upon the representative character of the PLO and its very legitimacy could thus be put in question. Such a situation will only benefit Israel as it continues its process of Judaization of the occupied lands. This situation will also allow for the interference of others in the internal affairs of the Palestinians because a house divided upon itself tactically and strategically cannot hope to stand firmly and prevent others from muddling in its affairs.

National unity helped the PLO gain recognition during the early stage of its development. Changes, however, were required after recognition was achieved. The fact that for a long time the PLO continued to depend on consensus in decision making eventually led to divisions within its ranks. Consequently, the next stage for the PLO development was to change its understanding of national unity. For sometimes it seemed that the PLO was condemned to have either unanimity without strategy or strategy without unanimity. By 1988, however, the PLO seemed to have acquired a new understanding of national unity. The program adopted at the November 1988 PNC meeting was passed by majority rather than consensus.

In spite of the differences and lack of unity among the commando groups, the PLO remains a solid framework for potential cooperation and mutual planning. Its unity of purpose has made this possible. The PLO today has its own well-trained, well-equipped forces, its own hospitals, schools, factories, social security system and even tax collectors. Its administration has grown from a small insignificant level to one which is as large and as effective as that of some contemporary governments.

ORGANIZATIONAL DEVELOPMENT

At its inception, the PLO was a weak and dependent organization. Today, the PLO has not only achieved a degree of independence but has become a recognized actor in Middle Eastern politics. Unlike other revolutionary bodies, the PLO does not conform to the usual rules of revolution. It began where revolutions ought to end, and then only if they are successful: with an administrative machinery comparable to that of a government.

At the time of its establishment, the PLO was developed out of a governmental model. By 1977, it had developed into a large establishment with representatives and regional offices throughout the world. Frank H. Epp, a professor of Middle Eastern politics, in his book, *The Palestinians*, portrays the PLO as a government. To some Palestinians, he reports, the National Council is the parliament of the Palestinians, the Executive Committee is the cabinet of ministers, and the regional offices are embassies.[21] However, the PLO does not perceive itself as a government in spite of all the structural similarities between itself and governments.

In order to trace the development of the PLO since its inception, it is necessary to study the sessions of the Palestine National Council. It is at these sessions that major organizational developments have been most apparent.

The significance of the First Palestine National Council cannot be exaggerated. It was at this meeting, held on May 28, 1964, that the PLO was born. The National Covenant and the Fundamental Law that stated the mission as well as the guidelines for the operation of the PLO were drawn up at this meeting. The Fundamental Law laid down the bases for the organizational framework and interrelationships constituting the PLO. The earlier discussion of the Fundamental Law in this chapter points to its significance for this study.

The second session of the council was held on May 31, 1965 at Cairo. One of the significant resolutions of this session was the decision to impose a mandatory draft upon all Palestinian males who became eighteen years of age, as had already been initiated in the Gaza Strip. The council also paid attention to Palestinian women and urged their incorporation into the activities of the organization. As a result of this call, the General Union of Palestinian Women was later established. However, the most important resolution may have been the adoption of the Popular Mobilization Law. This law, as will be discussed later, aimed at activating the Palestinian masses in support of the PLO.

Due to conflicts within the PLO and with various other parties like the Jordanian regime, the third session probably was the least important of all sessions. This session was held in May 1966 at Gaza. The leadership had promised the election of a new National Council, but none was elected. Council members witnessed a military display of live ammunition put on by the Liberation Army, heard speeches by the leadership, and carried no resolutions of major significance.

If the third session was the least productive, the fourth session may have been the most important in the short history of the PLO. Held on June 10–17, 1968 at Cairo, the session was the first after the 1967 Arab-Israeli War and came in the aftermath of the battle of Karameh. All of Palestine had now fallen under Israeli occupation. Shukairy had resigned as chairman of the Executive Committee and the Fedayeen (Commandos) had captured the hearts of the Arab people as the alternative to a regular army of liberation. As the previous sessions included almost 400 members each, this one had one hundred. This number was based on a compromise with the commando groups in order to incorporate them officially within the PLO. The old leadership had been integrated into the revolutionary movement. The new membership list included thirty-eight names representing the permanent officers of Fateh, and also included the following Palestinian guerrilla movements:

1. Palestine National Liberation Movement (Fateh).
2. Vanguards of the Popular Liberation War (Sa'iqah).
3. Palestine Liberation Movement.
4. General Committee in Support of the Revolution.
5. Palestinian Revolutionaries Front.
6. Palestinian Popular Liberation Front.
7. Movement of Revolutionary Young Palestinians.
8. Vanguards of Sacrifice Movement.[22]

The membership also included ten representatives of the Popular Front for the Liberation of Palestine. The front incorporated three groups: The Vengeance Youth, Heroes of the Return, and the Palestine Liberation Front. Twenty members represented the Palestine Liberation Army and the Popular Liberation Forces, the official military organs of the PLO. Only three members represented the unions: one for the General Union of Palestinian Students, one for the General Union of Palestinian Workers and one for the General Union of Palestinian Women.

It is clear that a major shift had occurred in the makeup and emphasis of the PLO at this juncture. Forty-eight percent of the delegates of the council came directly from the commando groups. The rest of the delegates generally supported the guerrillas. Therefore, guerrilla groups rather than a political leadership became the spokesmen of the Palestinians. Guerrilla warfare rather than conventional warfare had taken the forefront of the PLO strategy.

As a result, it was inescapable that other shifts should occur. The National Covenant was amended to incorporate some radical changes. The Fundamental Law and the Popular Mobilization Law were also changed. It must be pointed out here that, from a technical point of view, the amendments to the covenant did not properly conform to Article 33 of the covenant, which stipulates: "This Charter is not to be modified except with a majority of 2/3rds of the National Council of the Palestine Liberation Organization in a special session to be convened for that purpose." Since the amendments were adopted at a regular session and not a "special session" they were technically improper.[23]

As was mentioned earlier, the revised covenant stressed guerrilla warfare as the new strategy of liberation. As will be seen in the next chapter, Fateh's "style is recognizable in the new covenant."[24] This version of the covenant remains in force today, and no new changes have been adopted since.

Members attending the fourth session of the council felt that the old Popular Mobilization Law was not adequate due to the new conditions brought about by the 1967 war. The new version of this law stressed the organization of the Palestinians according to profession rather than their place of residence.

The Fundamental Law changed the least. Article 30 replaced the old council with the new one in its membership; Article 31 limited the term of office of the council to two years. It also stipulated that, in case elections for a new council were not held within two years, the present one would meet and decide the matter. A new article was also added to give the council the right to add new members to its body. Article 8 regarding annual sessions of the council was changed to require semi-annual meetings. Jerusalem, which now was under Israeli occupation, was made the permanent headquarters of the National Council.

The fifth session of the council was held in Cairo in February 1969. At this session, the first election for the Executive Committee took place. As noted earlier, prior to this session the chairman of the committee was the only elected member who, in turn, named all members of the committee. The newly elected chairman of the Executive Committee was

Yasser Arafat, the leader of Fateh. Also for the first time, the council president was a different person from the chairman of the Executive Committee. Mr. Yahya Hammuda remained as president of the council, but his office was upgraded to equal that of the chairman of the Executive Committee in duties as well as pay. The newly elected Executive Committee of eleven members included "four members of Fateh, three Fateh sympathizers, two Sa'iqa representatives and one Sa'iqa sympathizer, as well as a holdover from the old PLO executive committee.[25]

One hundred and twelve members attended the sixth session of the council held in Cairo between September 7 and 9 of 1969. The council adopted a resolution granting eight seats to the Popular Democratic Front for the Liberation of Palestine (PDFLP) and raised the number of seats granted to the General Union of Palestinian Workers from one to five. The General Union of Palestinian Students was also granted two seats in addition to their previous single seat. A seat representing the General Union of Palestinian Women was also added, giving this union its second seat on the council. The Palestine Liberation Army, on the other hand, lost five seats and was to be represented by its general commander only, thus bringing about a greater separation between the military and politics. Four new independent members were also added to the council.

A significant resolution of the sixth session was the creation of a revolutionary court under the PLO. The Executive Committee was empowered with the authority to appoint a panel of judges known as the Palestinian Revolutionary Court. The court was given the task of trying any Palestinian brought before it by the Executive Committee on matters relating to Palestinian national interest. Thus, at this session the PLO completed the establishment of its governmental institutions by introducing the third branch of government: a judicial system.[26] The court was charged with litigating cases that relate to discipline within the PLO and those relating to treason against the Palestinian people.

The seventh session of the council met in Cairo from May 30 to June 4, 1970. Its 115 members established a Central Committee, which, as noted earlier, was an attempt to unify all guerrilla groups. The Central Committee included all members of the Executive Committee and representatives of all Palestinian guerrilla groups. The seventh council also established a unified military command for all Palestinian military forces, including the commandos.

Soon after the session ended, developments in Jordan reached a level whereby a confrontation between the guerrillas and the regime was imminent. The Central Committee called for an extraordinary session of the council. That session was held in Amman in August 1970. It produced no organizational changes but issued a proclamation condemning American peace initiatives and urging the Central Committee to establish a joint commission with other Arab revolutionaries to lead the fight against "imperialism, Zionism, and all traitors."[27]

Soon afterwards, the confrontation with the Jordanian regime took the shape of a civil war. The PLO and the guerrillas were eventually ousted from Jordan. It was with this background that the eighth session of the National Council was held. This session was officially opened in Cairo on February 28, 1971, and lasted until March 5, 1971. The Ansar Organization—a new guerrilla group—participated, and for the first time Palestinians under Israeli occupation were represented. Three Arabs from Occupied Palestine attended as representatives of the Palestinians under occupation. In this session, it was resolved that a unified military establishment be founded among all Palestinian groups at all levels of training, organization, arms, and action. The Palestine National Fund was also proclaimed the fund of all the Palestinian people and their revolution. All financial matters of the guerrilla groups and the PLO were to become a part of the fund. Thus, a greater unity among the Palestinians was achieved, at least for the time being.

It was the relationship of the PLO with the Jordanian regime that preoccupied the ninth session, held in July 1971. Because of the military defeats in Jordan, it had become evident to the council that there should be more emphasis on Palestinian civic and professional mass organizations. Therefore, union representation was expanded from ten to twenty-six representatives. At this session, the Central Committee was eliminated because of new tensions among the commando groups.

The tenth session, which followed a popular conference of 500 Palestinian members, was held at Cairo on April 6–12, 1972. The council adopted the recommendations of the conference, the main topic of which was national unity.[28] The resolutions called for total unification of all Palestinian military entities within one institution, unification of all tax and collection systems and expenditures within the Palestinian National Fund, unification of all news and public relations agencies into a centralized system, and the merger of the foreign offices of all Palestinian groups under the PLO. The council also resolved to expand its membership of 180 representatives to incorporate all sectors of the Palestinian population.

To implement its resolutions, the council established a special National Unity Committee of twenty-two members to follow up and aid the Executive Committee in this matter. Unity of the media centers and tax collections was implemented soon after the council recessed. Also, an Arab front of all parties and groups sympathethic to the PLO was formed in November 1972. However, unity at other levels was not achieved to the satisfaction of the council.[29] Serious disagreements over tactics remained. Those disagreements centered on issues of international operations such as the hijacking of planes. Fateh opposed such activities while the PFLP refused an outright rejection of them.

It is for this reason that the eleventh session again took up the issue of national unity in its January 1973 meeting. It resolved to establish a Higher Military Council, headed by the chairman of the Executive Committee. The council included the military department head of the PLO and a representative of each commando group. It became the supreme commander of all Palestinian military and guerrilla units. The session also decided to establish a Central Council as a link between the National Council and the Executive Committee. It was deemed necessary for this council to meet quarterly to see that resolutions of the National Council are being implemented and to aid the Executive Committee in such matters. The Central Council was headed by the president of the National Council and its membership of nineteen to twenty-three included four from Fateh, two from Sa'iqah, two from the PFLP, two from the Arab Liberation Front, six from the unions, and five independents.

One of the consequences of the Arab-Israeli War that occurred in October 1973 was Arab (Jordanian, Syrian, and Egyptian) acceptance of U.N. Security Council Resolution 338—which reiterated Security Council Resolution 242—and a rise in Arab willingness to sign a peace treaty with Israel. Obviously, such moves were considered contrary to the objectives of the PLO National Covenant and led to the deterioration of PLO-Arab relations (specifically with Egypt). Such developments forced a delay in the convening of the twelfth session of the National Council. But by June 1974 the PLO was able to patch up its deteriorating relations with Egypt, which facilitated the convening of the session on June 1–6, 1974 with about 150 delegates attending. Naturally, the main topic of discussion was the peace initiatives. The council proclaimed its rejection of U.N. Resolutions 242 and 338, which were considered the basis for the negotiation of an Arab-Israeli peace. It also rejected Jordanian claims to represent the Palestinians and called for the establishment of an independent national authority over any part of Palestine that may be liberated.[30]

This session revealed a major shift both in the PLO's goal and tactics. The council authorized the chairman of the Executive Committee to attend any Geneva Conference on the Middle East. Presumably, this meant an authorization to Mr. Arafat to accept a peace settlement with Israel if Palestinian rights (at least in the West Bank and Gaza) were recognized. This could be interpreted as the PLO's first move away from its position on the necessity of armed struggle for the purpose of creating a secular, democratic state in all of Palestine. Consequently, diplomacy became an acceptable option and an independent Palestinian state in the West Bank and the Gaza Strip became an alternative and, perhaps, acceptable objective. This authorization so outraged some commando groups that the Popular Front for the Liberation of Palestine (PFLP) and the Arab Liberation Front (ALF) refused to put forth nominees for seats on the Executive Committee.

At the organizational level, the council resolved to expand the Executive Committee to include three members of the newly found National Front for the Liberation of Palestine. This front was founded among the Arabs of the West Bank in cooperation with the PLO.

The thirteenth session of the National Council was held in Cairo on March 12–20, 1977. "While that meeting was [held] about a year and a half later than scheduled, those familiar with the traumatic events that afflicted the Arab world need no explanation of the underlying reasons for the delay..."[31] Professor Ibrahim Abu-Lughod, who attended the council session as a Palestinian-American delegate, cites the Lebanese War and the Sinai pact as the factors behind the delay.

The council was expanded to include 293 members. The additional members represented occupational and geographic concentrations. "More emphasis was given to individuals who were outside the mainstream of existing political/military organizations."[32] However, politically, the "membership reflected the dominance of Fateh on the Palestinian scene."[33] Political issues dominated the discussions. These included the Lebanese crisis, peace initiatives, rapprochement with Jordan, and contacts with Israeli elements. The council adopted a political program of fifteen resolutions that "projected once more the progressive orientation of the Palestine Revolution and its affirmative posture."[34] Only thirteen votes allotted to the PFLP were cast against the program. These votes were "directed against the Executive Committee's rapprochement with the Jordanian regime and its interaction with the Arab states (Egypt and Syria)."[35]

Most significant in the program approved at this session was the emphasis placed upon the Palestinian right to self-determination as well as their right to establish their independent national state on their soil. This objective has since been interpreted to mean a state on the West Bank and Gaza. The program also stressed the necessity for PLO participation in "all" international conferences related to the Palestine question and formally accepted a specific U.N. General Assembly resolution. That resolution, 3236 of November 22, 1974, reaffirmed the Palestinians right to self-determination and their right to national independence.

The fourteenth session convened in Damascus at the heels of the Camp David agreements. It met from January 15 to January 23, 1979. Naturally, this session was preoccupied with drafting a response to the Camp David Accords. The Program rejected the Camp David agreements as a "conspiracy" against the Palestinians and reaffirmed Palestinian rights to self-determination and independent statehood. Interestingly, the Camp David agreements also helped normalize Jordanian-PLO relations. The council's resolutions affirmed the Jordanian-Palestinian "fraternal" relations and requested that solidarity between their peoples should continue. Moreover, the council dealt with internal Palestinian affairs. Most significant among those was the issue of bureaucratization of the PLO structures. By now, the various departments of the PLO had developed a clear bureaucracy that was burdened with many of the ailments inflicting third-world bureaucracies. Corruption, mismanagement, and even nepotism had become a not so unusual feature of the PLO's institutional infrastructures. Consequently, the council empowered the Executive Committee to review the departments and organs of the PLO in a manner that will take "merit" and "quality" into account in order to achieve "optimal performance" from these departments and organs.

The next session was also held in Damascus. It took place on April 11–16, 1981 and culminated in a political statement that reaffirmed previous resolutions regarding collective leadership, institutional efficiency, and a host of condemnations of "Zionism and imperialism." The meeting was held in Damascus, and Syria's influence upon the PLO was evident in the statement. Of all PNC sessions, this one, perhaps, was least significant in terms of setting new trends or initiating new policies.

The sixteenth session of the PNC met after the Israeli invasion of Lebanon and the commando exodus from South Lebanon and Beirut. By now, a PLO rift with Syria was beginning to become evident. But the meeting took place prior to the open rift within the ranks of Fateh. Because Mr. Arafat feared Syrian intervention in the affairs of the PLO, the meeting was convened in Algiers in February of 1983. Confronted with a serious setback in Lebanon, the various Palestinian factions needed to portray a semblance of unity. Therefore, the resolutions stressed Palestinian national unity and affirmed the desire of all commando groups to work within the framework of the PLO. Most significant, however, were the resolutions relating to the peaceful settlement of the Palestinian-Israeli conflict. Unlike previous resolutions condemning peace initiatives, this session can be considered a hallmark in that regard. The resolutions accepted the Arab peace plan proposed at the Fez summit of September 6, 1982. They also accepted the Brezhnev peace plan of September 16, 1980. Both plans called for Arab-Israeli peace in return for the establishment of an independent Palestinian state in the West Bank and Gaza. Moreover, instead of an outright rejection of the Reagan peace plan of September 1, 1982, the PNC only pointed to shortcomings as far as the Palestinians were concerned and refused to consider it. However, the conferees took a step in the direction of the Reagan peace plan when they authorized the Executive Committee to develop a harmonious relationship with Jordan with the objective of establishing a future confederation between an independent Palestinian state and Jordan.

In all, the sixteenth session can be seen as a landmark session whereby the PLO began a process of accommodation rather than rejection. While they historically rejected peace proposals, now they were accepting them—sometimes with serious reservations. Ironically, it was Israel that began its process of rejectionism as they rejected all three peace proposals.

At the administrative level, however, which is the main focus of this chapter, the sixteenth session adopted no resolutions and introduced no new programs. Soon after this session, Fateh was to face a major rebellion among its ranks. As will be discussed in Chapter 4, the rebellion had the effect of splitting the ranks of Fateh and contributed to a deeper split among the commando groups in general as well as widening the rift between Mr. Arafat, chairman of the Executive Committee, and the Syrian regime. Arafat and his loyal Fateh forces were even eventually evicted from their remaining strongholds in Lebanon by a coordinated Syrian-Palestinian (anti-Arafat factions) effort. With these developments, the very survival of the PLO came into question.

It was against this background that the seventeenth session of the council met in Amman, Jordan on November 22, 1984. The fact that Mr. Arafat was able to muster enough attendance to hold the meeting was, by itself, a personal victory for the PLO chief. It also provided him an opportunity to vindicate his policies. Aside from the political program adopted, the most significant contribution of this session to the functioning of the PLO was its departure from the practice of achieving consensus on resolutions. This practice had had the effect of giving a veto power to small factions within the PLO. This time, however, many commando groups did not attend the session and a consensus was not possible. Consequently, even more moderate resolutions were passed. These resolutions were worded in broad terms to avoid further alienation of the factions that boycotted the session. The council gave its support to the rapprochement between the PLO and Jordan, and it agreed to cooperation with Jewish democratic forces that support the struggle of the Palestinians—and no longer simply with those forces opposed to Zionism. They also accepted King Hussein's call for an international conference and insisted upon full PLO participation in it. The council even praised the Egyptian government for its support for the PLO and called for the return of Egypt to the Arab ranks. Moreover, the council authorized the Executive Committee to proceed with its negotiations with Jordan to find an acceptable formula for their mutual efforts at achieving a resolution of the Palestinian problem. Administratively, the council simply reaffirmed previous PNC resolutions and approved a budget that was designed to maintain all PLO infrastructures and rebuild those that were destroyed in Lebanon.

The eighteenth session was held in Algiers in April of 1987. This session was hailed as the session of national unity. The major groups that boycotted the Amman meeting attended and resolutions adopted called for an international peace conference, supported contacts with "democratic" Israeli forces opposed to the occupation, and elected, for the first time, a member of the Palestinian Communist Party to the Executive Committee. Organizationally, this session elected seventy-five-members to the Central Council and empowered it with authority similar to that of the PNC.

The outbreak of the intifada made the next session, held in Algiers in November 1988, the most significant since the creation of the PLO. At that session, the PNC proclaimed the state of Palestine. Subsequently, the central council elected Yasser Arafat to the post of president of the state of Palestine. The territorial boundaries of the state of Palestine were deemed to be those of the occupied Palestinian territories of the West Bank and the Gaza Strip, including the old city of Jerusalem. The political program adopted at this session recognized all U.N. resolutions, including Security Council resolutions 242 and 338. It was in the wake of this program and later clarifications that the U.S. began its substantive dialogue with the PLO.

It becomes clear to observers reviewing the developments of the PLO that there are many problems hindering its progress. However, it is also true that the PLO has achieved many successes since its inception in 1964. Administratively, the PLO is more complex today than it was in 1964. Its organizational pyramid incorporates many departments that carry out tasks comparable to those carried out by the ministries of a government.

The most important of these are: the Political Department; Military Department; Information Department; Department of Popular Mobilization; the Palestine National Fund; the Occupied Homeland Department; and the Department of Education. Also, there are a number of important semi-independent institutions within the PLO. These include the Palestine Red Crescent Society, the Research Center, the Social Affairs Institute, and the Samed Society.

In order to further understand the contention of this researcher that the PLO operates in a governmental fashion, a look at each of these departments and institutions is helpful. Obviously, the short reviews of these administrative operations cannot be considered as a complete account of all the activities of these entities. It is to be seen as merely a blueprint or a sketch of these operations.

The Political Department

Similar to a ministry of foreign affairs, the political department is responsible for relations with governments and international organizations. Being one of the earliest departments established by the Executive Committee, the political department has opened offices throughout the world. Today, its offices extend all the way from Tokyo to New York. The political department also participates in many international conferences and organizations, including the United Nations. Mr. Farouk Kaddoumi, head of the political department, summarizes the achievements of his office since 1964 by saying: "The independent Palestinian entity has developed in a clear fashion... to make the Palestinian feel his identity, personality, and belonging to the revolution with pride."[36] In fact, as will be discussed in Chapter 6, the PLO has been more successful at the international level than it has been in regional politics. Today, the PLO has offices with some diplomatic privileges in more than 100 countries and information offices in many more states.

The Military Department

Established at the fourth session of the Palestine National Council, this department is charged with supervising all military forces of the PLO and coordinating the activities of the Palestine Liberation Army and the guerrilla groups working within the PLO framework. The Liberation Army includes the following units:

1. The Sa'iqah ('Ain Jalut) Forces
2. The Qadisiyah division
3. The Hittin division
4. Popular Liberation Forces (these are guerrilla units established in conjunction with the regular military forces).

Most of these forces have, since the evacuation of Lebanon been moved to Syria, South Yemen, and Jordan. Their effectiveness is minimal at best.

Information Department

This department is in charge of public relations, information, and Palestine education. Prior to 1967, this department managed a Cairo radio program and a daily newspaper, *Akhbar Falastin* (Palestine News), in Gaza. By 1972, the information department was in charge of the unified media center that included all Palestinian groups. The unified media center has its own news agency: The Palestine News Agency (Wafa), which is quoted regularly by the media centers of the world. The center also produces the central magazine of the PLO, *Falastin al-Thawra* (Revolutionary Palestine). The weekly issue of this magazine normally exceeds 25,000 copies given free to the fighters and sold in the Arab markets.

Also under the control of the unified media center are the Institute of Palestinian Cinema, the Folklore Group, and the Theatre Group. But most important are the radio broadcast operations managed by the center. These include central broadcasting operations located in Cairo, and the regional operations in Baghdad, Yemen, Algeria, Libya, Sudan, Syria, and Lebanon. However, PLO broadcasting operations are maintained at the sufferance of the Arab governments. It is usual for Arab government displeasure with the PLO (Syria and Egypt in particular) to lead to temporary denial of broadcasting facilities.

Department of Popular Mobilization

This department was established in 1965 to organize the Palestinian masses within the PLO. As its functions and structure will be discussed later, it is sufficient to indicate that this department has established general unions for the Palestinian masses and organized councils in refugee camps. It also supervises a Higher Council for the Palestinian unions, which incorporates among its membership the general unions for students, women, workers, teachers, artists, doctors, pharmacists, writers, journalists, and engineers.

Palestine National Fund

Not unlike a treasury department or ministry of finance, the fund is charged with all financial matters of the PLO. It is headed by an official elected by the PNC to the Executive Committee. Its administrative council of eleven members is appointed by the Executive Committee and serves for a three-year term. The administrative council regulates and supervises all financial matters. It sets the general budget and oversees its implementation. As noted earlier, a large source of income comes from withholdings from salaries paid to Palestinians working in the Arab world. Such withholdings are in effect in Iraq, Syria, Egypt, Libya, Kuwait, United Arab Emirates, Saudi Arabia, and Algeria. Arab governments also contribute to the Fund.

Occupied Homeland Department

This department follows the development in occupied Palestine. It studies and reports on the various developments in Israel, especially with regard to the Palestinians living under Israeli occupation. Its periodic reports give full details on the political, social, and economic conditions of these Palestinians. This department is also reported to fund certain projects for the benefit of those Palestinians living under occupation.[37] Such projects include improving town and village services, as well as educational and social service activities. Since the beginning of the intifada, this department has channelled a large amount of funds to aid those Palestinians facing Israel's repressive measures designed to end the uprising.

Department of Education

The functions of this department are similar in nature to those performed by ministries of education in the various countries around the world. However, because of political and geographic considerations, its job is more difficult. Palestinians normally to go public schools in the countries where they reside. Through the League of Arab States, the Department of Education coordinates the educational needs of the Palestinians with those of the countries where they reside. In addition, it runs Palestinian schools in some areas. It also obtains scholarships for higher education for needy Palestinian students, and helps secure admission to Arab universities for Palestinians living under Israeli occupation. At one point, this department entertained the idea of establishing a university in the West Bank. Currently, it is studying the feasibility of the establishment of a free Palestinian university with campuses in a number of states in the region. Its first campus was planned to open in 1983 in Beirut. But the Israeli invasion of Lebanon contributed to the return of that project to the drawing board.

The Palestine Red Crescent Society

Established in 1969, the society provides medical aid to civilian and military personnel. Authority in the society resides in the executive council, which serves the wishes of the council of the society. The executive council is made up of nine members, six of whom are elected by the PNC, with the remaining three appointed by those elected. The activities of the society include medical assistance to those Palestinians and others in need and the operation of hospitals under its administration. It also oversees the medical training of Palestinians and secures medical scholarships in various universities for Palestinian students. The society operates fifteen hospitals in Syria, Egypt, Lebanon, and Yemen. It also operates central medical clinics for outpatient services and for dentistry in Lebanon and Syria. Moreover, the society has established forty-four major medical clinics in various refugee camps and other concentrations of Palestinians in other countries, including Egypt, Syria, Lebanon, and Sudan. In addition, the society has built hygiene centers in many refugee camps. Reports of the society hospitals indicate a high level of modern technology and a professional staff exceeding in quality that of many countries in the region.[38]

The PLO Research Center

The Palestinians often say their motto is "The Gun and the Pen," indicating their pride in their literary and scholarly achievements as well as their military ones. The PLO Research Center embodies these literary and scholarly achievements. Established in 1965, the center has produced a host of publications that have proved beneficial to the PLO and to researchers as well.

The center is divided into three general areas: documentation, research, and information. Each of these is subdivided into specialties. The documentation division includes the general library, the Hebrew library, the documents library, and the media archives. The research division includes the Israeli research office, the Palestinian research office, and the military research office. The information division incorporates the Palestinian Diary section, which records daily events, and the Israeli radio stations section.

The center also produces many books, pamphlets, a journal, and a daily publication. The center has put out hundreds of books classified as follows:

1. Palestine Studies Series.
2. Palestine Book Series.
3. Palestine Research Series.
4. Facts and Figures Series.
5. Palestine Diary.
6. Maps and Pictures Series.

The center translates many of its publications into foreign languages, including English, French, German, Dutch, Spanish, Italian, Japanese, and even the international language, Esperanto. After the Israeli invasion of Lebanon, the center moved to Cyprus.

The Social Affairs Institute

Initially, this institute, founded in 1969, only cared for the families of those commandos killed in action (martyrs). Today, however, it has grown into a large operation, encompassing such a variety of social, medical, and educational services that it can truly be called a ministry of welfare and social services. It is run by a main committee whose members include a general director, and by regional committees. The regional committees are located in areas of Palestinian concentration and function directly at the local level. Other than the original task of caring for the families of the "martyrs," the institute operates in the following areas:

1. Social Welfare: The committees work in areas of family affairs. These include counseling and services. They also run a "fighter's mail" service where mail is delivered directly to the fighters and their families.
2. Health Care: The committees insure that medical attention is given to the needy. Popular clinics operate for this purpose in areas of Palestinian concentration.
3. Education: Financial assistance is provided by the committees to needy Palestinian students. Also, teachers are assigned to aid students' achievement levels in areas of weaknesses. The Sons of the Martyrs School also falls under the responsibility of the institute. In addition, kindergartens have been founded by the institute for the care of young Palestinians.

Samed Institute

This is the Organization of the Palestinian Sons of Martyrs originally founded in 1970 by the Social Affairs Institute as an institute of technical training. Today, Samed is an independent entity within the PLO and operates a chain of production plants.[40] Samed is intended both to train Palestinians for work in the private sector and to provide secure jobs for those Palestinians who otherwise cannot find employment, especially those disabled in action. A total of forty-three industries, including sewing, weaving, carpentry, food, plastic products, and construction equipment fall under the institute's auspices. There have also been some agricultural developments, and plans have been made to establish light industries based on agricultural production. Samed also publishes a Palestinian economic journal. Samed is run by an executive committee composed of three elected workers. In addition, a revolutionary committee of workers is elected in every plant to manage it and to care for the needs of its employees. Finally, a workers' profit-sharing program is in operation at all Samed facilities.[41] In 1984, Samed was placed within an Economic Department, established specifically to incorporate all Samed activities and oversee Palestinian economic development.

These are the major departments, institutes, and ad hoc operations of the PLO. Other sections do exist, though. Some are formed from time to time to care for specific needs of the moment; others are relatively permanent. These include the center for planning; and the trade and supplies commission. It is through such departments and agencies that the PLO best interacts with the Palestinian masses. The Department of Popular Mobilization was set up for the purpose of interaction. A look at its system of operation gives the investigator a better understanding of the popular Palestinian involvement in the PLO.

POPULAR PARTICIPATION IN THE PLO

Soon after its inception, the PLO initiated the Popular Mobilization Department. This was in accordance with Article 4 of the covenant, which granted all Palestinians natural membership in the PLO. After a brief period of study and planning, the second session of the PNC adopted the Popular Mobilization Law which, in theory, placed the PLO itself under the supervision and direction of the Palestinian people. The organizational pyramid of this department was based on the geographic locale of the masses. Members were organized in local units in cities, towns, villages, and camps. In each unit, numbering no more than 500, a local assembly of all active members met at least quarterly. An executive committee of the local unit, consisting of only seven members, was elected by the assembly annually and met at least once a week. Subcommittees for various activities were organized by the executive committee, which also participated in the work of a division office.

The division constituted a number of local units. It also had an assembly of all members in the unit and a committee of all officers of the participating units. Higher in the organizational pyramid was the regional assembly and office. The highest authority in the Department of Popular Mobilization was the Higher Assembly and the General Office. The assembly was constituted of all members of the regional offices, who elect the General Office membership.

This Higher Assembly was charged with checking on all agencies of the PLO. It also had the power to recommend legislation to the Palestine National Council and had often been assigned various organizational and technical duties by the PNC.[42] The third session of the PNC adopted a resolution that stipulated that members of the council should be active members in the popular mobilization units. This, in effect, made this department the most significant, if not the most powerful, in the PLO. The establishment of this department has had the effect of placing the authority in the PLO in the hands of active Palestinian people and may have facilitated the eventual dominance of the guerrilla groups.

After the 1967 Arab-Israeli war, however, the department lost a large number of its units which fell to Israeli occupation. Units under occupation were disbanded by the occupying enemy. A search for a new system was in order. The fourth session of the PNC, held in 1968, adopted a reorganization scheme based on occupational groups rather than geographic ones. This made mobilization possible even under occupation, since professional and labor unions were not disbanded. General unions of the various professions and occupations were established and encouraged to participate in the PLO. Each general union has its own hierarchy and participates in the Higher Council of the unions. The Higher Council in turn works closely with the Popular Mobilization Department to mobilize the Palestinian masses. In addition, a special office for the Occupied Territories was established, and regional offices were maintained. A regional unit now incorporates representatives of all organizations, as well as the general unions.[43] Today, there are general unions for more than ten professional groups (see the Organization Chart of the PLO on p. 52). These unions are formed around political and social issues rather than work-related questions. These unions do not concern themselves with worker-management matters, but function mainly to mobilize their membership behind the Palestinian cause. Their activities include educational, economic, social, and medical assistance to their membership. Their programs are basically political and supportive of the PLO. The constitution of every one of these unions specifies the relationship of the union with the PLO as an organic one.

The general union experiment seems to be successful, and more so than that of the local units. This success has led to greater pressure on the governing bodies of the PLO to maintain a popular political line. In effect, popular participation, then, has resulted in greater limitation on the actions and policies of the leaders of the PLO. This experiment in popular participation by the PLO has been called "an example for democracy in exile."[44]

DEMOCRACY OR AUTOCRACY?

PLO officials often present their organization as a democratic movement. This claim is not without basis. PLO antagonists, on the other hand, charge that the organization's leadership has shown some autocratic tendencies. Their charges, too, are not without basis.

The fact is that the PLO today has many democratic features, as well as indications of autocratic behavior. To this observer, both tendencies are natural to a movement like the PLO. To aspire to a purely democratic commando and exile movement is unthinkable. A certain level of autocracy is characteristic of a guerrilla movement.

In the PLO, autocracy is fermented by the environmental conditions under which the organization operates. These conditions have set limits to the degree of freedom the PLO enjoys in areas of Palestinian concentration. It is understandable that PLO interaction with the Arabs of Israel or those living in the Occupied Territories is limited. Moreover, those familiar with the Middle East also will realize the limitations imposed by the Arab regimes. In fact, of all the areas where the Palestinian masses are found in concentration, only Lebanon gave the PLO the freedom it needed for proper interaction and mass mobilization. However, after the Lebanese crisis and a Syrian and Israeli entry there, the PLO found itself in a position similar to that of its position in Syria, where its activities are seriously restricted and even banned.

Another factor contributing to autocracy within the PLO is the multiplicity of the resistance groups. With conflicting ideologies and many competing smaller guerrilla units, it is understandable that the leading group (Fateh) would exhibit certain autocratic tendencies. It is the contention of this observer that such tendencies are tactical moves designed to safeguard the survival and development of the PLO. The need for national unity is undisputed among guerrilla groups. To achieve this unity, many attempts were made. These attempts have always failed when based on the basis of equality or democratic guidelines. The autocracy of the powerful has been employed to maintain the smaller groups in line and to prevent uncalculated actions they may carry out that can be of harm to the PLO.

A third factor permitting a level of autocracy is the esteem given the PLO by the Palestinian masses. As their only representative since the loss of their country in 1948, and as commando fighters, the PLO leaders are seen by many Palestinians to possess charismatic characteristics. Charismatic leaders have always exhibited some autocratic features.

One can also argue that the PLO is a democratic movement. In fact, by looking at other movements of national liberation, one can conclude that the PLO is fairly democratic. The Algerian, the Cuban, and the Vietnamese revolutions were each dominated by a strong faction and were less democratic than the PLO.

Another testimony of PLO democracy has been evident in this chapter: the PLO interacts with the Palestinian masses at many levels. Examples of such interaction can be seen through the Ashbal (Cubs) training, the Popular Mobilization Department, Samed Institute and its worker-management programs, and all the other departments and activities.

The Palestine National Councils have also been quite representative in character, under the circumstances. Direct elections for PNC membership are understandably difficult. Nevertheless, the council membership has included representatives of all commando groups, general unions, localities, and ideological trends. Even the Palestinians of Israel are represented at the PNC. Those of the Occupied Territories also have their representatives not only in the council chambers, but also on the Executive Commrittee.

In addition, one can argue that the PLO represents the popular will of the Palestinian masses. Evidence of Palestinian support of the PLO is overwhelming. The Palestinians of Arab countries financially support the PLO. Those in the Occupied Territories have indicated their support of the PLO through their municipality elections, public pronouncements, and lately, through the Unified Leadership of the Uprising and its communiqués.

Finally, if autocracy in the PLO was more evident during its early stages, today there is a clear trend toward greater democratization and popular participation. The election of the Executive Committee rather than its appointment by the chairman underscores this point. The process of separation of powers has also grown in the PLO structure. The military establishment is less dominant now than it had been in the past. The executive branch is separate from but responsible to the legislative branch. Popular participation has also grown from a mere symbolic gesture to a solid front that is ready to defend the PLO and the Palestinian revolution as was evidenced during the Jordanian and Lebanese confrontations. On the whole, it appears that the PLO has been a successful experiment in revolutionary democracy.

NOTES

1. Fateh, *Tahir al-Aqtar al-Muhtallah* (Liberation of Occupied Territories), September 1967, pp. 5–6.
2. For the text of the Palestine National Covenant, see Appendix 2.
3. William B. Quandt et al., *The Politics of Palestinian Nationalism* (Berkeley: University of California Press, 1973), p. 68.
4. Leila Kadi, *Arab Summit Conference and the Palestine Problem* (Beirut: PLO Research Center, 1966), p. 21.
5. Walter Lehn, *The Development of Palestinian Resistance* (Detroit: Association of Arab-American University Graduates, 1974), p. 18.
6. Mehmood Hussain, *The Palestine Liberation Organization* (Delhi, India: University Publishers, 1975), p. 18.
7. Quandt et al., *Politics of Palestinian Nationalism*, p. 58.
8. *Al-Hurriyah* (Beirut), 20 February 1967, quoted in Ibid., p. 69.
9. Quoted in Hussain, *Palestine Liberation Organization*, p. 18.
10. Kadi, *Arab Summit Conferences*, p. 23.
11. For a discussion of the guerrilla organizations, see Chapter 4.
12. *The Times* (London), 15 June 1969: emphasis added.
13. Hisham Sharabi, *Palestine Guerrillas: Their Credibility and Effectiveness* (Washington, D.C.: Georgetown University, 1970), p. xi.
14. Voice of Fateh (Cairo), 8 June 1968, quoted in Quandt et al., *Politics of Palestinian Nationalism*, p. 70.
15. Y. Harkabi, *Palestinians and Israel* (Jersualem: Israel Universities Press, 1974), p. 50.
16. Sharabi, *Palestine Guerrillas*, p. 29.
17. A. Yaniv, *P.L.O.: A Profile* (Jerusalem: Israel Univerisities Study Group for Middle Eastern Affairs, 1974), p. 9.

18. For the full text of the agreement, see *Fateh* (Beirut) 2, no. 9 (29 May 1970), p. 4. Also *Al-Hadaf* (Beirut) 1, no. 41 (9 May 1970), p. 3.
19. Quandt et al., *Politics of Palestinian Nationalism*, p. 73.
20. *Free Palestine* (Washington, D.C.), August/September 1970.
21. Frank H. Epp, *The Palestinians* (Scottdale, Penn.: Herald Press, 1976), p. 128.
22. Rashid Hameed, "Munazzamat al-Tahrir al-Filastiniyah fi 'Ashar Sanawat" (The Palestine Liberation Organization in Ten Years), *Shu'un Filastiniyah* 41 (January, February 1975), p. 250.
23. Ibid., p. 250.
24. Harkabi, *Palestinians and Israel*, p. 50.
25. Quandt, et al., *Politics of Palestinian Nationalism*, p. 71.
26. *Watha'eq Filastiniyah 1969* (Documents on Palestine) (Beirut: The Institute of Palestine Studies, 1969), p. 360.
27. Hameed, "Munazzamat al-Tahrir al-Filastiniyah," p. 523.
28. Sa'id Hammoud, "Al-Mu'tamarat al-Qawmiyah al-Filastiniyah Wal-Wihdah al-Wataniyah" (Palestinian National Congresses and National Unity) *Shu'un Filastiniyah* 18 (February 1973), p. 89.
29. Hameed, "Munazzamat al-Tahrir al-Filastiniyah," p. 524.
30. *Watha'eq Filastiniyah* (Documents on Palestine) (Beirut: The Institute of Palestine Studies, 1974), p. 321.
31. Ibrahim Abu-Lughod, *The Thirteenth Session of the Palestine National Council* (Detroit: Association of Arab-American University Graduates, 1977), p. 1.
32. Ibid., p. 2.
33. Ibid.
34. Ibid., p. 11.
35. Ibid. For more details see the PFLP monthly *Al-Thawra Mostamerrah* 1, no. 9 (March 1977), pp. 1–34.
36. *Falastine al-Thawra* (Beirut) 1 January 1977 (Special Issue), p. 40.
37. Hameed, "Munazzamat al-Tahrir al-Filastiniyah," p. 529.
38. Assad Hamouri, "Al-Hilal al-Ahmar al-Filastini: Nathrah 'Ala Nashatateh" (The Palestine Red Crescent Society: A Look at Its Activities), *Shu'un Filastiniyah* 41 42 (January/February 1975), pp. 179–188.
39. For more details on the center, see Anis Sayegh, "Markaz al-Abhath: 'Ashar Sanawat Min al-Tajribah" (The Research Center: Ten Years of Trial), *Shu'un Filastiniyah* 41 42 (January/February 1975), pp. 179–188.
40. *Falastin al-Thawra* (Beirut) 1 January 1977 (Special Issue), pp. 159–161.
41. Ibid., pp. 140–149.
42. For the text of the Popular Mobilization Law see *Watha'eq Filastiniyah* 1965 (Documents on Palestine) (Beirut: The Institute of Palestine Studies, 1965), pp. 294–306.
43. *Watha'eq Filastiniyah* 1968 (Documents on Palestine) (Beirut: The Institute of Palestine Studies, 1968), pp. 523–533.
44. Anis Al-Qasim, *Al-I'dad al-Thawri li-Marhalat al-Tahrir* (Revolutionary Preparations for the Liberation Stage) (Beirut: PLO Research Center, 1967), p. 179.

4

Strategy and Tactics

"If there is to be a revolution," Mao Zedong wrote, "there must be a revolutionary party. Without a revolutionary party, without a party built on the Marxist-Leninist revolutionary theory and in the Marxist-Leninist revolutionary style, it is impossible to lead the working class and the broad masses of the people in defeating imperialism and its running dogs."[1] Some Palestinian groups within the PLO agree with Mao. However, the predominant line of the PLO views ideology at this juncture of the struggle as disruptive. Abu Omar, a former Fateh leader, summed up this majority view when he said, "The only ideology we hold is to liberate Palestine."[2]

Prior to 1967, the PLO National Covenant adhered to the common Arab strategy of regular military warfare. Article 14 stressed the need to "mobilize (Arab) military" potentialities for the liberation of Palestine. The common Arab belief that Arab unity is the road to liberation was affirmed in the convenant (Article 13). However, this strategy was soon to be shattered with the humiliating defeat of the Arab armies in the 1967 Arab-Israeli war.

After 1967, the PLO became dominated by revolutionary commandos and their supporters. Its strategy thus shifted to reflect this domination. Article 9 of the revised convenant clearly points out that "armed struggle is the only way to liberate Palestine." The same article goes on to stress that popular armed struggle is "a strategy not a tactic." Article 10 goes further to explain that "commando action is the nucleus of the Palestinian popular liberation war." In fact, the revised convenant reflects the political thought and strategy of the dominant commando group, Fateh.

Even the declared objective of the PLO was modified as a result of the influence of the commando groups. The slogan of the PDFLP became the official policy of the organization. Instead of the old objective of establishing an Arab state in Palestine, the new objective aims at the dismantling of the "Zionist State of Israel" and its replacement with a secular democratic state in which Moslems, Jews, and Christians are to live in peace and equality. As Fateh moderated its position further, the PLO also adopted the new Fateh objective of setting up an independent Palestinian state in the Occupied Territories next to Israel. To better understand the objectives, strategies, and tactics of the PLO, a look at the major commando groups dominating it is in order.

PALESTINE NATIONAL LIBERATION MOVEMENT (FATEH)

The Palestine National Liberation Movement, also known as Fateh, has not defined its ideology in explicit terms. Generally, it is opposed to formulating an ideological program at the present stage of its struggle to liberate Palestine. In explaining why they have not defined an ideology, Fateh leaders assert that their group "is neither a Party nor a Front. It is simply a movement." They go on to explain that a "Party has a fixed social ideology and the Front unites organizations within the context of a specific plan of action. The basic element of a movement is dynamism. It accepts principles as well as assumptions but subjects its thoughts to practices and experience. Through motion and dynamism the movement builds its intellectual content."[3] Moreover, Fateh fears that if it adopts any one ideology, it would contribute to more splits within the Palestinian national movement.

Fateh's origins can be traced back to 1958, when a small number of Palestinians living in Gaza and elsewhere founded small secret societies dedicated to the objective of Palestinian liberation. By 1959, they merged in Fateh and began to publish their analyses of the Arab-Israeli conflict and to advocate the idea of armed struggle. "The Algerian war of liberation was often cited as an example of what might be done in Palestine."[4] In fact, the Algerian example had such a great influence upon Fateh's thinking that Franz Fanon's approach of colonial people's violence as a means of self-liberation was adopted almost without reservations.

By the early 1960s, Fateh was gaining popularity among the Palestinians, especially those with higher education. Its secret cells were growing in the Gaza Strip and were even founded in Jordan, Syria, Lebanon, and Egypt. On January 1, 1965, Fateh initiated its military operations against Israel. It issued its communiqués announcing its operations under the name *al-'Asifah* (the storm), the name given the military division of Fateh. The very first communiqué pledged a continuing struggle. It also asserted Fateh's belief in "armed revolution as the means for return (of the Palestinians to their homeland) and freedom, (and) to prove to the imperialists and their running dogs, the international Zionist movement, that the Palestinian people are still on the battlefield, that they did not die and will not die."[5]

In the short period between 1965 and mid-1967, Fateh carried out increasingly provocative acts of sabotage against Israel. The 1967 War helped Fateh succeed in the first stage of its plan for liberation: "It created a climate in which the Palestine question became again the principal issue in the Arab world."[6] Professor Michael Hudson contends that Israel helped make this possible by convincing the Arabs that it intends to keep the Occupied Territories. Hudson reports a conversation with a resistance leader as follows:

"I knew we were going to lose the war," said a resistance leader, "but that didn't bother me as much as the possibility that the Israelis might withdraw immediately. If they had, our cause would have been set back for years: The Palestinians would have been further demoralized, Israel would have won a tremendous moral victory, and the Arab governments would have agreed to suppress the resistance as part of the price for withdrawal. Fortunately, the Israelis gave us break."[7]

Another break given by Israel to Fateh occurred on March 31, 1968. On that day, Israel attacked the town of Karameh, east of the Jordan River. As a center of Fateh concentration, Israel had hoped to wipe out this guerrilla base. However, the Israelis were surprised by the unexpectedly stiff opposition from the commandos, who were aided by Jordan's armed forces. They retreated, leaving behind equipment and casualties. Israel may have expected the commandos to conform to the rules of guerrilla warfare set down by Mao Zedong by retreating when the enemy is advancing. By relying on the objective conditions of their environment and not the theory of general guerrilla warfare, Fateh fighters were able to defend themselves in the "first decisive battle ever waged by Palestinian guerrillas."[8]

The battle of Karameh, though hardly a military victory for the Arabs, gave the Palestinian commandos a huge boost. Less than ten months after the total Arab defeat in the 1967 War, the guerrillas were seen since Karameh as the living alternative to regular warfare. After suffering so much humiliation in the 1967 War, the Palestinian and Arab masses finally could point to a "victory." The Battle of Karameh, therefore, induced major psychological consequences leading to greater popularity of the commandos in general and Fateh in particular. Professor Hudson reports that, before the June 1967 War, Fateh numbered no more than 200–300 fighting men, by the time of the Karameh battle their number had increased to around 2,000, but that in the three months after Karameh it had burgeoned to 15,000.[9] Soon after Karameh, Fateh established its dominance over the PLO.

The guiding principles for Fateh's strategy were set down in 1958 as follows:

1. Revolutionary violence is the only available means of liberating the homeland.
2. This violence must be exerted by the masses.
3. The object of this revolutionary violence is to liquidate the political, economic, and military institutions of Zionism over the whole occupied territory of Palestine.
4. This revolutionary action should be independent of all party or state control.
5. The revolutionary struggle will of necessity continue over a long period of time.
6. The revolution is Palestinian in origin, Arab in development.[10]

Clearly, these guiding principles cannot be read as an ideological blueprint. As noted earlier, Fateh insists that ideology is destructive at this stage. In its publications, Fateh writes: "The establishment of revolutionary doctrines without maintaining and achieving the first step of our goals (the liberation of Palestine) inevitably leads to the destruction of our revolution and the destruction of both its meaning and its content."[11] Clearly, Fateh stood for a broad Palestinian base. A rich capitalist can be a member of Fateh if he believes in the objective of liberating Palestine just as a poor farmer can. Fateh's basic thesis is that armed struggle is essential to spark the revolution and to liberate Palestine. In this regard, Fateh writes: "The basis and propellant of the Palestinian movement is armed struggle. . . . Let our slogan for this phase be: Let the Palestinian revolution begin. . . . "[12]

There are indications that Fateh's concept of armed struggle is influenced by the writings of Che Guevara. Two basic themes are specifically adopted from Guevara. These come from Guevara's 1960 book, *Guerrilla Warfare* where he asserts that (1) popular forces can win a war against an army, and (2) it is not always necessary to have to wait for a revolutionary situation to arise; this can be created by a revolutionary focus.[13] In this regard, Professor Sharabi writes:

According to Fateh, the revolutionary vanguard must, in order to succeed, transform itself into a mass movement. To do this, the vanguard must awaken the Palestinian masses "not by verbal propaganda" but by "concrete example." Armed struggle is the only way to awaken mass consciousness.[14]

In fact, Fateh built its strategy by borrowing from other successful guerrilla movements. The influence of the Algerians, the Cubans, the

Vietnamese, and the Chinese is evident in Fateh's strategy and tactics. From the Algerian experience, Franz Fanon's works are the most prominently influential. "The description of a colonial people and the need to resort to violence is taken from Fanon, texts preaching the necessity of armed struggle from Guevara, the notion of the extended war from Mao."[15] Even Fateh's opposition to ideology is not original. "Its leaders ... argue with Debray's position, that to form a political party at the outset of the struggle (is) superfluous—the guerrilla is the party nucleus in the making."[16]

Just as it emphasizes armed struggle, Fateh believes in the necessity of political struggle. "Armed struggle," Fateh contends, "is political struggle in its peak."[17] Armed struggle is complemented with the political struggle against the enemy. It is, moreover, the means to mobilize the masses. According to Fateh, the revolution is a leadership and a base; "a leadership represented in the revolutionary vanguard and a base represented in the popular masses."[18] The political struggle aims at maintaining a proper level of interaction between the leading vanguard and the popular base. This continuous interaction leads to a higher level of recruitment and revolutionary mobilization where the popular base would carry on the people's war of national liberation.

In a pamphlet entitled *Al-Nidal as-Siyassi wal-Askari* (Political and Armed Struggle), Fateh asserts that "the revolutionary war which Fateh advocates has clear political objectives and a well-known means of struggle."[19] The objectives are "to liberate the people of Palestine, to restore their homeland, and to establish a legitimate political authority."[20] This authority in the liberated land will establish "a progressive, democratic, and nonsectarian Palestine."[21] In order to achieve these objectives, a popular war of national liberation must be employed. Such a liberation war entails political and armed struggle.

In analyzing the details of armed struggle, Fateh cites Mao and Giap to argue for an extended and long-term popular war. It is pointed out that these two leaders have shown in theory and experience that armed struggle passes through three stages: (1) strategic defense, (2) strategic balance, and (3) strategic counterattack.[22] Fateh, however, concluded that Palestinian conditions limit their revolution to two stages, one being the stage of avoiding decisive battles, and the second that of waging decisive battles.[23] The strategic balance stage, which is dropped, calls upon the revolutionaries to attack and seize the enemy's weakly defended fortified points and cities. Since Fateh knows that there are no such points in Israel and that it cannot hope to achieve such military victories and hold onto them at this stage, its strategists appropriately dropped this revolutionary phase from Fateh's program.

Fateh refers to the first stage as that of "birth, growth, and sinking of roots. It is launched with the understanding that we are weak and the enemy is strong."[24] The objective of this stage is "self-development and expansion to allow a defeated people to change the balance of power in their favor."[25] This stage is characterized by a strategy of extended defensive war on internal fronts and the tactic of lightning offensive war on the external fronts; creation of the people's army, and finding a safe base from which the second stage can be launched.[26]

The second stage aims at annihilating the enemy and destroying its forces and institutions. It is to be achieved by the following means: (1) forcing the enemy into a defensive posture, (2) spreading the revolution in such a manner that it can strike the enemy at any desired point, (3) striking at the experienced fighting elite of the enemy to make it difficult to compensate for losses in the ranks of the elite, (4) rendering the enemy incapable of working in accordance with the rules and means that serves its strategy, (5) gradually destroying the morale of the enemy, and (6) winning over world public opinion for a potential revolt within the enemy's camp among the Israeli Jews.[27] This potential revolt would come about when the Israeli population is overburdened by continuous war. That war will make Israel's population realize the "oppressive and exclusivist" nature of their system and conclude in favor of a just solution.

The ultimate objective of Fateh's struggle is the liberation of Palestinian lands and the "establishment of an independent democratic Palestinian state with the sovereignty and the capability to preserve the legal rights of all citizens without discrimination based on religion or faith."[28] This objective was repeated, explained, and amplified by Fateh representatives in almost every international or national gathering they attended. The boundaries of that hoped-for state, however, have been modified over the years. Today, they seem to be limited to the Occupied Territories.

Critics of Fateh charge that it is fundamentally a conservative movement. Professor Sadek al-'Azm contends that Fateh did not make the fundamental break with the past, and maintained a traditional link with the conservative Arab regimes.[29] The PFLP also is a critic of Fateh. It charges Fateh with lack of political awareness because it advocates ideological neutrality and rejects a class base for its revolution. As noted, Fateh rejects ideology and contends that the Marxist class struggle theory does not apply to the Palestinians. Abu Omar, a former Fateh leader, explained that Marx did not talk about a refugee class and went further to say that "whatever classes or differences do exist socially, they are not very sharp and they are not the basis for the struggle."[30]

Generally, the leftists accuse Fateh of conservatism, the conservatives accuse it of radicalism, and some charge it with idealism. Fateh's and the guerrilla groups' aim of establishing a democratic secular state in Palestine was viewed by most Arab leadership as utopian. In time, Fateh and many of the Palestinians came to the same conclusion. Because Fateh believes that "the only security for the people of Jewish faith in that area is not to live there on the basis of force and dominance and superiority of arms, but to live in a system that relates them in a human way to the rest of the population of the area," it, since 1974, began to advocate a new objective.[31] Fateh's objectives came to emphasize the "legitimate rights" of the Palestinian people, including their right to form their own independent state. While Fateh leaders assert that they will be ready to form a state on any land "liberated" or "returned," it is understood that the geographic location of such a state would be the West Bank and the Gaza Strip in accordance to the Fez Summit Peace Plan. That Arab peace proposal advocated the establishment of an independent Palestinian state in the West Bank and Gaza (including Jerusalem) in return for Arab-Israeli peace. Consequently, Fateh leaders are willing to indulge in peace negotiations aiming at such a resolution. By 1985, Fateh leaders even went further to advocate the confederation of the emergent independent Palestinian state with Jordan. This was done in response to Jordanian and American overtures after the Reagan Peace Plan of 1982. While such prospects failed, the fact that Fateh leaders even considered them indicates their pragmatic nature and flexible style.

These leaders have included a core group of a few individuals who shared their college years in Cairo and later formed Fateh. This group included Yasser Arafat, Khalil Wazir, and Salah Khalaf, Fateh's top three leaders. Yasser Arafat is the chairman of Fateh's "general command." Mr. Wazir was his deputy until he was assassinated in April 1988, and Khalaf is the group's chief security officer.

Born in Cairo on August 24, 1929, Mohammed Yasser Arafat was soon to leave Cairo for Palestine to live with his uncle in Jerusalem after the death of his mother in 1933. His family had moved to Cairo from Gaza in 1927. Arafat, then known to the Palestinians as Abu Ammar, lived in Jerusalem for only four years, after which he rejoined his father in Cairo. His interest in the Palestinian problem was evident in his activities as early as 1939. By 1946, Arafat was already involved in smuggling arms to Palestine. By 1952, he was elected to the presidency of the Union of Palestinian Students at Cairo University, from which he received a degree in civil engineering. Later, he worked in Kuwait where Fateh was formally founded in 1959. Since then, Arafat has been the leader of Fateh. By 1969, Arafat was elected to serve as the chairman of the Executive Committee of the PLO as well, a position he has held since.

Arafat and Wazir formed the first Fateh call. Wazir was born in Ramleh on October 10, 1935. At the age of thirteen, he witnessed the ejection of his family from their hometown. He grew up as a refugee in Gaza.

By the early fifties, Wazir had met with Arafat and their work eventually produced the largest Palestinian commando group. To the Palestinians, he was known by his code name, Abu Jihad.

Salah Khalaf, better known as Abu Iyad, met with Arafat in Cairo, and together they led the Union of Palestinian Students. Of all Fateh leaders today, Khalaf is the one who is most likely to replace Arafat should he retire from the scene.

Khaled Hassan, alias Abu Sa'id, also met with Arafat in Cairo. Today, he is a close advisor to Arafat. By all accounts, he is the number-three man in Fateh's hierarchy. His brother, Hani, is also among that small group of Fateh's leading circle. This core group remains in charge of Fateh in spite of all its difficulties.

Perhaps the most significant difficulty faced by Fateh's leaders came at the heels of the Israeli invasion of Lebanon, when a rebellion took place among its ranks. This rebellion was declared against Arafat's leadership by two of Fateh's military commanders, Nimer Saleh and Sa'id Musa. The rebels complained of autocracy within Fateh and the PLO. Aided by Syria and other Palestinian commando groups, the rebels were able to force Arafat out of his stronghold in Tripoli in northern Lebanon. They later joined other anti-Arafat groups to form their own "Salvation Front," as will be discussed later in this chapter. But here again, Arafat was able to weather the storm and maintain his control of Fateh and the PLO.

THE POPULAR FRONT FOR THE LIBERATION OF PALESTINE (PFLP)

Although established in late 1967, it would be inaccurate to conclude that the Popular Front for the Liberation of Palestine (PFLP) emerged suddenly as a result of the June 1967 War. "The PFLP represents the transformation of the Arab Nationalist Movement (ANM)."[32] Established in the early 1950s, the ANM regarded the entire Arab world as its field of activity. The movement had established itself in many Arab countries including Syria, Iraq, Lebanon, Egypt, and South Yemen. In fact, the ANM "was a major force behind the Front for National Liberation (FNL) takeover of Southern Yemen in 1967."[33]

The ANM had established a Palestinian guerrilla branch in 1964 known as the National Front for the Liberation of Palestine (also known as the Vengeance Youth). Their commando operations began as early as November 1964. Their program advocated Palestinian armed struggle in coordination with Arab revolutionary action. After the June 1967 War, this group joined with two other commando groups—the Palestine Liberation Front and the Heroes of Return—to form the Popular Front for the Liberation of Palestine. The final form of the front was shaped after meetings between the three groups in November 1967. The leader of the front, George Habash, is a Christian Palestinian medical doctor who was among the founders of the ANM and later called himself an "Asiatic Marxist-Leninist."[34]

As a Marxist-Leninist organization, the front has made a thorough study of the role of political ideology and acquired a Marxist vision of the forces of the revolution as well as those of the enemy. In arguing for the necessity of political thought for their revolution, the front explains the meaning of fighting without ideology as follows:

It means to fight in a manner that lacks planning, to fall into errors without realizing how serious they are or how to deal with them, to improvise political positions not based on a clear view. When political positions are improvised, there is usually a multiplicity of positions which means dispersed forces, with the result that the revolutionary forces of our people are dispersed along many paths instead of all converging on one path as one solid force.[35]

According to their weekly, *Al-Hadaf* (The Objective), revolutionary political thought does not exist in isolation nor is it a luxury or an intellectual exercise. It is based on scientific thought that aids the masses in identifying their enemies and friends.[36] It also promotes a complete revolutionary change among the peasants, workers, and refugees. The PFLP ideology starts with Mao Zedong's analysis of the classes of Chinese society and asks the question of who is the enemy and who are the friends of the revolution. Accordingly, the enemy is identified as Israel, international Zionism, international imperialism, and Arab reactionary regimes.

PFLP's analysis of Arab capitalism ties the capitalist class to the existing reactionary regimes and to international capitalism. Therefore, the PFLP is of "the opinion that Arab capitalists are a comprador bourgeois class and the regimes are comprador bourgeois-feudal regimes which can never stand on the side of revolution."[37] In fact, the PFLP argued that revolution in the Arab world was a prerequisite for attaining their goal in Palestine.

On the Palestine level, the PFLP identifies the forces of the revolution on the basis of class. Its argument is as follows:

It is essential to define the forces of revolution on the Palestinian level from a class angle. To say that the Palestinian people with all their classes are in the same revolutionary position with regard to Israel and that all classes of the Palestinian people have the same revolutionary capacity because they find themselves without a territory and live outside their country, would be unrealistic and unscientific. Such a statement would be correct had the entire Palestinian people been experiencing the same material living conditions. As it is, the Palestinian people do not all live under these same conditions but rather under different living conditions, a fact which we cannot scientifically ignore.[38]

The workers and farmers, according to the PFLP, are the backbone and mainstay of the revolution. These two classes, along with the dispossessed bourgeoisie who live in the refugee camps, constitute the majority of the Palestinian people and are the main force behind the revolution. The PFLP also contends that the petit bourgeoisie class can be the ally of the Palestinian revolution but should not be allowed to lead it. Moreover, the revolutionary classes should lead a national democratic revolution that incorporates all the revolutionary forces on the Palestinian, Arab, and international levels.

Unlike Fateh, the PFLP lays strategic emphasis on the mobilization of the Arab revolutionary classes. In this regard, the PFLP writes:

Although we do not say that the mobilization of the forces of the revolution in the Arab field is one of the immediate tasks of the Palestinian revolution, we may say that the fate of the Palestinian revolution and the armed struggle—commando action—now being carried on by the Palestinian people depends on the extent of their coalescence with a revolution in Jordan, Lebanon, Syria, Egypt, Iraq, and the rest of the Arab countries.[39]

The reason for the necessity of this coalescence with the Arab revolutionary forces is based on a PFLP prediction of clashes with the Arab reationary forces. Also, this cooperation serves the "Arab Revolution," provides the Palestinians with an "Arab Hanoi" and forms a "firm foundation for the Palestinian and Arab national liberation movement which would enable it to stand in the face of the enemy camp and gain superiority over it."[40] However, the creation of an "Arab Hanoi" is yet to take place. Moreover, it is doubtful that any concerned Arab country would be willing to become an "Arab Hanoi."

Like Fateh, the PFLP strategy called for armed struggle and guerrilla warfare against Israel. But unlike Fateh, the Popular Front adopted unique tactics that entail striking the enemy interests wherever they are. These strikes were directed against economic as well as military targets of the enemy camp. Clearly, these tactics entailed skyjacking and bombings in and out of Israel and against not only Israel but also imperialism and Arab reactionary forces.

Leila Khaled, a PFLP member who carried out skyjacking missions in Europe, defended her acts by saying that the real enemy is imperialism. She went on further to explain: It should be clear that my act (skyjacking) cannot be evaluated in isolation of the situation and the underlying causes behind it, nor on the basis of the Western value system which forgives the enemy of all crimes and considers me an outlaw.[41]

These acts are said to have put the Palestinians in the limelight of the Arab-Israeli conflict. However, the tendency today is to avoid such acts of skyjacking and international terrorism. Even the PFLP has (since 1972) denounced skyjacking, considering it an individualistic and adventurous act that gives the enemy an excuse to strike at the resistance movement.[42] By 1972, a body of opinion within the PFLP held that such operations did not constitute Marxist-Leninist tactics.

Critics of terrorism are many and include the rightist elements of Arab society as well as the ideological leftists. Professor Al-Azm, a Marxist author, contends that it is unrevolutionary to commit such acts. He disputes Leila Khaled's analysis and asks the question: "Is it a sound revolutionary act to blame a single Western person or a group of persons, selected at random, of all the crimes of Western imperialism to the degree of endangering their lives?"[43]

In discussing terrorism as a weapon, Brian Crozier observes that "terrorism is a weapon of the weak."[44] However, he equates it with violence emanating from government acts. He writes: "The violence of the strong may express itself in high explosive or napalm bombs. These weapons are no more discriminate than a hand-grenade tossed from a rooftop; indeed, they will make more innocent victims."[45] Crozier then gives examples of terrorism and concludes that these acts are "generally a useful auxiliary weapon rather than a decisive one."[46]

Prior to 1972, George Habash, leader of the PFLP, defended these acts:

When the Jews were doing this sort of thing (terrorism) in Palestine you did not call it acts of terrorism, but a war of liberation. . . . the attacks of the Popular Front are based on quality, not quantity. We believe that to kill a Zionist far from the battleground has more of an effect than killing 100 of them in battle; it attracts more attention. And when we set fire to a store in London, those few flames are worth the burning down of two kibbutzim. Because we force people to ask what is going on, and so they get to know our tragic situation. You have to be constantly reminded of our existence. After all, world opinion has never been either with us or against us; it has just kept ignoring us. . . . Where was the world opinion in 1917 when the British decided to give land that was 90 percent populated by Palestinians as a gift to the Jews?[47]

Until its conference of 1972, the PFLP believed in selective terrorism. Selective terrorism was defined as carefully planned acts of violence against specific targets and for a specific purpose. PFLP's acts had been directed mostly against Israel, however, many were carried out in Europe and elsewhere. The Popular Front also has carried out some acts of sabotage in the Arab world. In May 1969, the PFLP blew up a section of Tapline, the pipeline transporting Saudi oil to the Mediterranean. However, its leadership ousted Dr. Wadi Haddad from its ranks. Dr.

Haddad, who died in 1974, was known to have been the man who masterminded PFLP skyjacking operations.

In a pamphlet entitled *Al-Muqatel al-Thawri* (The Revolutionary Fighter), the PFLP discusses the need to mobilize the masses, and advocates the creation of a leading political party as the vanguard of this revolution of the masses. On mobilization, the pamphlet states:

To prepare the entire people for war means to create an armed people. This requires popular unity and mobilization of all people's capabilities within a national front.... The Vietnamese have given us the concrete example of national unity within a front joining together national groups which differ from one another in social orientation, religious background, and class interest. This front fights the enemy under the slogan: "Unity: a great unity for a great victory." A slogan that has become the cry of all struggling people elsewhere.[48]

To lead this revolution, the PFLP, unlike Fateh, insists that a revolutionary party with correct thoughts must be formed. This party will provide a valid doctrine and strategy for the liberation of Palestine. The PFLP writes:

The basic lines of the wars of national-democratic liberation having socialism as a goal are now clear and well known throughout the world: the leadership of a revolutionary Marxist-Leninist party, a broad Arab national front, and the principal of armed struggle are the most effective weapon against the enemy. The party mobilizes the workers and the peasants and builds the movement of scientific socialism; the front mobilizes the various national classes and groups to participate in the battle of liberation; and the principle of armed struggle transforms guerrilla warfare into a people's war for the liberation of Palestine.[49]

As Fateh did, the PFLP had adopted the goal of establishing a "democratic national state in Palestine."[50] In this state, "both Arabs and Jews will live as citizens with equal rights and obligations and ... will constitute an integral part of the progressive democratic Arab national presence living peacefully with all forces of progress in the world."[51] By 1978, however, the PFLP had reconciled itself to Fateh's later position of calling for an independent Palestinian state in the Occupied Territories. In 1983, the PFLP, along with all other commando groups attending the Algiers 16th PNC session, adopted a resolution accepting the Fez Summit Peace Plan. That plan calls for the establishment of an independent Palestinian state in the West Bank and Gaza (including Jerusalem) in return for peace with Israel.

Led by a man recognized as the intellectual giant of the left in Palestinian politics, the PFLP has gained a reputation for its leftist tendencies as well as its pragmatic understanding of inter-Palestinian politics. Dr. George Habash, the PFLP's secretary general, was born in Lydda

(Lod) in 1926 to a Greek Orthodox grain merchant. By 1948, the Habash family, like most others of Lydda, was dispossessed of both their town and country. He joined with other students at the American University in Beirut, where he studied medicine, to form the Arab Nationalist Movement (ANM) in 1953. The ANM was a political party that aimed at Arab unity and the liberation of Palestine. Basically, it was a Nasserite movement. Nasser's failure in 1967, however, led the ANM to pioneer a front of Palestinian commandos under the leadership of Habash. Today, even after having suffered a serious heart ailment, Habash is still in command of the PFLP. In this role, he is aided by young intellectual Marxists like Ahmad Yamani and Abu Ali Moustafa.

THE POPULAR DEMOCRATIC FRONT FOR THE LIBERATION OF PALESINTE (PDFLP)

The Popular Democratic Front for the Liberation of Palestine (PDFLP) is a breakaway group from the PFLP. Established in February 1969, this group is headed by a Jordanian Marxist, Nayef Hawatmeh. Prior to its split from the PFLP, this group was a radical faction within the PFLP that opposed the "petit bourgeoisie" leadership of the PFLP.

The existence of this radical faction was evident as early as August 1968. In a report to the PFLP Congress in August 1968, this faction called for: (1) The adoption of a revolutionary scientific ideology (the ideology of the proletariat) with its antiimperialist, anti-Zionist, antireactionary and antiunderdevelopment; (2) raising the basic national consciousness of the radical masses beyond the level of "demagogic slogans"; (3) rejection of all defeatist peace proposals and preparing the people for a war of popular liberation by organizing them into popular militia troops; and, (4) the initiation of a dialectical debate among all members of the Arab national resistance movement. Without this dialectic, "the resistance movement will remain captive of the wrong politics, which have been persistently followed and have made it a mere tactical pawn, to be used to apply pressure in the hands of the Arab regimes."[52]

It has been argued that the PDFLP does not differ in its program from the PFLP. True, both are Marxist-Leninist groups influenced by the Cuban and Vietnamese experiences; also, both argue for the need for a political party. However, the PDFLP faction maintains that the party must be committed to an ideology favorable to peasants and workers. The PFLP, on the other hand, realizes this but also recognizes that Arab society is constituted of a large segment of petit bourgeoisie. Thus, the PFLP attempts not to alienate that large portion of the populace.

The PDFLP, now known as the Democratic Front for the Liberation of Palestine (DFLP), argues that the scientific mass revolution cannot be dependent upon the petit bourgeoisie class. Its thinkers quote recent

Palestinian-Arab history to support this argument. "The 1967 War has proven the weaknesses of the petit bourgeoisie class," the PDFLP argues; "when faced with the choice of a popular war of liberation and the defeatist UN peace resolutions, this class retreated to accept the defeatist resolutions in order to safeguard its selfish class interests."[53]

The PDFLP, unlike the PFLP, had been a more enthusiastic supporter of the PLO. Hawatmeh, its leader, was an active member of the PLO Executive Committee. However, this support has not been without critical comments and strong recommendations. In this regard, this group recommended in 1969 the following changes in the PLO:

1. The forming of the National Council from fighting progressive elements.
2. The forming of the Executive Committee from the fighting forces.
3. The elimination of all bureaucratic features of the PLO.
4. The transformation of the Palestine Liberation Army into an army of guerrilla fighters.[54]

However, since Fateh and the resistance groups dominated the PLO in 1969, the PDFLP has come to defend the PLO. In fact, the PDFLP has developed by 1975 to the level of advocating publicly, as does the PLO, the establishment of a Palestinian state in the West Bank and the Gaza Strip.[55] This is not seen as contradictory to its ultimate objective of a democratic secular state in Palestine. In fact, this group was one of the earliest to proclaim this objective. However, their 1975 program attempted to define specific objectives as steps towards the final goal. In that program, the PDFLP proposed four specific conditions for peaceful solution:

1. The recognition of the Palestinian right to self-determination and to establishing an independent entity.
2. The recognition of the right of all Palestinian refugees to return to their homes and lands.
3. The abolition of the Israeli "Law of Return," the limitation of Jewish immigration to Israel, and the destruction of all Zionist institutions.
4. The elimination of all discriminatory features in Palestine, thereby insuring equality through legal means.[56]

Today, however, the group has dropped its third condition and has worked within the PLO on emphasizing the creation of an independent state in the Occupied Territories. As Fateh does, this group opposes external terrorist operations. Its leaders and cadres believe that such operations are "limited in objective and negative in results."[57]

Now simply known as the Democratic Front for the Liberation of

Palestine, the PDFLP is led by its founder and secretary general, Nayef Hawatmeh, and Yassir Abed Rabu, its deputy secretary general. They preside over a pyramid structure that includes a politburo and a central committee. Hawatmeh was born in Salt, Jordan to a Christian family in 1935. At the young age of thirteen, he was touched by the plight of the Palestinians and while studying at the Arab University of Beirut, he joined the ANM. His activities in the ANM created problems for him with the government of Jordan, which sentenced him in 1957 to death. Later, he escaped to Iraq, where he rejoined the ANM as secretary general of its Iraqi branch. Between 1959 and 1963, Hawatmeh was imprisoned in Iraq for his antiregime activities. When the PFLP was formed, Hawatmeh was one of the original members of one of its leading cadres, which split from the PFLP in February of 1969.

THE POPULAR FRONT FOR THE LIBERATION OF PALESTINE, GENERAL COMMAND

Originally, the Popular Front for the Liberation of Palestine, General Command was known as the Palestine Liberation Front. As noted earlier, this front joined the PFLP in November, 1967 only to split off again in October 1968. The original front was founded as a secret group of young Palestinians who advocated guerrilla warfare as early as 1959. Headed by a former Syrian officer of Palestinian origin, Ahmad Jibril, the front organized its cells of Palestinian Arabs regardless of class or ideological commitment. Essentially, the front saw itself as the symbol of a broad national unity.

When Fateh began its commando operations in January, 1965, the front sent its representatives to meet with Fateh leadership to discuss the merger of the two groups. These talks resulted in some coordination between them for a very brief period only. Soon afterwards, the talks of merger were halted.[58] However, after the Arab defeat of June 1967 and the emergence of other commando groups, the front joined the ANM's National Front and the Heroes of the Return group to form the PFLP.

By the end of 1967, it became evident that the ANM was attempting to control the newly formed PFLP. These attempts were rejected by the Jibril group, and eventually led to their split in October 1968. In a meeting of this group, it was decided to expel the ANM's National Front from the PFLP.[59] Thus, the name PFLP was retained and the title, "General Command" was added.

The General Command advocates national unity at this stage of the struggle: "The Palestinian revolution needs a coalition of all the elements that serve the goal of national liberation." However, this coalition is thought of as "tactical and secondary to the strategy" of a continuing class struggle.[60] Class struggle, according to this group, must come after long preparations and after the national coalition achieves its goals. Thus, the Marxist-Leninist groups are advocating a class revolution prematurely and without taking into consideration the actual conditions of the Palestinian people. The present task of the movement is to prepare the revolutionary cadres who will take the lead of the revolting masses.

In regard to external operations, the General Command advocates fighting the enemy wherever its exists. Since the enemy comprises Israel, Zionism, imperialism, and Arab reactionary regimes, such operations outside the Occupied Territories are justified. Therefore, this group, as did the PFLP earlier, directs its activities to the Western and Arab areas in addition to Israel.

The objective of the General Command was the liberation of Palestine from Zionism and imperialism. Any decision regarding the form of the new state to be founded in liberated Palestine "should be the result of a general Palestinian Council consisting of all fighting groups and representing all sectors of the Palestinian population."[61] As did other groups before it, this group also came to accept the new objectives of the PLO. By 1982, the General Command endorsed the Fez Summit Peace Plan at the 16th PNC in Algiers. In 1983, however, the group had become so vehemently opposed to Arafat's leadership of the PLO that they pioneered the drive, along with rebels from Fateh, to oust him from his last Lebanese stronghold in Tripoli. They later joined the rebels to form the National Salvation Front in Damascus. Their current opposition to Arafat has kept them outside the PLO.

The leader of the group, Ahmad Jibril, is assisted by his deputy, Talal Naji, in overseeing the small, but dedicated, group of commited Palestinian militants based mostly in Syria and certain areas of Lebanon. An engineer by training, Jibril studied at the Syrian Military Academy. After graduation, he was recruited by the Syrian Military Intelligence and, in 1961, he formed, with Syrian consent, the Palestine Liberation Front. Since then, Jibril became Syria's front man in its attempts to take over Fateh and, later, the PLO. Today, Jibril is seen by most Palestinians as a pro-Syrian renegade who is, perhaps, most outspoken in his opposition to Arafat's leadership of the PLO.

VANGUARDS OF THE POPULAR LIBERATION WAR (SA'IQAH)

The formation of Vanguards of the Popular Liberation War (Sa'iqah) was in accordance with a decision of the National Congress of the Syrian Ba'th Party, this group began organizing within the cadres of the party. Its ideology is identical to that of the Syrian Arab Socialist Ba'th Party.

The Ba'th was founded in 1947 by two secondary school teachers, Michel Aflaq and Salaheddin al-Bitar. It merged in 1953 with the Arab

Socialist Party to form the most powerful Arab party in today's Syria and Iraq. "This success," Professor George Lenczowski writes, "could be ascribed to a combination of ideology and manipulative skills."[62]

The party's ideology can be traced to its constitution of 1947. The constitution proclaims three fundamental principles that can be summarized as (1) unity and freedom of the Arab nation within the Arab homeland; (2) a belief in the special character of the Arab nation as exemplified in its repeated awakenings, inventiveness, and vitality and (3) a belief in a special mission of the Arab nation in promoting humanitarianism and opposing colonialism.[63]

The constitution describes the party as universal Arab, nationalist, socialist, populist, and revolutionary. However, an investigation of the Ba'th program finds the party advocating a representative and constitutional democracy where nationalism rather than socialism is the prime factor. The party, nevertheless, offers some socialist economic measures. These include agrarian reform; nationalization of public utilities, natural resources, large-scale industries and transportation; workers' participation in the management of factories; and promotion of unions. It also accepts the principles of private ownership and inheritance.

The party views the Palestinian struggle as an integral part of the Arab struggle against colonialism. Israel is seen as an extension of imperialism in the area and as a major center of imperialist interests in the Middle East. Thus, the liberation of Palestine is the main task facing the Arab liberation movement. "Because of the imbalance of power between imperialism and the small but growing Arab liberation movement," the Ba'th argues, "a popular war of liberation [is] the only alternative for the weak to defeat the strong."[64]

It was with this background and in accordance with such beliefs that the Sa'iqah group was formed. As an advocate of Arab unity, Sa'iqah advocates the unity of all commando groups within the PLO. However, the Sa'iqah-PLO relations were strained during the 1976 Syrian intervention in the Lebanese civil war. In fact, Sa'iqah's loyalty to the Syrian regime led its leadership to dispatch its units to fight other PLO factions on Lebanese soil. Sa'iqah attacked PLO headquarters in Beirut with the aim of capturing the leadership from Fateh. Instead of achieving this objective, Sa'iqah lost a number of its own commandos, who defected to the PLO. However, the ranks of Sa'iqah were augmented with recruits from the Syrian Army. As did Jibril's group, Sa'iqah also fought Arafat in Tripoli in 1983 and later joined the National Salvation Front.

Even though Sa'iqah officials may deny it, the fact remains that Sa'iqah's relationship with the PLO and Arab regimes is determined by the Syrian Ba'th regime. Moreover, it can be argued that Sa'iqah is merely a commando unit of the Syrian army. Its activities are highly coordinated with the Syrian army and its leadership is subject to Syrian pressures.

Regarding the goal of the Palestinian revolution, Sa'iqah rejects the democratic-secular objective because "it contradicts the cause of Arab unity."[65] Sa'iqah advocated the establishment of "an Arab country that has no borders" and as such "any resolution of the Palestine question that does not conform to this principle is rejected."[66] This belief did not mean that Sa'iqah was in favor of eliminating the Jews from Palestine. In this regard, the group saw the future of the Jews in Palestine as that of equal citizens within a united socialist Arab society. However, with Syria's acceptance of Security Council Resolutions 242 and 338 in the mid–1970s, Sa'iqah came to advocate the return of all Occupied Territories to Arab sovereignty.

OTHER GUERRILLA GROUPS

Other less significant guerrilla groups have emerged on the Palestinian scene. Some joined major Palestinian groups, some remained independent, and many have disappeared. Of these, the Arab Liberation Front (ALF), the Popular Palestinian Resistance Front (PPRF), the Working Committee for the Liberation of Palestine, the Arab-Palestine Organization, the Palestinian National Front (PNF), and the Popular Struggle Front (PSF), and Black September may be most significant.

The Arab Liberation Front was established by the Iraqi faction of the Arab Socialist Ba'th Party in April 1969. Like the Iraqi Ba'th, this front sees the revolution as an interaction between theory and practice. They quote Regis Debray on the need for this interaction: "the choice (of ideology and practice) is not between action without a head or a theory without legs...," for both must go together.[67]

Just as the Sa'iqah relies on and interacts with the Syrian regime, so the Arab Liberation Front is dependent upon the Iraqi regime for support and ideology. Therefore, it is understandable that the ALF's ideology is Ba'thist nationalist. Like Sa'iqah, the ALF often supports the PLO and advocates national unity. The ALF also opposed the democratic-secular solution for Palestine and advocated a national Arab unity including liberated Palestine. Moreover, the ALF does not exclude military operations outside Israel (international skyjacking and terrorism), but emphasizes the need for the proper timing and planning to avoid their negative results.

The Popular Palestinian Resistance Front, on the other hand, was established independently of any Arab regime. It began as a secret group in the Occupied Territories and spread to the neighboring Arab countries. It made its first appearance on January 17, 1968, when its representatives attended a Cairo conference for the guerrilla movements.

The PPRF advocated a class-oriented revolution to overthrow imperialism, Zionism, and Arab reaction in the Middle East. The leaders and

Strategy and Tactics | 97

thinkers of the PPRF supported the PLO as a framework of national unity and agreed with the more radical groups on the use of international terrorism to strike at all imperialist interests.[68] However, this group seems to have disappeared today.

The Working Committee for the Liberation of Palestine was established in 1967 as a reaction to the Arab defeat in the June war. Its ideology was similar to that of Fateh, and its goal was proclaimed as "the establishment of an Arab state in Palestine."[69] Moreover, it advocated external operations against Israeli interests if they were carefully planned according to a scientific strategy of liberation. The Working Committee, however, has eventually joined Fateh and ceased to exist as an independent unit.

The Arab-Palestine Organization was a splinter group that broke away from the PFLP (General Command) in August 1969. The organization supported the PLO and in turn was supported by the Egyptian regime. It advocated armed struggle and a "scientific Marxist-Leninist" strategy for the liberation of Palestine. This organization also rejected the democratic-secular solution and advocated the total liberation of Palestine.[70] This organization has dwindled in numbers and become insignificant. Today, it too, seems to have vanished.

The Palestine National Front is one of the more recent groups of the Palestinian resistance movement. Established by the Communist Party on August 15, 1973, the PNF operated only in the Occupied Territories. Its cells were secretive and were often exposed to Israeli penetration and punishment. Its position was clearly pro-PLO. It advocated total liberation of Palestinian lands occupied in 1967 and the establishment of a secular-socialist democracy there. In a pamphlet distributed in the Occupied Territories in November, 1973, the PNF rejected all peaceful solutions to the Palestine question, including the proposals for "a Palestinian entity, local autonomy, the Allon plan, King Hussein's plan or the American initiatives."[71] This group, too, accepted the Fez plan, but its activities were related more to building a mass political party than to armed struggle. Today, the PNF has disappeared and the Palestine Communist Party has emerged as one of the four major Palestinian groups. Its mass political organization in the Occupied Territories has given it a major role in organizing and participating in the leadership of the intifada.

One of the least understood and most publicized groups was the short-lived Black September movement. This group reflected a Palestinian desire to avenge the setbacks of the guerrillas and their eventual defeat in September 1970 at the hands of the Jordanian regime. Since the group did not publish any documents, no complete information is available about it. All other groups denied any connection with Black September, and Fateh denounced its terrorist tactics. Western observers, as well as

Israel's government, have concluded that Black September was a cover name for certain Fateh operations between 1971 and 1974.[72] Regardless of origin or philosophy, this group's actions demonstrated its strong belief in terrorism. Palestinian, Arab, and international reaction to its activities was one of shock and condemnation, and may have led to its disappearance.

A group that remains active today is the Popular Struggle Front. The PSF was founded in 1968 by an ex-Ba'thist Jerusalemite, Bahjat Abu Gharbiyyeh. Abu Gharbiyyeh spent many years as a school teacher in Hebron. In 1948, he lost two brothers in the war with Israel as he, himself, was injured. Today, after Gharbiyyeh's retirement, the PSF is led by a medical doctor, Samir Ghosheh. Its platform is nationalist and it advocates armed struggle for the purpose of liberating the Occupied Territories and establishing an independent Palestinian state.

Other groups have existed as well. It is clear from the previous discussion that all Palestinian commando groups advocate armed struggle and guerrilla warfare. Of course, these concepts are not of Palestinian invention. The Chinese, the Cubans, and the Vietnamese have inspired the Palestinians. Palestinian literature makes frequent reference to Marx, Mao, Guevara, Giap, and Fanon. The theories and tactics of these famous revolutionary thinkers form the backbone of Palestinian revolutionary strategies. Violence is an inherent doctrine in these philosophies. Armed struggle had been the guiding principle adopted by all groups with the PLO. Professor Hisham Sharabi tells us that "reliance on armed struggle is a fundamental strategic principle which ought to exclude all political compromise."[73] He further writes:

> In proclaiming armed struggle as the only way to a "just peace," the resistance movement envisaged a strategy of attrition based on protracted war. It based itself on the premise which held that since force is the basis of Zionist strategy, then the inescapable precondition of any settlement should be the invalidation of force as the instrument of achieving a Zionist peace. This could never be accomplished by persuasion, only by force.[74]

Today, however, most Palestinian commando groups have toned down their rhetoric on armed struggle and have, in practice, come to accept and appreciate the value of diplomatic and political activities. The Palestinian uprising in the Occupied Territories has raised the banner of compromise, and the Palestinian groups have rallied behind the intifada and its objectives.

POLITICAL VIOLENCE AND THE PALESTINIAN COMMANDOS

Literature analyzing the causes of violence and revolutionary change is voluminous. In their attempt to understand the causes of violence, scholars are normally led to generalizations and categorizations. Whatever perspective these scholars adopt, they generally agree that violence and revolutionary change usually stem from people's reactions and responses to the political, cultural, social, and economic conditions of the environment.

Violence is a complicated phenomenon. Therefore, it is often noted that "efforts to generalize about revolutionary causation have been criticized as faulty and unnecessarily restrictive."[75] Accordingly, the debate on the causes of violence could be limited if the scholars acknowledge that "there are various kinds of explanation, and their method and objectives are determined by the context of inquiry."[76]

Scholars in the field have distinguished between long-term factors that contribute to revolutionary change and immediate sources of irritation that lead to violent attempts to overthrow an order of things. Chalmers Johnson employs the concepts "dysfunctions" and "accelerators" in his analysis of revolution. Dysfunctions are defined by Johnson as "conditions that put a social system out of equilibrium." If the dysfunctions get to be severe and are not softened, revolution becomes the only alternative unless the elite declares its bankruptcy by abdication, resignation, or by terminating the older order nonviolently.[77] Johnson, however, warns that dysfunctions alone do not lead to violence. In order for violence to break out, "accelerators of dysfunctions" must be present. He defines accelerators as "occurrences that catalyze or throw into relief the already existent revolutionary level or dysfunctions. They do not of themselves cause revolution; but when they do occur in a system already bearing the necessary level of dysfunctions..., they will provide the sufficient cause of the immediately following revolution."[78]

Harry Eckstein employs two similar concepts: "preconditioning" and "precipitants." By the latter, he means an event that actually initiates violence; by the former he means the set of circumstances that make it possible for the precipitant to produce violence.[79] It must be noted here that Johnson, Eckstein, and most other scholars base their analyses on international violence or civil wars. Thus, their analyses apply only in part to the Palestinian revolution and may best explain the intifada and its rise as a revolution against Israel's occupation.

In order to deal properly with the voluminous amount of literature on the underlying causes of violence it is helpful to divide these causes into three types: long-term, middle-term and short-term.

Long-Term Causes

Those dealing with the long-term causes of violence provide us with a variety of theories that range from economic causes to those of foreign control. A common interpretation of the economic causes is provided

100 | The Palestine Liberation Organization

by Walter W. Rostow. Marxist thinkers too relate violence to the economic conditions of society.

Rostow delineates five states of economic growth: (1) traditional society, characterized by economic stagnation; (2) the preconditions for takeoff, characterized by the transformation of scientific discovery into advanced technology; (3) the takeoff, which occurs when modern economic means dominate the society; (4) the drive toward maturity, which comes when the economy begins to seek new areas for development; and (5) the age of high consumption, which is achieved with the production of durable goods and services. Violence occurs at the second stage, when advanced technology begins to disrupt the traditional economic conditions.[80]

A similar interpretation relates violence to the process of modernization. James N. Rosenau concludes that "the more rapid the rate of social change becomes, the greater the likelihood of intrasocietal violence."[81] Michael Hudson discusses Palestinian violence in the context of modernization and asserts that Palestinian modernization brought a new generation of leaders. This generation reacts to its frustrated national aspirations with calculated violence.[82] Secularization, which accompanies modernization, is also accredited with promoting violence by some scholars. Hagopian writes: "Secularization is an estimable factor in the genesis of modern revolutions."[83]

Another common interpretation relates violence to colonialism and nationalism. Rupert Emerson asserts that nationalism drives people to violent rejection of Western colonialism. The people's struggle for self-determination is essentially a response to the impact of the West. Emerson concludes that people "would rather be governed like hell by themselves than by their imperial rulers."[84]

Middle-Term Causes

It should be clear that middle-term causes of violence are in part ramifications of the long-term factors already discussed. Of these middle-term causes, scholars often cite economic depressions. James Davies writes: "Revolutions are most likely to occur when a prolonged period of objective economic development is followed by a sharp reversal."[85] Alexis de Tocqueville noted that, during the French Revolution, "it was precisely the most prosperous parts of France that had most enthusiastically supported the Revolution" and concluded that revolution occurs when an oppressive regime attempts economic reforms rather than when economic conditions are too harsh.[86]

Short-Term Causes

Short-term causes are generally noted by social psychologists. Most of their research on violence tends to revolve around a major hypothesis: Men have certain basic wishes, needs, or instincts which, if frustrated, contribute to aggressive behavior that may give rise to revolution and violence. Edwards points to this hypothesis when he adopts "four elemental types of wishes" and concludes that violence occurs when one or more of them is repressed.[87]

Ted Robert Gurr examines how changing conditions stimulate people's behavior and their responses. His major conclusion is that "relative deprivation" or the gap between what one gets and what he thinks he should get is a contributing factor to violence. Professor Gurr advances three patterns of relative deprivation. The first is called "decremental deprivation" and is a feature of small revolts prior to revolutions. With this pattern, the people's "value expectations remain relatively constant but value capabilities are perceived to decline."[88] Gurr calls the second pattern "aspirational deprivation." This occurs when "capabilities remain relatively static while expectations increase."[89] The last pattern is "progressive deprivation," in which "there [are] substantial and simultaneous increases in expectations and [a] decrease in capabilities."[90]

Where does the PLO fit into all these theories? In spite of the complexity of the PLO, it could be used to test the validity such scholarly hypotheses as these. While that is not the task of this book, it is possible to note certain preliminary relationships between the PLO and the theories on the subject.

Since the majority of the Palestinians live in diaspora and refugee camps, it would be unwise to attempt to analyze Palestinian violence according to Rostow's thesis, i.e., violence occurring during the preconditions for takeoff. However, a similar theory could be more applicable to the PLO case, that is, the modernization theory. As noted already, Professor Hudson relates PLO violence to modernization. Although empirical studies are lacking on this subject, Dr. Hudson asserts that the new Palestinian generation was more educated and more "modernized" than the old one of pre-1948. Thus, "it was inevitable that they should learn better than their parents about the loss of their land."[91] Drawing their lessons from the success of the Algerian revolution and the failure of the Arab regimes in the 1967 War, the new Palestinian generations, Professor Hudson concludes, chose to revolt. In fact, a similar case can be made for Palestinian disappointment in Arab states' military capabilities dating back to the 1948–1949 War, since Palestinian commando organizations began in the 1950s.

Another applicable hypothesis which may explain Palestinian violence is that concerning secularization. This thesis is best supported by the existence of the leftist groups within the PLO, the PFLP, and the PFLP's offshoots who adopted a Marxist line. These groups realized that old Arab sectarian ideologies have failed to get results and were inspired by the successes of the Chinese, Vietnamese, and Koreans.

The most applicable thesis, however, is that of colonialism and nationalism. Most scholars seem to agree on the simple notion that colonialism breeds violence when confronted with indigenous nationalism.

Since PLO armed struggle is directed mainly against Israel, one must raise the following question: How does the PLO perceive Israel? The objective here is not to determine the nature of Israeli existence but simply to clarify the Palestinian perception of Israel, since this could relate to the discussion of violence.

Maxime Rodinson, a French Jewish scholar often quoted by the PLO, traces the origin and mentality of Zionism to conditions prevailing in nineteenth- and early twentieth-century Europe. This was an era of empire-building, when the Europeans explored the rest of the world, annexing territories, transforming them into colonies, and exploiting the native populations. The Zionists were unlike other European colonists because they had to create a social base and take over a national territory.[92]

Herzl's theory embodied the colonial heritage. He wrote that the new Zionist state would be "an outpost to civilization as opposed to barbarism."[93] He even went further than the European colonists and sketched a blueprint for ridding the country of its natives. He wrote:

We must expropriate gently the private property on the estates assigned to us: we shall try to spirit the penniless population across the border by procuring employment for it in the transit countries, while denying it employment in our country; if we move into a region where there are wild animals to which the Jews are not accustomed—big snakes, etc.—I shall use the natives, prior to giving them employment in the transit countries, for the extermination of these animals.[94]

It goes without saying that the Zionists were as good as Herzl's blueprint. Unlike traditional European colonialism (which was based on continued exploitation of the native peoples), Zionism moved towards the eventual expulsion of the native Palestinians. Thus, it would be difficult to find any PLO publication on the nature of Israel that does not take the Israeli colonial setting as a basic premise. Palestinian violence, then, can be viewed as a reaction to Israeli colonialism. Similar violence occurred in Rhodesia/Zimbabwe and still occurs in South Africa, the two closest European colonial settler states that resemble Israel.

Another theory that may apply to the Palestinian case is that of the social psychologists, who claim that men have basic needs, wishes, or instincts which, if frustrated, give rise to feelings of aggression and revolutionary behavior. Unlike most people, the Palestinians lack a basic need—self-determination. Ever since the repression of the establishment of Israel, Palestinian society has grown both within Israel itself and in the refugee camps in the Arab host countries. One can also argue with Edwards that the "wish for recognition" instigated the creation of the PLO. Between 1948 and the mid–1960s, the Palestinians have been legally nonexistent as a significant political entity. The creation of the PLO could have been intended to fill this need.

The PLO case may also be explained in accordance with Ted Robert Gurr's hypothesis of relative deprivation. Obviously, there is a huge gap between what the Palestinians in the refugee camps get in terms of the necessary goods and conditions for a decent life, and what they think they should get. Palestinians strongly believe that they are entitled to a decent life on their lands and that they would have been able to attain it if expulsion had not been imposed on them. This gap is a factor contributing to PLO violence. This psychological need for self-determination is both individual and communal among Palestinians. It has further been reinforced by its acceptance in the international community, in President Wilson's Fourteen Points, the Covenant of the League of Nations (Article 22), the U.N Charter (Preamble and Article 1, especially subclause 2), and many countries as was noted in Chapter 2.

Palestinian violence has deep roots at many levels. First, it is a reaction to Zionist colonialism, which wanted the land without the people. Second, it is driven by psychological (both individual and comnunal) motivation to recover the land lost. Third, it is further supported by the general objectives of modernization and secularization. But, most importantly, Palestinian violence takes root in the lack of any peaceful means for legitimate change. In those colonies where mother countries provide independence on their own, there was no need for the kinds of violent armed struggle that took place in Indo-China and Algeria, where there was no other alternative in achieving independence. The same can apply to the Palestinians. If they are given peaceful means for achieving a homeland, they are not likely to feel the need for armed struggle.

PROBLEMS OF PLO STRATEGY

As violence is an inherent part of the strategy of the PLO, the art of diplomacy is a natural outgrowth of its environment. The Palestinians do not live in isolation; their acts are not without consequences in the region and, thus, they must deal with the political realities of their environment. The PLO then needed to master not only the art of guerrilla warfare, but also the art of diplomacy. Consequently, they shape and are shaped by their political environment.

Second, many Palestinian commando groups within the PLO were the creation of certain Arab regimes. These groups remain loyal to the regimes even at the expense of the PLO. The Sa'iqah's role in the Lebanese crisis was an indication of this. Sa'iqah commandos fought other PLO commandos in aid of the Syrian regime. Total unification and complete PLO independence cannot be achieved without the total separation of these groups from their foster-regimes.

Third, although efforts have been made to mobilize the Palestinian masses living in Israel or under Israeli occupation, more efforts need to be devoted to that objective. Clearly, mobilization of these masses is not an easy task. However, it should be clear also that these people form a significant concentration of the Palestinian masses within the "enemy camp." Their role is indispensible for the achievement of the PLO objectives. PLO activities among them need to be a primary task. The mobilization of the Palestinians there following the start of the intifada has given the PLO new avenues of struggles and great opportunities in diplomacy. Today, the intifada has made a profound impact on Israel and opened the door for a Palestinian peace initiative that could very well result in an eventual resolution of the conflict.

A fourth problem facing the PLO is the lack of a sanctuary for military operations. Military operations against Israel normally lead to Israeli retaliation or even encroachment. Thus, the need for a secure defensible sanctuary is prominent. This by itself is a problem since the Palestinians live not on their own land but under the rule of other regimes, some of which are not friendly ones. Syria, for example, wants to manipulate the PLO. Jordan opposes their commando operations and Lebanon wants to limit their independence. However, a level of popular support for the PLO exists in all three countries. Ironically, the intifada has relieved the PLO of this problem. Armed and diplomatic struggle can now continue without an "Arab Hanoi" or a sanctuary. The Occupied Territories are now transformed into the center of the confrontation with the enemy.

A related problem was the PLO's visible and armed presence in urban centers. This presence has proven harmful, especially in Jordan and Lebanon. Visibility in such centers gives the impression that the PLO is interested in political power in the Arab countries. The PLO cannot afford more wars with Arab armies. Its strategy is designed to struggle against Israel and not to fight the Arab armies in urban centers. The PLO military capabilities have been weakened during every confrontation with Arab armies, for example in Jordan and Lebanon.

On the other hand, urban warfare could be most effective in Israel and the Occupied Territories. Generally, the Middle East is not an ideal place for popular armed struggle and guerrilla warfare. The area lacks the swamps and the thick forests, or even the high mountains normally used as a sanctuary by guerrillas. This problem, however, does not negate the Palestinian strategy. Military operations in urban centers can be most successfully utilized to strike at the enemy. It is in the urban centers where the guerrillas can cause the greatest damage to Israel. These operations also can produce psychological effects on the Israeli population, leading to emigration and dissension. Moreover, in urban centers the commandos can "hit and run," hiding among the crowds. Such commando activities have been carried out in Latin America and other areas. In Uruguay such hit-and-run tactics used by the Tupamaros urban guerrillas have led to martial rule. But the Palestinians of the Occupied Territories need not worry about such results, since Israel already implements martial law. In fact, similarities between the two experiences—Palestinian and Tupamaros—are almost nonexistent, since the Tupamaros' guerrillas are committed Marxist nationals fighting capitalism within their own country while the Palestinians are fighting to "liberate their country" from a "settler-colonial" regime.

A possible problem the PLO has to consider resides in the nature of their target. While violence, such as that of the Tupamaros, may divide the population within the enemy's camp, Palestinian and Arab violence normally unites Israel. Therefore, violence must be supplemented with political action to widen rifts existing within Israeli society. Violence alone may only unite the Israelis behind their government's "fight for survival." Israel is known to have a heterogeneous society with many social, economic, and political rifts. The PLO has attempted to further these rifts by establishing a dialogue with the liberal elements of Israel's society. One can argue that such efforts have been fruitful and have influenced the rise and growth of the Israeli Peace Movement. Here again, the intifada has had a great influence. Besides furthering the polarization of Israel's society, it also directed the PLO toward diplomacy and away from violence.

Another major problem facing the PLO is the multiplicity of guerrilla groups. Historically, quite a number of revolutionary movements have exhausted their forces in factional quarrels waged in exile. The status of the Palestinian society contributes to this multiplicity of forces. Palestinians today are dispossessed not only physically but also politically, economically, and culturally. Unlike other colonized societies, where the existence of their state was only dominated but not denied, the Palestinian national existence and their territorial claims are totally denied. In fact, very few societies have been broken down as fully as the Palestinian society has. Naturally, societal factionalism leads to strategic divisions. Therefore, the very birth of the Palestinian guerrilla movement reflected these divisions. But, ironically, as these same pressures that cause divisions intensify, the Palestinians often reunite.

It is one of the more striking aspects of PLO politics that a paradox of divisions and unity exists. While ideological disparities among the guerrilla groups continue to grow, the movement has also seen periods of occasional political solidarity. On one hand, guerrilla groups are in competition with each other for leverage and influence and, on the other, they all feel uneasy about their relations with the Arab states. Thus, threats from the Arab countries, whether implied or explicit, tend to push the various guerrilla groups into greater cooperation.

Today, however, the divisions among the various commando groups, and even within single groups such as Fateh, have been put aside in their common objective of supporting the intifada. Thus, the intifada has saved the PLO from many of its dilemmas and forged its various factions into a new form of national unity. Even the Islamic elements, which have historically been antinationalist, are now coordinating with the PLO. The Islamic Liberation Movement-Palestine, known by its acronym, Hamas, has coordinated with the national leadership of the intifada and may soon be represented in the PNC.

FACTIONALISM AND NATIONAL UNITY

The idea of national unity has been the cornerstone of Palestinian political action since the six-day war of June 1967. Palestinian activists everywhere stress that Palestinian national unity is a necessary prerequisite for the achievement of their goals and the fulfillment of Palestinian aspirations. Consequently, the PLO became the framework within which national unity was achieved. This unity, which basically revolved around the idea of consensus among the various Palestinian commando groups on declared decisions, became a de facto notion which was accepted by everyone. To deviate from the accepted declared decisions (national unity) meant deviation from the principle of working for the national goals, and, in some cases, deviation meant treason.

It is clear today that such a situation is not acceptable to either side in the Palestinian national movement. The culmination of the Eighteenth Palestine National Council meeting in Algiers in 1987 has ended the dispute. No concerned Palestinian was pleased with this situation of dispute and disagreements. First, the dispute could possibly have led to a total split within the PLO at both the tactical and strategic levels. Second, it could have caused an internal struggle that will divert Palestinian resources from fighting their external enemies to fighting each other. Third, internal division at the national level could have jeopardized many of the Palestinian institutions in the Occupied Territories and on the outside, and deprived the Palestinian people of many of the necessary services that these institutions provide. Before 1987, serious divisions did occur in the ranks of the General Unions of Palestinian Workers, Teachers, Women, and Writers and Journalists.

Historically, the process of commando groups unity within the framework of the PLO has gone through a number of stages beginning with 1967.

The Idea of National Unity: 1967–1974

The period immediately after the 1967 War witnessed an emphasis on national unity under the banner of the PLO. All Palestinian commando groups began to join the PLO and to transplant gloom among the Palestinian people and Arabs in general into hope. The Arab defeat in the six-day war and the continuation of partisan warfare among the Arab regimes "had a unifying effect within the Palestinian ranks."[95] Palestinian national unity was understood to mean a consensus among all Palestinian commando and political groups on declared decisions. This emphasis was aimed at considerations at the Palestinian, Arab, and international levels.

At the Palestinian level, the period after the 1967 Arab defeat witnessed a Palestinian people so divided and separated with differing loyalties to various Arab governments that the PLO's initial task had to be that of unity under its leadership. Such a unity, it was argued, would give the PLO a legitimate representative role that could transform the Palestinians from helpless refugees into a people with recognized national rights.

At the Arab level, prior to 1967, the West Bank was ruled by Jordan while the Gaza Strip was controlled by Egypt. Therefore, Israel occupied them from Jordan and Egypt, leaving the Palestinians without political representation apart from these two countries. Consequently, the PLO had the task of acquiring an Arab consensus on the representative character of the Palestinian people. This task was fulfilled at the Rabat Arab Summit Conference in 1974, when all Arab leaders resolved that the PLO is the sole legitimate representative of the Palestinian people.

At the international level, the global community viewed the Palestinian people as refugees, and perceived the Middle East conflict to be over borders between existing independent states and not over the rights of a people who had lost their homeland. This vision was evident in United Nations resolutions, as represented in the now famous Security Council Resolution 242 of 1967. Henceforth, the PLO attempted to change this perception by seeking international recognition of Palestinian national rights as well as of its role as the representative of the Palestinian people. Here again, the PLO succeeded in achieving its objectives. By the time

Mr. Arafat attended the U.N. General Assembly meeting in 1974, the world community had come to the above conclusions.

The Palestinian, Arab and international situation, then, required Palestinian groups within the PLO to present a cohesive and unified position on all declared decisions in order to achieve that initial objective of recognition. But, in reality, the emphasis on national unity through declared decisions has left a lasting impact on the dynamics of the very structure and functions of the PLO. Therefore, the division between the armed and political branches of the Palestinian Resistance Movement which existed prior to 1969 had to make way for the emerging national unity. Prior to 1969, armed struggle was carried out by separate commando groups. Political activities, on the other hand, were the domain of the PLO itself. In the aftermath of national unity, both had to be subordinated to a single framework of action that, in essence, limited both directions. Consequently, diplomatic personnel often made military decisions and military personnel were to make political or diplomatic decisions. In fact, in many cases, it became very difficult to distinguish between political and military leaders.

While national unity, therefore, was significant in the period prior to 1974 for the achievement of recognition, it was nevertheless to cost the Palestinian Resistance Movement in dynamism. As the political and armed branches of the movement united, they both suffered the loss of a certain amount of freedom of action, they both became less dynamic. Ironically, after the achievement of recognition in 1974, no serious evaluation of the requirements of the new stage took place, and the PLO continued to stress national unity as an objective. Therefore, a consensus among the various resistance groups was still required for decision making, and any single group was able to obstruct decision making.

National Unity: 1974–1984

While 1974 ushered in a new era for the PLO, the practice of consensus in decision making limited both the diplomatic and military branches of the organization. During this era, new international initiatives were taken in search for a diplomatic solution to the Palestinian problem. In response to such initiatives, the Palestinian armed action was to suffer negatively. Even PLO diplomatic action suffered, because political conditions changed dramatically during this period while PLO decision making processes did not.

If one is to begin with the widely accepted premise that the PLO cannot hope to achieve its objectives independently of other regional powers, then, that premise necessitates that the PLO interact with its political environment. This political environment had changed drastically after 1974.

At the Israeli level, these change are represented by a number of factors that made the achievement of PLO objectives more difficult. First, Israel continued to occupy Palestinian lands (the West Bank and Gaza). Israel was also carrying out a process of Judaization of these lands. By 1984, more than forty percent of the Occupied Territories had been confiscated and 174 Jewish settlements had been erected on these lands. Moreover, the practice of expulsion of Palestinians was made more effective with the assumption of the Likud to power. This practice also became direct and open as Meir Kahane and others organized specialized public campaigns designed to expel the local Palestinian population. In addition, Israel formally annexed Jerusalem and declared the city as its "eternal capital." All of these actions made the achievement of even the minimal requirements for the fulfillment of Palestinian goals more difficult.

There is also the Palestinian political environment itself which has undergone serious changes. While Palestinians everywhere have reached a consensus on the minimal conditions for peace and the achievement of Palestinian national rights, there are differences over the means. Those Palestinians under occupation are most anxious to end the occupation. The majority of these people hope for a diplomatic solution to their ordeal. There are also those Palestinians who are not under occupation and are in no hurry to reach a settlement. Still others do not even approve of the consensus on the minimal requirements for peace. Many of those in the latter group come from the 1948 refugees, who believe that a Palestinian state in the West Bank and Gaza falls short of returning them to their lost homes and lands.

One also should not disregard the special relations that tie certain Palestinian communities to specific Arab regimes. Palestinians of the West Bank have a historic and rather close relationship to Jordan. This is in addition to the many Palestinians living in Jordan who advocate closer ties to Jordan. Such ties, in fact, have been strengthened during this decade (1974-1984) as represented in the reconvening of the Jordanian Parliament and the convening of the Palestinian National Council in Amman. There are also the Palestinians living in Syria with ties to its regime. The existence of such relationships makes the task of the PLO even more difficult. Arab countries with large Palestinian communities can take the diplomatic initiative away from the PLO should the PLO totally reject or fail to react to peace initiatives and plans.

There is also the Arab dimension of the Palestinian-Israeli confrontation. At this level, the Palestinians face this dilemma. They need to deal with the regimes as they do need to be independent of them.

From the beginning, a consensus emerged within the PLO that Palestinians should not get entangled in the Arab "cold war." Thus, the doctrine of noninterference was adopted as the strategy for the organization. PLO leaders felt that they have enough problems internally, between their own members—and between them and outside forces—to afford the luxury of being thus entangled. Also, some of the issues of the Arab "cold war," such as the ideological rift between Syria and Iraq, appear to them irrelevant to their condition.

Given the fact of Arab rivalries and shifting alliances, as well as differing Arab perceptions of a solution to the Palestinian problem, the PLO found itself entangled in inter-Arab affairs more than it had wanted to be. This was due, in part, to PLO insistence on Palestinian national unity. Consequently, the PLO found itself on one side or another of the Arab "cold war" most of the time.

In addition to the Arab dimension, there is the international dimension to the Palestinian question. At this level, there was a continuing conflict in East-West relations. This conflict resulted in varying proposals for peace (the Reagan Plan, the Brezhnev Plan, etc.). Even France had its own proposal, as did the European Community at Venice. The PLO needs to be always prepared to react to such proposals, even as it has to be able to react to changing global conditions such as the changes in the Communist bloc.

In sum, all of these dimensions of the Palestinian struggle require from the PLO a level of freedom and dynamism of response so long as the premise holds that there can be no solution to the problem without its help. National unity, as it has been practiced, deprived the PLO of such freedoms and dynamism. Consequently, the PLO became a prisoner of its own insistence on consensus. Attempts to escape from this dilemma, however, led to other problems. For example, Arafat's visit to Cairo in the aftermath of his Tripoli exit was carried out without this consensus, leading to serious problems even within his own commando group. Such attempts have historically created more divisions and threaten to lead to even more serious ones in areas of tactics and strategy in the future. In the long run, differences over strategy threaten the PLO with the potential loss of what it has already gained: Palestinian, Arab, and international recognition.

National Unity: Now and Beyond

The era of the balance of indecision is now coming to an end. Palestinian factions have come to realize that consensus on tactics is not necessary as a consensus on strategy. Therefore, the notion of national unity on both is now rejected, as it deprived the PLO of its freedom and flexibility.

The political-diplomatic struggle, which is perceived to be moderate, is now left to develop and take its course with the recognition of the existence of opposition to it. Such a tactic allowed the PLO to achieve whatever gains are possible from the intifada. There are many, even among the Palestinians, who are unhappy with the PLO's policy of compromise. Others feel that a political solution is possible. Therefore, the PLO is making room for political solutions and attempts to respond to peace initiatives in ways that do not give it a rejectionist outlook and allow it to capitalize on the achievements of the intifada.

Similarly, armed struggle, even though it is perceived to be extremist, has developed and taken its course with the recognition that there is opposition to it. The extremists within the PLO could be very significant in that they safeguard Palestinian rights in the case of the failure at the political-diplomatic level. Should flexibility at the political level lead to unacceptable compromises of Palestinian national rights, the extremists could always argue that they never consented to such compromises.

To attempt to limit the PLO to total consensus is self-defeating and counterproductive to Palestinian interests. The commandos have finally found a meaningful formula by which both trends may coexist within the PLO. Dialogue now aims at finding not tactics, but acceptable goals. The accepted strategic goal has become the Red Line that no faction should cross. Means and tactics, on the other hand, need not have a consensus. Each faction determines its own means so long as there is agreement on the strategic goal. This formula provided the PLO with flexibility of movement in both its political and military struggles.

Past revolutionary movements have sometimes operated in accordance with the above premises rather than on consensus. The Algerian Revolution, for example, had its own extremists and moderates. Mr. Farhat Abbas ran a political office and a government-in-exile, while Ben Bella and Boumedienne ran an effective armed struggle. Their agreement on the strategic goal of liberation and use of both diplomatic and armed tactics led to their eventual success. Consensus was never a guiding principle of the Algerian Revolution.

The intifada has now forged a new brand of Palestinian national unity. The Unified Leadership of the Uprising has given the Palestinians an example of unity in action. Since its inception, Palestinian factions have observed a code of conduct compatible with that example.

NOTES

1. Mao Tse-tung, *Selected Works*, Vol. 4 (Peking, China: Foreign Languages Press, 1948), p. 284.
2. From *Free Palestine*, August/September, 1970.
3. "Al-Fateh as a Movement," *Fateh* (Beirut) October 1, 1969, p. 2.
4. William B. Quandt et. al., *The Politics of Palestinian Nationalism* (Berkeley: University of California Press, 1973), p. 56.
5. Communiqué of the General Command of al-Asifa, No. 1, 1 January 1965. In *Watha'eq Filastiniyah 1965* (*Documents on Palestine*) (Beirut: The Institute of Palestine Studies, 1965), p. 1.

6. Michael Hudson, "The Palestinian Arab Resistance Movement: Its Significance in the Middle East Crisis," *Middle East Journal* 23, no. 3 (Summer 1969), p. 300.

7. Ibid., pp. 300–301.

8. "Fateh's Armed Struggle: Theory and Application," *Fateh* (Beirut), 17 April 1970, p. 2.

9. Hudson, "Palestinian Arab Resistance Movement," p. 301.

10. Gerard Chaliand, *The Palestinian Resistance* (Middlesex, England: Penguin Books, 1972), pp. 67–68.

11. Fateh, *Kayf Tanfajer al-Thawrah al-Shaibiyah al-Musallahah* (How Popular Revolution Breaks Out) (Amman: Fateh, 1967), p. 29.

12. Ibid., pp. 31–32.

13. Ché Guevara, *Guerrilla Warfare* (New York: Monthly Review, 1961), p. 2.

14. Hisham Sharabi, *Palestine and Israel: The Lethal Dilemma* (New York: Pegasus, 1969), p. 31.

15. Chaliand, *Palestinan Resistance*, p. 10.

16. Sharabi, *Palestine and Israel*, p. 31.

17. Ghazi Khurshid, *Dalil Harakat al-Mukawamah al-Filastiniyah* (A Handbook of the Palestinian Resistance Movement) (Beirut: PLO Research Center, 1971), p. 16.

18. Ibid.

19. Fateh, *Al-Nidal as-Siyassi wal-Askari* (Political and Armed Struggle) (Amman: Fateh, 1971), p. 5.

20. Ibid.

21. *Fateh* (Amman), 19 January 1969, p. 5.

22. Mao Tse-Tung, *Selected Works*, Vol. 1., and Vo Nguyen Giap, *People's War People's Army* (Washington, D.C.: n.p. 1965).

23. Fateh, *Al-Nidal as-Siyassi wal-Askari*, p. 21.

24. Ibid., p. 23.

25. Ibid.

26. Ibid., p. 24

27. Ibid., pp. 27–29.

28. Khurshid, *Dalil Harakat al-Mukawamah*, p. 28.

29. Sadek Jalal Al-'Azm, *Dirassah Nakdiyah Lifikr al-Mukawamah al-Falastiniyah* (A Critical Study of Palestinian Resistance Thought) (Beirut: Dar al-Tali'ah, 1973), p. 30.

30. *Free Palestine*, August/September, 1970.

31. Ibid., p. 1.

32. Robert Anton Mertz, "Why George Habash Turned Marxist," *Mid East* 10, no. 4 (August 1970), p. 31.

33. Sharabi, *Palestine and Israel*, p. 196.

34. Chaliand, *Palestinian Resistance*, p. 82.

35. PFLP, *A Strategy for the Liberation of Palestine* (Amman: PFLP, 1969), pp. 12–17.

36. *Al-Hadaf* (Beirut) 2, No. 30 (9 August 1969), pp. 14–17.

37. PFLP, *A Strategy*, pp. 12–17.

38. Ibid., p. 19.

39. Ibid., p. 47.

40. Ibid.
41. Leila Khaled, "Hakatha Khataft Ta'erat al-Boeing" (This Is How I Hijacked the Boeing), *Shu'un Filastiniyah* 13 (September 1972), p. 6.
42. Al-Azm, *Dirassah Nakdiyah*, p. 52.
43. Ibid., p. 53.
44. Brian Crozier, *The Rebel* (Boston: Beacon Press, 1960), p. 159.
45. Ibid.
46. Ibid., p. 160.
47. Oriana Fallaci, "A Leader of the Fedayeen: We Want War Like the Vietnam War," *Life* 48, no. 12 (22 June 1970), pp. 18–20.
48. PFLP, *Al-Muqatel al-Thawri* (The Revolutionary Fighter) (Amman: PFLP Information Department, 1969), p. 1.
49. Ibid., pp. 4–5.
50. PFLP, *A Strategy*, p. 80.
51. Ibid.
52. PDFLP, *The August Program* (Amman: PDFLP, 1969), pp. 25–27.
53. PDFLP, *Harakat Al-Muqawamah Fi Waki'ha Al-Rahen* (The Resistance Movement at the Present State) (Beirut: Dar al-Tali'ah, 1970), p. 25.
54. PDFLP, *Waq'i Harakat al-Muqawamah al-Filastiniyah* (The Reality of the Palestinian Resistance Movement) (Cairo: PDFLP, 1969), pp. 43–44.
55. Mahjoub Omar, "Sira' Min Ajl al-Widah" (Struggle for Unity), *Shu'un Filastiniyah* 56 (April 1976), pp. 18–30.
56. PDFLP, *Al-Barnamaj al-Siyassi* (The Political Program), (Beirut 1976), p. 32.
57. Khurshid, *Dalil Harakat al-Mukawamah*, p. 198.
58. PFLP, General Command, *Al-Jabhah* (The Front) (Beirut) 2, no. 10 (1970), pp. 20–21.
59. Khurshid, *Dalil Harakat al-Mukawamah*, p. 198.
60. Ibid., p. 205.
61. Ibid.
62. George Lenczowski, "Socialism in Syria," in Helen Des Fosses and Jaques Levesque, eds., *Socialism in the Third World* (New York: Praeger, 1975), p. 55.
63. Ibid., p. 62.
64. Khurshid, *Dalil Harakat al-Mukawamah*, p. 92.
65. Ibid., p. 102.
66. Ibid.
67. Arab Liberation Front, *Al-Tarik al-Kawmi li-Tahrir Falastin* (The National Path to Palestinian Liberation) (Beirut: Dar al-Tali'ah, 1970), p. 2.
68. Khurshid, *Dalil Harahat al-Mukawamah*, p. 223.
69. Ibid., p. 238.
70. Ibid., p. 258.
71. Quoted in *Al-Hadaf*, 15 November 1973, p. 10.
72. Dana Schmidt, *Armageddon in the Middle East* (New York: John Day, 1974), p. 186.
73. Sharabi, *Palestine and Israel*, p. 198.
74. Ibid., p. 206.
75. Carl Leiden and Karl Schmitt, *The Politics of Violence: Revolution in the Modern World* (New Jersey: Englewood Cliffs, N.J. 1968), p. 37.

76. Mark Hagopian, *The Phenomenon of Revolution* (New York: Dodd, Mead, 1974), p. 122.

77. Chalmers Johnson, *Revolution and the Social Systems* (Stanford: Hoover Institution, 1964), p. 8.

78. Ibid., p. 12.

79. Harry Eckstein, "On the Etiology of Internal Wars," *History and Theory* 4, no. 2 (Spring 1965), p. 140.

80. Walter W. Rostow, *The Stages of Economic Growth: A Non-Communist Manifesto* (Cambridge: Cambridge University Press, 1960), pp. 4–11.

81. James N. Rosenau, ed., *International Aspects of Civil Strife* (Princeton: Princeton University Press, 1964), p. 5.

82. Hudson, "The Palestinian Arab Resistance Movement," pp. 291–305.

83. Hagopian, *Phenomenon of Revolution*, p. 143.

84. Rupert Emerson, *From Empire to Nation* (Boston: Beacon Press, 1967), p. 43.

85. James G. Davies, ed., *When Men Revolt and Why?* (New York: The Free Press, 1971), p. 136.

86. Quoted in Melvin Richter, "Tocqueville's Contributions to the Theory of Revolution," in Carl J. Friedrich, ed., *Revolution* (New York: Atherton Pres, 1966), pp. 118–120.

87. Lyford Edwards, *Natural History of Revolution* (Chicago: Chicago University Press), pp. 3–4.

88. Ted Robert Gurr, *Why Men Rebel* (Princeton: Princeton University Press, 1970), p. 46.

89. Ibid., p. 51.

90. Ibid., p. 46.

91. Hudson, "Palestinan Arab Resistance Movement," p. 296.

92. Maxime Rodinson, *Israel: A Settler Colonial State?* Trans. David Thorstand (New York: Monad Press, 1973), pp. 31–41.

93. Theodore Herzl, *The Complete Diaries of Theodor Herzl*, Vol. 1 (New York: Theodor Herzl Foundation, 1960), p. 55.

94. Ibid., p. 88.

95. Abdallah Frangi, *The PLO and Palestine* (London: Zed Press, 1984), p. 108.

5

The PLO and the Arab States

"Whatever happens in Palestine," PLO leaders claim, cannot but have its repercussions and its echoes in all the Arab world."[1] Abu Omar, a former Fateh leader, explained this claim in these terms:

Our revolution is the first sustained mass movement in the Arab world. And the enemy we are fighting, imperialism, does not threaten only Palestine—it threatens the Arab world as a whole. Therefore, we consider our revolution to be the vanguard of the Arab revolution. It creates the revolutionary climate for changes in the neighboring countries. It also has pointed the right path for facing colonialism and imperialism and oppression.[2]

While it is true that the Palestinians and the Palestine question have their repercussions on the Arab people and governments, it is also true that Arab regimes play a major part in determining the fate of the Palestinians. As noted in previous chapters, the creation of the PLO was decided at an Arab summit conference. The Palestinians who make up the active PLO membership and its fighting forces live and are stationed in several Arab countries.

The Palestinians face this dilemma: If they want to develop themselves into a viable force capable of achieving its goals, they must have the ability to act independently from the Arab regimes; in order to maintain and strengthen their independence, they must deal with the Arab regimes and play a balancing act between them. If the Palestinians refuse to deal with the regimes in this way, they jeopardize their development and, in the end, their independence if not their very existence as an organized force.

There is, of course, always the possibility that if the Palestinians befriend or even deal with one Arab country more than others they will incur the others' wrath. As a result of bitter experiences with the Arab regimes, the Palestinians have come to learn that "state interests take precedence over Arab national interests in the Arab world."[3] Arab regimes have generally and understandably placed the interests of their regimes above those of the Palestinians. The Palestinians and the Arab nationalists, on the other hand, perceive the Palestinian problem as the major Arab issue, preceding any and all regional or internal state problems. This contradictory perception of national priorities has been the most significant single factor that characterizes Palestinian-Arab relations. Arab perceptions of the Palestinian revolution are related to this dichotomy of perceptions.

Regardless of perceptions to the contrary, the Palestine problem has been a major unifying factor among Arabs, perhaps the only real one. It is a unifying factor not only in inter-Arab relations, but also in terms of domestic relations within the Arab states. Therefore, any discussion of Arab perceptions of the Palestinian revolution must take into consideration the fact that the Palestine conflict serves the interests of Arab regimes, diverting their attention from internal and domestic inequities. Israel provides those regimes with the foreign enemy needed for the purpose of political socialization in authoritarian societies. Thus, while Arab leaders would like to solve the Palestinian problem, the absence of a solution does serve their purpose as well.

A second premise that one needs to address when dealing with Arab perceptions of a solution to the Palestine problem is that the absence of peace with Israel does not mean the presence of war. In fact, today, all Arab regimes have de facto peace with Israel. This is not a costly price to pay for the absence of peace. Should the alternative to lack of peace be real war where full mobilization and sacrifice are needed, then the Arab regimes will be more likely to opt for accommodation with Israel. Thus, every Arab leader has the potential of being a new Anwar Sadat, provided that a new Arab consensus for it emerges.

A third premise is that Palestinian nationalism has, in time, evolved to that point where some Palestinians perceive themselves as members of a Palestinian rather than Arab "umma" or nation. In the process, they have come to be seen as a potential threat to Arab regimes. Palestinian nationalism has become so strong that Palestinian loyalty to the PLO far exceeds their loyalty to the states in which they live or even to the Arab Umma. While the reasons contributing to the growth of Palestinian nationalism take root in their diaspora, it is clear that bitter experiences at the hands of Arab regimes have contributed substantially to this phenomenon. It is understandable, then, that Arab regimes are suspicious of their own Palestinian populations. These Palestinians are likely to take PLO orders and disrupt their fragile systems, should their regimes and the PLO enter into a phase of conflict. Therefore, Arab regimes with a large Palestinian population are more likely to seek an accommodation with Israel satisfactory to the Palestinians than those with little to or no Palestinian population. On the other hand, Arab regimes with no significant Palestinian population are free to go to extremes.

A fourth influence on Arab perceptions of the Palestinian struggle is the fact that the Palestinian Revolution is not a classic case of a guerrilla insurgency. While its activities have significant implications for the countries of the region, its power is negative. It cannot hope to achieve its objectives independently of other regional powers. It can, however, prevent these powers from resolving the Palestine conflict in a manner that excludes the Palestinians. In fact, a number of peace initiatives have been foiled by the PLO. Therefore, proposed accommodations by the Arab countries reflect this reality. Any serious effort at a solution must, then, have "face-saving" elements acceptable, at least in part, to the Palestinians. Sadat's major problem was that his accommodation with Israel seemed to "save Egypt's face" but not the "Umma's face."

To analyze the links between the above premises and Arab-Palestinian relations, one would have to review the policies of the Arab states developmentally, beginning, at least, with the June 1967 War. Because an examination of the entire period and for every Arab state is beyond the scope of this study, I have chosen to identify trends and discuss their ramifications. This chapter will also examine the development of Arab policies for a selected number of states. These states will include Egypt, Jordan, Lebanon, Syria, and Saudi Arabia. The aforementioned states are selected because of their perceived significance in regard to the Palestine conflict. Four of them—Egypt, Syria, Jordan, and Lebanon—have common borders with Israel. Saudi Arabia is significant because of its newly acquired regional role.

THE DEVELOPMENT OF ARAB PERCEPTIONS

While all Arab states recognize the PLO as the sole legitimate representative of the Palestinian people, differences in the extent of their support for PLO objectives exist. After the initial defeat of the Arabs in 1967, the number of Arab countries calling for a political accommodation with Israel was very small (mainly Jordan, Tunisia and Saudi Arabia). Their voices were merely whispers. However, they became bolder as they were joined by the voices of the major Arab decision makers. While Jordan had not hidden its desire for a peaceful settlement, Nasser's acceptance of the Rogers Plan in 1970 gave the accommodationist position in the Arab world recognition and legitimacy. By 1971, the movement toward accommodation reached a peak as a result of three developments. First was Sadat's assumption to power in Egypt. Sadat, a more temperate man than his predecessor, based his policy on a recognition of the importance of the United States' role in any accommodation with Israel. Thus, he pursued a deliberate policy to cultivate friendlier ties with the U.S., and to loosen his ties with the Soviet Union to win American confidence.

Second was the Jordanian civil war, which crushed the Palestinian guerrillas there and temporarily contained them. This gave the accommodationist forces in the Arab world an opportunity to gather momentum.

Third, the political struggle in Syria between the Ba'th factions was finally settled in favor of the moderates under the leadership of Mr. Hafez el-Assad. For the first time since the inception of the Arab-Israeli conflict, Syria now was ready to pursue the course of political accommodation.

Within the camp of accommodationists were the states of the Arabian Gulf (except for South Yemen): Egypt, Jordan, Lebanon, Morocco, Tunisia, and the Sudan. The opposing (nonaccommodationists) camp included Iraq, Libya, Algeria, and South Yemen. Syria fluctuated between the two camps.

The accommodationist camp perceived a settlement of the Arab-Israeli conflict along the lines of U.N. Security Council Resolution 242 of November 22, 1967. That resolution emphasized "the inadmissability of the acquisition of territory by war and the need to work for a just and lasting peace..."[4] Resolution 242 includes the following operative provisions:

1. Withdrawal of Israeli armed forces from occupied territories.
2. Termination of all claims of belligerency, and respect for sovereignty, territorial integrity, and political independence of every state in the area, and their right to live in peace within secure and recognized boundaries.
3. Freedom of international navigation.
4. A just settlement of the refugee problem.
5. Guarantees for the territorial inviability and political independence of every state in the area, including demilitarized zones.[5]

Arab regimes that sought accommodation at that time perceived an eventual exchange of territory for peace. Palestinians in the Occupied Territories were seen as having the option of rejoining the Arab states that had sovereignty over their areas. Some, like Nasser, discussed the possibility of a Palestinian state in the West Bank and Gaza.

While the PLO was opposed to political settlement and generally allied to forces within the nonaccommodationist camp, it nevertheless had its own moderates and hardliners. The moderates were represented by Fateh, Sa'iqah (when Syria was moderate), and other less significant groups. Although the Palestinian moderates opposed any political settlement that would have entailed recognition of Israel, they nevertheless wanted to maintain an open line of communications with all Arabs and feared confrontation with any major Arab states. The hardliners, on the other hand, were led by the Popular Front for the Liberation of Palestine (PFLP) and considered even the call for negotiations with Israel treasonous. Thus, the PLO reflected the developments in the Arab world as it also influenced them.

While these internal differences within the PLO were considered harmful to the Palestinian cause of unity, they have also proven helpful to the moderate majority. Saudi Arabia, for example, feared the rejectionist Palestinians. Its government feared that radicalization of the Middle East would cause instability that would threaten the Saudi regime itself. Therefore, in order to contain the radicals, Saudi Arabia cooperated with Fateh and gave the PLO a large dose of financial assistance. This assistance, however, has not prevented occasional discord between the two parties. PLO-Saudi relations at times have sunk very low and seemed at their lowest during the Jordanian and Lebanese civil wars when Saudi Arabia played a role supportive of anti-PLO forces. Similar lows occurred in the aftermath of the Iraqi invasion of Kuwait.

The October 1973 War marked a historic shift in Arab perceptions. Arab military capabilities seemed to have become a surprising match to Israel's might, and Arab oil was added to the list of weapons in the Arab struggle against Israel. One of the most important features of this war, however, may have been the degree to which Egypt and Syria were able to "pan-Arabize" it. Until 1973, the Arab-Israeli military conflict was limited to few Arab countries. Such was not the case in 1973, when the war resulted in unprecedented Arab cooperation. Even more basic than military solidarity has been the willingness of the Arab oil-producing states to use the "oil weapon" in a meaningful way in relation to the Arab-Israeli conflict.

This meant, therefore, that in the absence of an early resolution to the conflict, the number of Arab states involved would expand and the conflict would intensify. In fact, the ramifications of the 1973 War went beyond the balance of relations between Arabs and Israel. It threatened the policy of detente between the U.S. and the Soviet Union and almost involved the two superpowers in the conflict. Even more important, the war created serious strains between the U.S. and its NATO allies—and Japan—who depended heavily on Arab oil for their economic survival.

"A victor's peace, history teaches us, is seldom lasting. Neither is total defeat."[6] In his study on the causes of war, John G. Stoessinger concludes that peace, to be durable, "must be constructed on a measure of equality."[7] Unlike the 1967 War, the war of October 1973 ended without any party suffering total defeat and none claiming total victory. When fighting ceased, there was a sense of equality. It was within this context that Dr. Henry Kissinger began his "step-by-step" diplomacy to reduce the possibility of another confrontation in the area. With the U.S. president increasingly preoccupied with domestic scandals, Dr. Kissinger had extraordinary latitude in shaping the details of American policy in the conflict. His consequent "shuttle diplomacy" resulted in partial agreements and gave the misguided impression that peace was almost at hand. By 1976, it was clear that even Dr. Kissinger had failed in bringing about a lasting peace in the region. Perhaps, however, peace was not so much his real intention as was the avoidance of war.

Just as the limits of the Kissinger approach were becoming evident, Mr. Carter was assuming power in Washington. It was natural then for the new president to abandon the Kissinger approach in favor of an attempt to achieve a comprehensive accommodation. Two phases in the evolution of the Carter Mid-East policy may be discerned: "The first extends from the time Carter assumed office in January 1977..." and the second commences with the Sadat journey to Jerusalem.[8] During the first phase, emphasis was placed on a Geneva-style conference attended by all parties for the purpose of negotiating a comprehensive settlement. To carry out this objective, and in recognition of the premise that "lasting peace" would have to involve the Soviet Union, the United States issued a joint declaration with Moscow in October 1977, calling for a Geneva meeting. Procedural questions, however, impeded progress. Central to these questions was the involvement of the Palestinians. Having recognized the centrality of the Palestine question to the conflict, Mr. Carter was under Soviet and Arab pressure to invite the PLO to the conference. Israeli pressures as well as congressional demands to fulfill the 1975 Kissinger promise to Israel not to recognize the PLO so long as it does not recognize Israel,[9] placed Carter in a difficult position diplomatically. While he and his advisors knew that "there is no room for agreements without an attempt to tackle the central problem of the Middle East conflict, the relationship between Israel and the Palestinians, which almost certainly means, in practice, the PLO,"[10]—they could not directly involve the PLO.

The impasse which ensued was interrupted by President Sadat's trip to Jerusalem on November 19, 1977. Sadat's trip to Israel solved Mr. Carter's dilemma by refocusing diplomatic maneuvers on bilateral negotiations between Egypt and Israel. Thus, the call for a Geneva conference was dropped and the second phase of Carter's policy began.

The Sadat trip exposed the erroneous prevailing assumptions about Arab desire for peace; in fact, it showed that Sadat wanted peace at any price. Sadat gave his reasoning for the trip in the following manner:

My reasoning was that you cannot hope to succeed if you proceed from a stage A in a given plan to stage C direct; no stages, however brief, can be bypassed. So, if we really wanted the Geneva Conference to be a success, we had to make full preparations for it—at stage B, so to speak. Earlier attempts at such preparations had fallen through; and my proposal that a working committee be set up ... failed to receive any response because of the Arab-Israeli climate of mistrust and suspicion. In short, preparations had to take a different form and proceed along entirely new lines.[11]

The new line Mr. Sadat was talking about was to include a unilateral Egyptian initiative aiming at erasing the "climate of mistrust and suspicion." Speaking before the Israeli Knesset, Mr. Sadat made it clear that he was "not after a bilateral agreement on Sinai ... but to seek a wider peace, based on justice to all concerned."[12] Sadat went on to explain that a "just peace in the region" will include "the restoration of the Arab territories occupied in 1967, and the solution of the Palestinian problem through the establishment of a national Palestinian state, or—to use Carter's term—homeland."[13]

As efforts to negotiate a comprehensive settlement between Egypt and Israel had reached an impasse by fall 1978, Mr. Carter took a major gamble, inviting Sadat and Begin to meet at Camp David. After thirteen days of negotiations in total isolation, the three leaders emerged to announce agreement on two accords: "A Framework for Peace in the Middle East," and a "Framework for the Conclusion of a Peace Treaty between Egypt and Israel."

The Camp David agreements were not a final settlement but merely one stage in a process of negotiations. In March 1979, and after Carter had engaged in "shuttle diplomacy," the two countries signed a bilateral peace treaty. The second stage called for negotiations by Egypt, Jordan, Israel, and Palestinian representatives to determine the future of the West Bank and Gaza Strip. These negotiations took place with only Egypt and Israel participating. Jordan and the Palestinians did not participate mainly because "the Camp David framework [went] against the basic elements of a just solution."[14] Consequently, negotiations broke off.

In light of our earlier premises, namely, that of Arab incapability of achieving peace with Israel unless the peace formula would be acceptable to the Palestinians, how could Sadat have reached a bilateral treaty that was so unacceptable to the Palestinians?

The answer to the question is multidimensional. First, Egypt has no large Palestinian population. Palestinians residing in Egypt are estimated to number less than 50,000. Compared to a population of over fifty million, the Palestinians in Egypt make up a very insignificant portion of the population. Therefore, the fear of internal disruptions by the Palestinians is less significant to Egypt than it is to some other Arab states, such as Jordan. Perhaps it was partly because of this that Jordan declined the invitation to participate in the negotiations.

Second, the Camp David Accords seemed to have had the necessary "face-saving" formula for Egypt in that they placed the Sinai back under Egyptian sovereignty. The accords, however, did not provide the same for the Arabs. Given Egypt's unique sense of nationalism, it was possible for the president of Egypt to accept a formula that favors Egypt over the other Arab States. Unlike most other Arab countries, Egyptians have a sense of Egyptian nationalism. For centuries, the Egyptian masses did not have a strong commitment to Arab nationalism, although Nasser attempted to change that. If nationalism is measured by symbols, then, in Egypt, one should notice more prevalent symbolism relating to Egyptian nationalism than to Arab nationalism. While the speeches of Egyptian leaders often employ the term "Egyptian umma" (nation), the speeches of other Arab leaders use terms like "Jordanian family," "Syrian people," and "Iraqi people." Even the names of stores, streets, banks, and companies in Egypt suggest more of a sense of Egyptian nationalism than of Arab nationalism. Major political parties in Egypt rarely have the word "Arab" in their names, unlike most other Arab political parties.[15]

Egyptian history reveals that strong and ambitious Egyptian leaders had sometimes favored an Arab policy over an Egyptian one. While this might seem to be Arab-nationalist, in fact it was more Egyptian than Arab. Mehemet Ali, for example, followed such an Arab policy and thereby expanded his rule in Syria. During this century, Nahhas Pasha, along with Nouri Said of Iraq, championed the call for the establishment of the Arab League, not because he was an Arab nationalist but mostly because the call served Egypt's interests. In all cases of Egypt having championed Arab causes, one can see that Egypt maintained its own interests above all others. Therefore, "Arab nationalism in Egypt is predicated upon Egyptian leadership."[16]

Of course, this discussion is not meant to indicate that Egypt is not Arab, because it is, nor is it to imply that Egyptian nationalism means enmity toward Arab nationalism, because it does not. Rather, there exists an inherent contradiction within Egypt when it comes to nationalism, since it is impossible for two equally dominant nationalisms to coexist. While Egyptian nationalism is not a threat to Arab nationalism, it does pose a problem to it. Egyptian leaders in conflict with other Arabs can always appeal to their people's sense of Egyptian nationalism. This gave Sadat the opportunity to violate the basic elements of Arab consensus for peace with Israel so long as his actions seemed to serve Egypt's immediate interests. Because this contradiction does not exist in the same degree in other Arab countries, their leaders cannot deviate too far from whatever Arab consensus exists at the time.

The Camp David Accords themselves helped create a new Arab consensus. Soon after Egypt signed its bilateral peace with Israel, Arab leaders met in Baghdad to establish a unified Arab front in opposition to Sadat's action. Ironically, their resolutions at Baghdad represented "the victory of Arab accommodation."[17] Arab leaders agreed at Baghdad to assert "the Arab nation's commitment to a just peace based on... Israeli withdrawal from the territories occupied in 1967...."[18]

The Camp David Accords further neutralized Egypt and opened the way for Israel to invade Lebanon in the summer of 1982. This invasion, which was, among other things, aimed at destroying the PLO, gave the Palestinians their first vivid encounter with loneliness. They learned that Arab regimes are either not able or, perhaps, not willing to provide the Palestinians with military support. For during the invasion Arab support was limited to diplomacy and rhetoric.

The Arab divisions that followed were also reflected among the Palestinians. As opposition within the PLO became vocal, the PLO had another encounter with Arab gun diplomacy. This time the Syrian regime, in support of some Palestinian dissidents, attempted to dominate the PLO while other Arab countries stood by watching. This brief encounter in Tripoli was followed by a Palestinian attempt to balance one Arab regime against another. It was in this context that Mr. Arafat visited Egypt and, in practice, ended its brief isolation in the Arab world.

PLO RELATIONS WITH SELECTED ARAB STATES

Egypt

The PLO was born in Jerusalem, but the seed that germinated it was planted in Cairo. As noted in the first chapter, it was President Nasser of Egypt who first advocated the formation of a "Palestinian entity" and who pushed for the creation of the PLO. Analysts seem to agree that Nasser's initiative was not all too innocent. It was the unrest of the Palestinians in the early sixties which moved the Arab governments into action. The Palestinians were disillusioned with the incapability of the "progressive" Arab regimes to fulfill their national aspirations. Guerrilla organizations such as Fateh began to emerge in Palestinian refugee camps. In sum, Nasser began to fear that he would lose the support of the Palestinians, and other Arab leaders wanted to maintain control over them.

The establishment of the PLO succeeded for a while in perpetuating Palestinian dependence on the Arab governments, particularly on Nasser's Egypt. The enthusiastic Palestinian reception of the PLO even isolated the guerrilla groups momentarily. However, the establishment of the PLO did not free the Arab regimes of their Palestinian problems; in fact, it only complicated them. As a spokesman for the Palestinians, the

PLO had to bend to radical pressures from guerrillas who appealed to the Palestinian masses.

Three major developments caused serious strains in PLO-Egyptian relations: (1) The Rogers Peace Proposal, (2) The second Sinai Disengagement Agreement, and (3) The Sadat trip to Israel. In fact, ever since the guerrillas took over the PLO, relations with Egypt have plummeted. But each of these three developments caused a major breakdown in relations. Each time Egypt broke off diplomatic relations with the PLO, it closed the Voice of Palestine radio broadcasting facility in Cairo. All three breakdowns were also characterized by moderation of Egypt's position toward Israel.

The first setback in PLO-Egyptian relations occurred on July 23, 1970, when Egypt accepted the Rogers Plan for a Middle East settlement. The result of this U.S. initiative was that the war of attrition that had been waged along the Suez Canal ended in a cease-fire on August 7, 1970, and the United Nations renewed its efforts to implement Security Council Resolution 242 (November 1967). Resolution 242 was not acceptable to the PLO because of its lack of reference to the national rights of the Palestinian people, as will be noted in Chapter 7.

The Palestinians saw this as an American device to defuse their revolution, to isolate them from their supporters in the Arab states, and to freeze the status quo in Israeli-Arab relations. Accordingly, they denounced the Rogers Plan and Egypt's acceptance of it. The PLO Executive Committee even announced on the day the cease-fire went into effect that its fighters would not abide by it. The PLO media attacked Nasser and accused him of falling into an imperialist trap. Anti-Egyptian demonstrations were organized by Palestinians in Amman and Beirut.

President Nasser responded by closing PLO offices in Egypt and suspending its radio broadcasts from Cairo. Apparently for the same reason, Nasser did not intervene immediately when the Jordanian forces launched as all-out attack on the Palestinians in September. The PLO attack on Nasser may have been a tactical error. As one PLO official put it: "We should have denounced the Rogers Plan, but not Nasser's acceptance of it—recognizing that he was in a difficult position. By denouncing Nasser, we gave Hussein the opportunity to destroy us using Nasser's sword."[19] This was in reference to the civil war in Jordan in that year.

However, the PLO confrontation with the Jordanian regime helped to reconcile Egypt and the PLO. Egypt mediated agreements between the two warring parties, and the PLO "no longer opposed the efforts of Egypt and other regimes to recover through peaceful means the territories occupied in 1967."[20] When it became clear to Egypt that Jordan was determined to rid itself of all armed Palestinians, Cairo severed its relations with Amman.

The next confrontation with Egypt also was the result of an American initiative. Henry Kissinger, then U.S. Secretary of State, mediated the second Sinai Disengagement Agreement between Egypt and Israel in September 1975. The agreement failed to mention the Palestinian issue. The Palestinians saw that agreement as "an imperialist attempt to suppress Arab cooperation and to shatter all features of a unified Arab fighting front after the October 1973 War . . . and to freeze the struggle with the enemy in order to liberate Israel from its isolation at the international level."[21] In a message to the Arab people, the PLO Executive Committee warned that the Egyptian leadership had fallen into an imperialist trap and urged all Arabs to unite in order to defeat U.S. designs.[22] The PFLP even went further to refer to Sadat as a "traitor" and to call for his overthrow.[23]

Most important to the Palestinians, were the secret accords between the United States and Israel. Prior to accepting the disengagement agreement, Israel asked for a huge sum ($3.3 billion) in U.S. economic and military aid.[24] Also, the United States agreed to send its technicians to man an early warning system at the entrance to the Sinai passes and to provide Israel with sophisticated military equipment. Furthermore, the United States pledged to Israel that the U.S. government would not deal with the PLO so long as the organization did not recognize Israel's right to exist. It may have been this pledge that angered the PLO most.

The Palestinian leadership saw the agreement as a dangerous step that threatened their interests. Pro-PLO analysts discussed the accord as a part of a U.S. policy of containment designed to rid the Middle East of any Soviet influence at the expense of Arab interests.[25] The Palestinian leadership saw the accord as an open invitation to American military intervention and a cause for splitting the united Arab front that emerged after the 1973 War. The leftist resistance groups discussed the accord as an "imperialist ploy to impose surrender upon the Arab regimes" and to eliminate all sources of revolutionary sentiment in the area.[26] In fact, it was not long after the accord was signed that the Lebanese crisis took the shape of a civil war. These events were seen by the leftist groups as a continuation of a joint plan by the United States, Israel, and Arab reactionaries to suppress the Palestinian resistance movement.

In fact, events in the Lebanese civil war of 1975–76, as events in the Jordanian civil war before it, led to the easing of tensions that had built up between the PLO and the Egyptian government. While fighting the Syrians in Lebanon, the Palestinians needed strong Arab allies, and Egypt was the alternative. PLO attacks on Sadat were halted and the Voice of Palestine broadcast was allowed to resume its operations from Cairo. Arafat travelled to Egypt and met with Sadat, who gave him verbal support and began a campaign of anti-Syrian propaganda in his country.

The third major confrontation between the PLO and Egypt was soon to follow. On Saturday, November 19, 1977, President Sadat went to Israel on a mission of peace. The trip was the first by an Arab leader and, as one Arab diplomat put it: "In one stroke, Sadat has, in effect, recognized Israel as a state and recognized Jerusalem as its capital, something not even the Americans can do."[27] This trip initiated a new process of direct negotiations between Egyptian and Israeli officials.

The PLO quickly denounced the trip. Mahmud Labadi, a PLO spokesman, scoffed at Sadat's visit to Israel and his speech at the Knesset. The Democratic Front for the Liberation of Palestine issued a more violent condemnation: "He has sold his soul, Egypt, and the Arab struggle to the Zionist-American devil."[28]

In fact, the Sadat trip to Israel and his ignoring the PLO in his Knesset speech were severe blows to the Palestinian leadership. In inviting all parties to attend the follow-up meeting in Cairo the following week, Sadat forced the PLO into an unpleasant corner. The organization has always insisted that it alone has the right to speak for the Palestinians. A PLO rejection of the Cairo invitation could be seen as a self-imposed freezing out of negotiations. It would also be bypassing an opportunity to confront Israel with a dilemma. Israel has maintained for years that it would never negotiate with the PLO. But if Israel, having agreed to go to Cairo, were suddenly to switch gears and drop out because of a PLO presence, it would leave itself open to world criticism. If, on the other hand, the PLO decided to join the Cairo meeting, it would have implied PLO acceptance of the Sadat trip and its recognition of Israel. Moreover, it would have caused a rupture in the PLO's relations with other Arab countries such as Syria and Iraq, and made many new adversaries within its own ranks. Thus, it was inevitable for the PLO to reject the Sadat initiative and his call for direct negotiations with Israel at Cairo. Even Sadat himself had concluded while in Israel that the PLO was not about to support his policy.

Accordingly, while in Israel, Sadat attempted to exclude the PLO from the peace process. Through overtures to West Bank and other Palestinians who were seen as not being members of the PLO, he tried to drum up credible Palestinian support for his efforts. His meeting with West Bank notables during his visit to Israel produced no such support. Instead, his trip resulted in an anti-Sadat uproar in the Occupied Territories. Karim Khalaf, the late mayor of Ramallah, proclaimed while Sadat was in Jerusalem that "Sadat's visit to Israel was a stab in the back of the Palestinian people."[29] Hikmat al-Masri, a Nablus notable who met with Sadat in Jerusalem, addressed the Egyptian leader: "You have a great heart... [but] of course, the PLO is our only representative."[30] The then Mayor of Halhul, Muhammad Milhem, said: "The PLO has not given us back our land and our homes, but it has made the world realize that we are not just refugees, but a nation."³¹

Some West Bankers did come out in support of Sadat, but that support was so mild that Sadat seems to have reached the same conclusion that had been reached earlier by Israeli leadership, namely, that an alternative to the PLO cannot be found in the Occupied Territories. Aziz Shihadeh, a Ramallah lawyer, said: "For ten years, nothing was done to rid us of the Israeli occupation; now Sadat is moving."³² However, Mr. Shihadeh could not but recall that a few months earlier another Ramallah lawyer who attempted to form a group of independents was denounced so roundly by other West Bankers that he suffered a nervous breakdown before he could hold his first press conference. Soon that lawyer was taking out large newspaper advertisements to recant.³³ Years later, Mr. Shihadeh himself was assassinated.

A week later, the Cairo meeting was delayed, but another meeting took place not in Cairo, but in Tripoli, Libya. This meeting included an anti-Sadat Arab front of Libya, Algeria, Iraq, Syria, South Yemen, and the Palestinians. The PLO thus chose to oppose Sadat's policies, and their relations with Egypt were once more dramatically severed. A large number of PLO leaders were expelled from Egypt and their radio broadcasting service there was once more closed down.

The subsequent Camp David summit meeting and its proclaimed accords were also opposed by the PLO as a sell-out of Palestinian rights. While the accords promised the return of Sinai to Egypt, they fell short of returning the West Bank and Gaza to the Palestinians. Instead, Palestinian residents of these areas were to have self-rule under Israeli suzerainty for five years. Moreover, the Egyptian-Israeli peace treaty permanently froze the Egyptian front and furthered Egypt's rift with the PLO.

As the ramifications of the Camp David Accords will be discussed in the next chapter, it is sufficient to point out here that the PLO leadership saw the accords as a dangerous plot against its very existence. By dealing separately with the Palestinians of the West Bank and Gaza, the Camp David Accords have, in effect, attempted to delegitimize the PLO as a representative of the Palestinians and to break Palestinian solidarity behind the PLO. At Camp David, as in the following talks, an Israeli, an American, and an Egyptian negotiated the future of the Palestinians in the absence of the Palestinians. As a result, the rift between Egypt and the PLO reached its climax.

The death of Sadat in 1981 gave the Palestinians and other Arabs new hopes of the return of Egypt to the Arab fold. This did not materialize immediately. Instead, Israel invaded Lebanon, and inter-Palestinian rifts, as well as the PLO's rift with Syria, occurred. Subsequently, it was

Arafat who went to Egypt and, in effect, ended Egypt's isolation in the Arab world. The Egyptian role in Lebanon did contribute to Arafat's move. During the Israeli invasion, Egyptian-Israeli relations reached a very low ebb. Later, Egypt helped Arafat during his seige in Tripoli. Consequently, Egypt became supportive of Arafat's position as well as his leadership of the PLO. Since then, Egypt has come to play the role of a mediator between the PLO and Israel. During the intifada, Egypt's role as a mediator became even more important. But events in the Persian Gulf led to yet another ebb in relations.

Jordan

At the opening session of the Palestinian Council that gave the PLO its birth certificate, King Hussein of Jordan was an honored guest and the keynote speaker. The PLO itself proclaimed Jerusalem, then a Jordanian city, its headquarters. Peaceful relationship between the PLO and the Jordanian regime lasted until 1966.

This peaceful coexistence was ended after Israel attacked the village of As-Samu in the West Bank in November 1966. The Israeli attack was said to be in retaliation against commando operations emanating from that area against Israel. The PLO, which incorporated many commando supporters, demanded a permit to train the Palestinian masses in Jordan. Fearing that such an operation would create a separate army and undermine Jordanian unity, King Hussein rejected the demand, attacked the PLO, closed its headquarters, and suppressed its activities.

The loss of the Jordanian regime's popularity among the Palestinians and the destruction of its military power in the 1967 Arab-Israeli War, coupled with the dislocation of its military and police establishment, led to a rapid growth of the commando movement in Jordan. The regime felt compelled to tolerate Palestinian activities on its soil. The commandos rapidly established bases, and training and supply centers along the central Jordan valley and in refugee camps.

The Battle of Karameh on March 28, 1968, launched the commandos into a wave of popularity in the Arab world. Fateh was the main beneficiary of this Arab enthusiasm. Its forces grew rapidly and its dominance over the PLO became possible. Given this growth and popularity after Karameh, the guerrillas "were unable to resist the temptation to abandon more or less underground activities and to operate openly."[34]

Under such circumstances, conflict developed with the Jordanian regime. Jordan was interested in keeping the guerrillas under its control, but they wanted freedom of action. The two objectives were clearly contradictory. By the end of 1968, the PLO had assumed many of the functions of a state and had developed the appropriate infrastructures to carry out such tasks. It took over security in the refugee camps, organized schools, built clinics and a hospital, and provided financial and material aid to the families of their martyrs. In fact, some commandos began to abuse their role, thus offending and alienating the Jordanian government and people.

The commandos had also become a threat to Israel. Their military operations were growing in frequency and significance. These operations had reached the heart of Israel, into cities such as Jerusalem, Tel Aviv, and Haifa. This in turn was creating problems for Jordan. Israeli retaliation against these operations took the form of air and land attacks on Palestinian refugee camps and towns in Jordan. If the intention of the Israelis was to turn the Palestinian people against the PLO and the commandos, then they failed badly. But if their objective was to hasten a Jordanian-PLO confrontation, then they had scored a success.

The first clash between the guerrilla and the Jordanian regime occurred on November 4, 1968, when Tahir Dablan, a close associate of the Jordanian intelligence services, who had set up an "independent" guerrilla group called Kata'ib il-Nasr (Battalions of Victory), provoked an incident with the Jordanian security forces that led to several deaths on both sides. The incident was used by the regime as a pretext for suppressing the Palestinian resistance movement.[35]

Given the openness with which the commandos operated, they made it easy for the government to infiltrate them and even establish its own cover guerrilla groups such as Dablan's. The regime even established its own Jordanian militia, known as the Saiqa Brigade. "Reputed to be about 45,000 strong (but more likely less than half that number), this semiclandestine, part-time force had been raised by Sharif Nasser ben Jamil, the commander-in-chief, in the previous year, to combat subversion."[36]

Feeling that his powers were strengthened, King Hussein, in February 1970, issued a decree restricting commando activities. The decree prohibited, among other things, carrying weapons in populated areas, demonstrations, and all other political activities and publications without legal authorization. The decree also demanded that all weapons carried or stockpiled by the commandos be surrendered.[37] The PLO immediately formed a Unified Command of guerrilla groups and rejected the decree. Armed conflict between the commandos and Jordanian army units took place in scattered areas. The tense situation continued until King Hussein, realizing the strength of the guerrillas, suspended his decree and signed an agreement with the PLO defining the areas of PLO control and the limits of governmental intervention in Palestinian affairs.

During the following uneasy truce, scattered clashes occurred and both sides were preparing for a major inevitable confrontation. The occasion for the confrontation was soon to come with Nasser's acceptance of the Rogers Plan in June 1970. King Hussein seized the opportunity of PLO-Egyptian impasse and announced his own acceptance of the Rogers Plan. This action outraged the Palestinians and led to daily clashes between them and the Jordanian troops in the streets of Amman and other major towns.

The situation was getting worse almost daily, and on August 16, 1970, Yasser Arafat, at a graduation ceremony of Fateh recruits, alleged that the Jordanian regime was moving troops to surround Amman as a prelude to an all-out attack on the guerrilla movement.[38] The confrontation with the Jordanian army was becoming more and more likely and the civil war was at hand.

At this critical point, the PFLP put into effect plans to hijack several foreign aircrafts. Three international aircraft were flown with their crews and passengers to Jordan. This drastic policy of the PFLP caused a split among Palestinian commandos. In spite of pressures from the PLO to release the aircraft, the PFLP blew them up after releasing the hostages. The Jordanian government was embarrassed by the hijackings because they demonstrated its inability to effectively control its territory and population. The hijackings, "probably as much as Israeli attacks, forced King Hussein to conclude that the Jordanians would have to choose either their government or the guerrillas."[39] At this point then, it became clear that the King had chosen to confront the guerrillas.

On September 15, 1970, King Hussein dismissed his civilian cabinet and appointed a military government of twelve senior officers, naming Brigadier Mohammad Daoud, a Palestinian, as prime minister. He also appointed Field Marshal Habis al-Majali as military governor of Jordan and commander-in-chief.

In response, the commandos appointed Arafat as "general commander of all the armed forces of the revolution" and accused the king of implementing an American-Israeli plan to liquidate the Palestinian Revolution.[40] On September 17, 1970, the Jordanian Army moved with its tanks and armored vehicles into the center of Amman and attempted to surround the refugee camps on the periphery of the city.

Heavy fighting erupted and continued for ten days. When the Jordanian army began to have the upper hand, Syrian tanks advanced fifteen miles into Jordanian territory in a bid to protect the Palestinians. King Hussein appealed to Britain and the United States to take action against Syria. Israel massed its troops on the Syrian border, and the United States moved its Sixth Fleet east toward the Israeli coastline.[41]

Under heavy criticism from many Arab governments, King Hussein justified his attack on the Palestinian commandos in the following manner:

We have reached the point where my people living in Jerusalem under foreign military occupation were ten times more secure in their homes than people living in Amman.... When people see the amount of arms and ammunition the guerrillas had in Amman, and the preparations they made for fighting here, they may well ask, how did we allow things to reach this pass. I can only answer that after the June war—the June disaster—I was so concerned with rebuilding the army, for the recovery of our lost territory.... The Fadayeen talked about resisting Israel but it was not a question of Israel at all. It was a question of takeover here.[42]

The king may be right in his comments about security in Amman, but there is no evidence to indicate that the Palestinian leadership, especially that of the PLO, had any intentions of a takeover in Jordan. Some radical groups such as the PFLP may have advocated a takeover, but it was clear that Arafat and the PLO leadership opposed any such moves. The problem is obviously more fundamental. In order to understand the underlying factors behind the civil war, one has, for instance, to review the history of the Jordanian regime since its inception and its role in suppressing national liberation movements. In fact, Jordan was, and still is, committed to eradicating any revolutionary movement. Evidence of this before 1967 is represented by the regime's actions against the PLO and Fateh. After 1967, Jordan attempted on many occasions to suppress the Palestinian Resistance Movement.

While analysts may disagree with the above conclusion, they do, however, agree that the essential factor leading to the outbreak of the civil war lies in the nature of the Jordanian regime and the contradictions between such a regime and a revolutionary movement as that of the Palestinians.[43] Although the Palestinians made mistakes as well, their gravest miscalculation lay in the fact that they did not realize soon enough that the confrontation with the Jordanian regime was likely to occur.

While the civil war resulted in many casualties on both sides and among the civilian population, no one knows exactly how many. Jordan claimed that its army lost 200 men, and that 541 civilians died in Amman alone. The PLO figures included 3,490 civilians, 3,000 soldiers, and 900 commandos killed, and about 14,000 individuals in all wounded. The United Nations estimated that 20,000 people had been killed or wounded.[44]

On September 26, 1970, Ja'afar Numeiry, then president of Sudan, arrived in Amman on a peace mission. Numeiry returned the next day to report: "We left Amman with one impression that there was an overall plot for the annihilation of the brave Palestinian Resistance.... The Jordanian authorities have a prearranged conspiracy to crush the Palestinian people, and they will go on deceiving and eluding until they have carried out their conspiracy."[45]

The months to come proved Numeiry correct. Even though the PLO and Jordan signed the Cairo Agreement on September 27, the day before

President Nasser's fatal heart attack, Jordanian army units maintained their squeeze on the guerrillas. Another agreement was reached on October 13, 1970. But like the one before it, this agreement did not lead to complete harmony. It called for commando evacuation of the cities. In complying with this provision Arafat said, "Our policy of evacuating the towns would prove ... that we do not have any intention to overthrow the Jordanian regime."[46]

Arafat's decision to withdraw from the cities may have been a mistake. Both the PFLP and the PDFLP warned him not to evacuate because "the reactionary Jordanian regime will not leave the resistance alone." "If we evacuate the towns," the PFLP wrote, "we would tie the ropes around the neck of the resistance movement, mainly because the resistance would be separated from the population. If the separation happens, this would lead eventually to the liquidation of the movement."[47]

The PDFLP, on the other hand, opposed the move on the basis that:

It is a big mistake to evacuate the towns. This will lead us to confront the Jordanian regime in a conventional war. We are not capable of doing that; our material power is inadequate. We were and still are able to fight the Jordanian regime for a long time, perhaps for many years, using guerrilla warfare inside the towns and cities. Moreover, the common people will become more educated to fight and bear the burden of the battle themselves if the resistance (movement) exists beside the common man.[48]

The PFLP and the PDFLP were proven right. Having evacuated the towns, the commandos had to struggle for survival. The Jordanian army extended its grip on the country and by mid-July 1971, it had cleared Jordan of all Palestinian commandos.

The relationship between the PLO and Jordan, if any, became one of accusations and counter-accusations. When in March 1972 King Hussein announced a plan for what was to be called the United Arab Kingdom, the PLO flatly denounced him. The proposal envisaged a union between two autonomous regions, Jordan's East Bank and the occupied West Bank, plus "all other parts of liberated Palestine willing to join" (i.e., Gaza Strip).[49] In essence, Hussein's proposal denied the PLO the right to Palestinian representation. Even after the Algiers Arab Summit of 1973, when all other Arab states recognized the PLO as the only representative of the Palestinians, Hussein maintained his attacks on the organization. But when the next Arab Summit met the following year at Rabat, Hussein was pressured to consent to the legitimacy of the sole PLO representation of the Palestinian people. His attitude toward the PLO did finally change. Now, he had come to accept its representational character. However, he maintained that "as far as [the Jordanians] are concerned, [the Resistance Movement] has no chance of appearing in our land with its suspect leadership."[50]

It was only after the Camp David Accords were signed that Jordan and the PLO began to talk openly again. Jordan joined the Baghdad summit and began a dialogue with the PLO. Abu Iyad (Salah Khalaf), a major Fateh leader, discussed these reconciliation negotiations: "We are working to resume all activities in Jordan in an organized way, and taking into account the lessons of the past. It will be difficult to say when that will occur, or even that it is a matter of months."[51]

Jordan's political orientation and its demographic position impose powerful constraints on its policy. Any organized Palestinian movement is perceived with uneasiness in Jordan. In fact, Jordan's fears are the mirror image of the uneasiness that prevails among PLO leaders. A good deal of this fear is over the question of representation. Being the only Arab country to grant citizenship to the Palestinians, Jordan perceived itself to have acquired a right to speak on behalf of the Palestinians. This perception was diametrically opposed to that of the PLO. Moreover, as far as the Jordanian regime is concerned, a Palestinian state on the West Bank and Gaza may provide a focus of identity for the Palestinians on the East Bank. This, in return, can undermine Jordan's authority over more than half of its own population. Therefore, the PLO's existence and legitimacy challenge not only Jordan's right to represent even the East Bank Palestinians, but also the very basis of Jordan as a state. Hence, Jordan's policy in regard to the Palestinians stems from its fear for both its domestic position and its very existence as a legitimate state.

Jordan's perception of Palestinian sovereignty remained tied to Jordan's perception of its own legitimacy, which would entail a degree of control over parts of Jordan (West Bank and East Bank). To that end, Jordan required a camouflaged political formula to grant the Palestinians a sense of participation while isolating and suppressing those who advocated the end of the Palestinian/Jordanian connection. To this end, Jordan attempted to discredit the PLO in 1970, and later, in 1972, advocated a federation scheme. Today, however, this scheme has PLO consent. The sixteenth PNC held in Algiers affirmed the historic relations between the Palestinians and Jordan, and called for the continuation of the dialogue between the two parties. The nineteenth session issued a political program that aims at an independent state confederated with Jordan.

With the rupture of PLO-Syrian relations after Arafat's departure from Lebanon and free from the limits imposed upon him by the old emphasis on Palestinian national unity, Arafat had more flexibility to push his dialogue with Jordan forward. Accordingly, Arafat proceeded to hold the seventeenth PNC session in Jordan in November of 1984. Soon afterwards, Arafat signed an agreement with the king of Jordan for joint diplomatic action. This agreement provided for PLO acceptance of all UN resolutions and called for a UN-sponsored international peace conference where a joint Palestinian-Jordanian delegation would represent both parties. The agreement called for full Israeli withdrawal from the West Bank, Gaza Strip, and Jerusalem in return for full Palestinian-Jordanian diplomatic recognition and peaceful relations with Israel. Moreover, the agreement endorsed Jordan's plan of association between the future independent Palestinian state with Jordan through a confederal arrangement.

While the agreement signalled PLO moderation at many levels, it failed to generate sufficient enthusiasm in Israel or the United States. A year later, King Hussein declared his abandonment of the agreement and blamed its failure upon the PLO leadership. The PLO, in turn, blamed the United States for the failure of this agreement to achieve the anticipated results. In fact, while the agreement only implied the PLO's recognition of Security Council Resolution 242 and 338, the U.S. insisted upon a specific acceptance by the PLO of these two resolutions. The PLO, in turn, insisted on an American acceptance of a Palestinian right to self-determination as a condition for its acceptance of the above-mentioned resolutions. Consequently, no progress was achieved.

The Palestinian intifada, however, was a final blow to the Jordanian aspirations concerning the West Bank. West Bank and Gaza Palestinians quickly displayed their allegiance to the PLO and denounced any links to Jordan. Communiqué No. 10 of the Unified National Leadership of the Uprising even requested the resignation of all Parliament members still residing on the West Bank. Realizing that the West Bank had changed forever, King Hussein issued a declaration on July 31, 1988 extricating himself from the West Bank and asserting that the PLO had full responsibility to the area. This declaration removed once and for all the Jordanian challenge to the PLO's representative character. Consequently, Jordanian-PLO relations improved dramatically.

With the Jordanian challenge removed, the PNC session of 1988 found it possible to conclude that a Palestinian-Jordanian confederation should not be opposed. This Jordanian move also cleared away any remaining obstacles to their Declaration of Independence on November 15, 1988.

Lebanon

Even though many Palestinians found asylum in Lebanon after the establishment of Israel and their displacement from Palestine, the Palestinian guerrillas did not appear in Lebanon in significant numbers until October 1968. Their presence there some seven months after the important battle of Karameh in Jordan was seen by Israel as a threat to its northern settlements. "In November, commando raids brought Israeli retaliation into Lebanon. Then, on December 28, 1968, Israeli commandos destroyed thirteen commercial aircraft at Beirut International Airport, ostensibly in reprisal for a terrorist attack on an El Al plane in Athens."[52]

These Israeli raids alarmed the Lebanese regime—just as they had the one in Jordan—and its political and economic establishment, as represented by the Maronite Phalange Party. The Lebanese army was embarrassed by the Israeli attacks, which went unchallenged. In fact, Lebanon's army was constituted as a police force rather than a defense force. Unlike the other Arab states, Lebanon avoided strengthening its military forces against possible Israeli aggression, and depended on Western "commitment" to protect it from Israel. To many people, the Lebanese army seemed impotent against Israel. There were reports that "as a result, Major General Emile Bustani ordered a crackdown on guerrilla operations."[53] Again, Israel's policy of retaliation had worked to hasten a confrontation between the Palestinian commandos and the host country. But unlike the case of Jordan, Lebanon's regime and its army were fragmented and desperately weak.

Among the population of Lebanon, many elements became convinced that coexistence with Israel was impossible as a result of the raids. They further called upon their government to assume its "proper" role in the Arab struggle against Israel. In fact, discontent with the failure of the regime to thwart the airport raid toppled the cabinet on January 7, 1969.

Lebanon's system is unique among the Arab states. It was designed to cope with the cleavages between Christians and Moslems and their sectarian subdivisions. This design "was mechanistic: fixed proportional representation according to religious sect . . . specified in all the institutions of government."[54] Unfortunately, this proportional representation solution for sectarian tensions aggravated other problems and led to governmental inefficiency and vast social inequality. In other words, Lebanon had the ingredients for a civil war prior to the emergence of the Palestinian commandos. In fact, since the creation of the system in 1943, Lebanon has had two civil wars—the first of which had no relationship whatsoever to Palestinian commandos and took place in 1958.

The emergence of the Palestinian commandos on the Lebanese scene and their commando raids on Israel represented a new challenge to the shaky sectarian balance of power. The Moslem and underprivileged elements of the population saw in the commandos a strong new ally against the ruling elites who represented the status quo. The upper classes of the country, mostly dominated by the Christian Maronite sect—which enjoyed undue influence in the seats of power—feared the commandos and viewed them as a threat to the system. As a result, Lebanese opinion was increasingly polarized into pro- and antiguerrilla positions.

Events took a serious turn in 1969 when the guerrillas made efforts to establish themselves in South Lebanon adjoining the Israeli border.

Several clashes with the Lebanese army occurred as a result. Palestinian commando attacks on Israel brought Israeli raids on southern Lebanese villages, which complicated the crisis. Egyptian mediation led to the signing of the Cairo Agreement on November 3, 1969 by the PLO and the Lebanese government.

The Cairo Agreement gave the PLO responsibility for Palestinians in the refugee camps, the right to establish armed posts within the camps, and the right to free movement in the border area. In return, the PLO was to control the actions of all its commandos to insure their noninterference in Lebanese affairs. Under the terms of the agreement, Palestinian commandos were to occupy certain areas near the Israeli border as bases for training and posts to launch military operations.[55] The major base in Arquoub region became known by Israel and in the Western press as Fatehland.

Friction between the commandos and the Lebanese government was appreciably reduced as a result of the Cairo Agreement and the Jordanian civil war. However, the truce was not long-lived. Increased guerrilla presence in Lebanon after their ouster from Jordan led to an escalation of their operations against Israel from Lebanon. This was followed by increased Israeli raids on Lebanon.

The Lebanese government's relations with the commandos, publicly cordial and restrained, had by 1972 become very tense. The regime wanted to avoid a clash with the commandos and to restrain their activities in order to limit Israeli reprisal attacks. This objective, however, was not to be met. In spite of Palestinian restraint, Israel "still had hopes of provoking a clash between the authorities and the commandos in Lebanon, and laid plans to this end."[56] The murder by an Israeli infiltration group of Kamal Nasser, Kamal Adwan, and Abu Yusef, three prominent PLO leaders, in their homes in Beirut on April 10, 1973, strained relations between the PLO and the Lebanese army leadership to the breaking point. The PLO was unhappy because the army had not responded to the attack, although the army barracks on Rue Verdun were close by.

Various attempts to reach accords between the regime and the commandos were only temporarily successful. Continuous Israeli raids on Lebanon, however, heightened tensions after every accord. By mid-April 1975, hostilities between the two parties had become severe. The Lebanese society had by now been fully polarized and the underprivileged groups had aligned themselves with the Palestinians in what came to be known as the "Palestinian-Moslem-Leftist Alliance." The civil war had begun.

It must be emphasized that while the Palestinians were a contributing factor to Lebanon's ensuing tragedy, the civil war had its own internal and external root causes. "While on the internal level the class and regional conflicts have been partly hidden by sectarian manifestations," the civil war was understandably hastened "by the impact of the Palestinian-Israeli conflict and the Arab-Israeli conflict on Lebanese politics."[57] The presence of the Palestinians on the Lebanese scene has only unmasked the contradictions within the Lebanese system and set the stage for the confrontation. In essence, the civil war "has been caused by the reluctance of the dominant elements in the country to recognize and accept the changed and changing circumstances which necessitate a new and different political formula."[58]

The savage war, which lasted 19 months and took perhaps 60,000 lives, resolved nothing. There were no winners, only losers and survivors. The civil war practically partitioned Lebanon and threatened to draw the Arabs into a war with Israel. These may have been the main reasons that led to a Syrian intervention. By the end of November 1976, the overwhelming Syrian presence had terminated the internal armed contest. The Syrian presence was backed by the Arab League and actually made a part of an Arab peacekeeping force there.

As a result of the Syrian role and its subsequent termination of the armed contest, Syria's regime became the major power broker in Lebanon. The PLO survived the war, but was badly bruised. Its independence had been curtailed in Lebanon north of the Awali river, which the Syrians did not cross, so that Israel would not invade the country and a Syrian-Israeli war be imposed upon Syria.

At that juncture, then, the PLO was completely out of Jordan, its relations with Egypt were worse than they had ever been, and its freedom was curtailed in Lebanon. In fact, PLO relations with the Arab regimes present a paradox: while the PLO was gaining steadily in its international standing and respectability, its actual independence of movement was being reduced. Verbally and diplomatically, the Arab regimes have given the PLO firm and even fervent support. But when interests of states have clashed with Palestinian interests, Arab leaders have, understandably, thought of themselves first.

Having been limited in their armed activities to southern Lebanon, the Palestinian commandos diverted their attention almost totally toward Israel. Their shellings of northern Israel and frequent attacks upon it led to an Israeli invasion of southern Lebanon in March of 1978. Five days later, the Security Council adopted resolution 425, calling for a cease-fire, an Israeli withdrawal, and the dispatching of a new UN force to the area to oversee and maintain the peace.

Peace, however, was not achieved. Unfolding events led to an all-out Israeli invasion of the country in June 1982. In spite of an American negotiated cease-fire between the Palestinian commandos and Israel, Israeli leaders went on with a plan to invade the country. Israel's war was principally directed against the PLO, its constituency in Lebanon, and its Lebanese allies.

The first eight days of the war witnessed an Israeli-sweep through southern Lebanon. Palestinian commandos and their Lebanese allies fought hard but were no match to Israel's might. By the ninth day, Israeli troops were surrounding West Beirut, where Palestinian and Lebanese forces had joined together under Arafat's leadership to resist the Israeli advance.

Rational military calculations would have suggested a brief battle followed by the immediate Israeli entry into West Beirut. This was not to be. The joint Palestinian-Lebanese forces resisted a deluge of bombs and blockades for almost three months. In mid-August, an agreement was reached that called for Palestinian fighters to leave with only their personal arms and for Israel to withdraw from Lebanon's capital. This agreement was to be supervised by a multinational force of American, French, and Italian troops. Consequently, by September 1, 1982, the evacuation of Beirut by Palestinian commandos was complete.

Those who had hoped that the evacuation of the Palestinian commandos would settle Lebanon's problems were quickly disappointed. Sectarian and political confrontations continued even after the withdrawal of Israel to the extreme south. Neither the assassination of Basheer Gemayel—president-elect of Lebanon in 1982—nor the massacres at Sabra and Chatilla refugee camps settled Lebanon's crisis. Today, the country is effectively divided along sectarian lines. Palestinian presence is basically limited to the refugee camps and the Bekaa valley under Syria's control. Some commandos have attempted to return, leading to the so called "camp wars" between these Palestinians and the Amal—the largest group of Shi'ite militia-fighters. The Amal hoped to be the only military presence in West Beirut. While agreements were reached at Taif, Saudi Arabia, to settle the Lebanese civil war, the settlement is still a dream.

Syria

Among the Arabs, the Syrian people may be the most outspoken supporters of the Palestinians. This support may be attributed as much to the strong sense of Arab nationalism in Syria as to Palestine's history as a part of Syria. Syrian support of the Palestinians has been forthcoming even before Syria acquired its own independence. However, not unlike other Arab governments, the Syrian regimes have taken every opportunity to insure that the Palestinian guerrilla movement remains limited at home. Domestic political considerations have been a major factor in Syrian-Palestinian relations.

"The Syrians have always linked their own struggle against Western imperialism to the Palestinian struggle against Western imperialism and its imported instrument of control, political Zionism."[59] Since independence, the Syrian armed forces have been critical in determining who controls the country. Between 1949 and 1968 alone, Syria experienced eleven attempts (some successful) by the military to take over the government. The successive Syrian regimes have not failed to reflect "the people's suspicion and distrust of the West, particularly the United States for its heavy material and political support of the Zionist state, and the U.S. attempts in 1957 to subvert the National Front regime...."[60]

While for the Arab world the loss of Palestine was an Arab tragedy, for Syria it was a particularly painful loss since Palestine constituted southern Syria. It has been noted that:

Of all Arab states, Syria has been among the most deeply influenced by the creation and existence of Israel. The Palestine defeat of 1948 put the army on the road to its dominating role in Syrian life and politics. Whether it likes it or not, Syria's evolution remains a function of continuing Israeli pressure and the permanence of the Palestine tragedy.[61]

The 1967 Arab-Israeli War was also painful for Syria. In that war, Syria's territorial integrity was violated, leaving the Syrian people to feel both emasculated and unprotected. For them, the loss of the Golan changed the nature of the conflict. Consequently, they became ambivalent. They feared further Israeli advances toward Damascus; yet, at the same time, they hold an unshakable determination to liberate the Occupied Territories.

A primary function of a state is to protect its territorial integrity. A secondary function is to recover territory it might have previously lost. Certainly Syria is no exception. After 1967, Syria had to establish priorities, with the emphasis being on her territorial integrity. Therefore, Syria's primary concern became the protection of the Syrian heartland from the threatening Israelis. Secondary to this is the recovery of the Occupied Territories and the restoration of Palestinian national rights.

Perhaps in the minds of many Palestinians the distinction between Syrian and Palestinian territories is only superficial. However, for Syria, as for Egypt, the distinction is clear.

The 1967 defeat and its ramifications heightened Syrian anxiety and gave rise to a tense debate among the ruling Ba'th party. This debate developed into an outright power struggle between the two factions of the party: civilian and military. The civilian group, led by Salad Jadid, saw in the results of the war the end of the classical war option and called for a popular war of liberation with unconditional Syrian support for the Palestinian guerrillas. On the other hand, the military group, led by General Hafez El-Assad, demanded a free hand on all matters dealing with the issue of confrontation. It wanted to keep the activities of the

Palestinians under check lest they provoke Israeli retaliations. It also wanted to establish a credible eastern front composed of Syria, Jordan, and Iraq.

During the 1970 civil war in Jordan, the issue of debate concerned the Syrian role in the war. The civilian faction wanted to rescue the resistance movement from the onslaught of the Jordanian army. The military leadership, on the other hand, had no desire to fight Jordan, a potential ally in the next inevitable war with Israel. Although the civilian faction succeeded in sending Syrian forces into Jordan on September 20, General Assad, who was opposed to intervention, denied these forces the needed air protection, which forced their hasty retreat. It was noted that:

This decision by General Assad [not to send air protection] reflected the basic thinking; he did not believe that the Palestinian guerrillas could do any serious damage to Israel, and saw no reason why two Arab nations should fight each other on their behalf. Assad did not particularly like the Jordanian regime, but he did not care for the men at the top of the PLO much more.[62]

One could probably add that General Assad feared that Syrian intervention in the Jordanian civil war would precipitate Israeli retaliation if not another major war like that of 1967. He may have also feared the U.S. reaction. Therefore, while the intervention underscored Syrian commitment to the Palestinians, its limited nature and fast withdrawal underscored Syrian fear of Israel.

The internal power struggle that had been brewing for years in Syria exploded during the Jordanian civil war. It was finally settled when General Assad carried out a swift coup in November 1970. He arrested the opposition's leadership and eliminated its power base. Thus, the Palestinians, having suffered a bloody setback in Jordan, were faced with an immediate political setback in Syria. Their activities there were put under firm military control. General Assad, now president of Syria, "had no desire to have the timing or extent of a battle (with Israel) forced on him when he did not want it by ... acts of guerrillas."[63] Nor would he "tolerate a Palestinian movement independent of his control."[64]

The outcome of the October 1973 Arab-Israeli War was not the liberation of the occupied Arab lands, but rather the initiation of a process of political settlement. While this process seemed possible at first, it proved to be futile by 1975 as a result of Israeli obduracy. However, the negotiations led to the isolation of the Syrian front from Egypt with the signing of the second Sinai Disengagement Agreement in 1975. Therefore, Syria's position became more precarious, and Syrian fear of Israel also became greater. As a result, Syrian control of the Palestinians became more important for Assad lest they provoke an untimely war with Israel.

It was at this juncture that the Lebanese civil war was intensified. Syrian policy in Lebanon was motivated by its perception of its own security vis-à-vis Israel. This is not to preclude other Syrian motivations, but it is reasonable to conclude that Syria's role in Lebanon was influenced by its fear of Israel. Other motivations accounting for Syrian policy in Lebanon could include Syria's image of its role in inter-Arab politics; Syria's concern for religious minorities; its determination to maintain the PLO under check; and its hope to establish a friendly and cooperative government in Lebanon.

The Syrian leadership believed that the second Sinai Disengagement Agreement had frozen the Egyptian front, if not permanently eliminated it. Their perceptions of this agreement and its relationship to the Lebanese civil war were noted by a commentary broadcast over Damacus radio as follows:

The escalation of fighting (in Lebanon) is connected with the activation of the negotiations on the Sinai Agreement. It is clear that the plan [American-Israeli-Egyptian] for events was aimed at the following:

- To cover up the Sinai Agreement;
- To create a new situation in the area that would draw the attention of the Arab citizens away from the basic struggle between the Arab nation and the Zionist enemy;
- To throw the Palestine Resistance into an internal Lebanese battle of a hateful sectarian nature and submerge it in the events in Lebanon in order to prevent it from carrying out its duties in confronting the enemy . . . ;
- To keep Syria preoccupied with the Lebanese problem . . . ;
- To create division among the Arab people in Lebanon. . . . [65]

It was feared in Damascus that Palestinian and leftist successes would inevitably lead to both a partition of the country and unrestricted PLO activities against Israel. Either of these developments would give Israel an invitation to invade Lebanon on the pretext of destroying "terrorist" bases and/or protecting a mini-Christian state. Any Israeli move into Lebanon would expose the Syrian western flanks and open the way to the encirclement of the Syrian army on the Golan and the fall of Damascus.

With such calculations, the Syrian leadership was determined to contain the conflict and maintain the internal balance of power in Lebanon. When it became evident that the balance of power "turned in favor of the Progressive-Palestinian alliance" in January 1976, Syrian mediation worked out an agreement and a cease fire.[66] But when this failed, Syria sent in the PLA and Sa'iqa troops to establish the hoped-for equilibrium. By June, Syrian troops advanced on Lebanon and finally reversed the military balance in favor of the rightist forces. With the blessing of an Arab mini-summit at Riyadh, the Syrian troops, which became official

Arab peace-keeping forces, established hegemony over the country.[67] The Syrian presence in the country forced not only a temporary cease-fire, but also halted the bloodshed for some time. The Palestinian guerrillas were kept in the camps and in the southern part of the country, where fighting with the Israeli-backed rightists persisted.

The PLO, having its independence curtailed in what could be its last possible sanctuary, was to face new and more determined peace initiatives soon after the civil war. The Sadat-Israeli talks, although rejected by Syria, put the PLO in a precarious position and opened the way for United States, Israeli, and some Arab leaders to search for an alternative to the PLO in peace negotiations. An alternative was not found, but the Camp David Accords were signed and Egypt was legally frozen out of the Arab-Israeli conflict.

The Camp David Accords, however, did contribute to the conciliation between Syria and the PLO. Both saw the accords as a momentous challenge that must be faced by joint action. Even before Camp David, Syria and the PLO had reached an understanding that was designed to face Israeli challenges in South Lebanon. But this reconciliation, while strengthened briefly during Israel's invasion of Lebanon, fell apart soon after Arafat's exit from Beirut.

The mutiny within Fateh completed the split between Arafat's PLO and Assad's Syria. Arafat accused Syria of organizing the mutiny, while Syria saw it as a Palestinian reaction to Arafat's "inept" leadership and questionable political moves. Consequently, Syria gave its blessing to the convening of a conference in Tripoli, Libya for the anti-Arafat Palestinian factions, where they denounced Arafat and demanded that he be removed from office. Since that time, both the PLO and Syria continue to engage in a war of rhetoric in which each condemns the other's behavior. Anti-Arafat Palestinian commandos consider Syria and the Lebanese territories under Syrian control as their haven. But here again, the intifada cooled down the rhetoric and may still bring about yet another reconciliation. The Iraqi invasion of Kuwait, however, has put any potential reconciliation on hold for the time being.

Saudi Arabia

For a long time, Saudi Arabia was able to stay away from Arab-Israeli politics, but by 1973 the country found itself at center-stage in Arab-Israeli relations. Whereas Cairo had been the focal point in resolving regional problems during the 1960s, Riyadh became the new meeting ground where such disputes were settled in the mid- and late 1970s. Negotiations for the disengagement agreements had to be carried out with the blessing of Saudi Arabia, as evidenced by Kissinger's continued "shuttles" to Riyadh.

Saudi Arabia's rising influence made it central for the resolution of the Arab-Israeli conflict. Perhaps Saudi rejection of the Camp David Accords was one of the most significant blows for their makers. Inasmuch as the country was considered to be so conservative and so committed to close relations with the United States, the American leaders as well as Sadat had taken Saudi support for granted. In fact, both the United States and Egypt anticipated that, while Saudi Arabia may not like the accords or the treaty, it would soon afterwards seek to minimize any Arab measures against Egypt and would eventually come to support the Sadat position. This hope soon proved to be false. Saudi Arabia not only condemned the Camp David agreements but joined "radical" Arab regimes in imposing sanctions against Sadat's regime.

A number of factors combined to bring about this Saudi rejection. First was the fear of Soviet penetration of the region. The Palestine problem had, for some time, been the Soviet bridge to the Middle East. Arab regimes that oppose U.S. accommodation schemes tend to establish closer ties with the Soviets. By joining the displaced camp, Saudi Arabia was able to strengthen the principle of accommodation through pressure on the U.S. rather than break with it. Thus, the Camp David Accords did not lead to a major Soviet "victory" in the Arab world. In fact, the Baghdad summit seemed to lead to the further isolation of the USSR in the region. Second, the Saudis feared that, had they embraced it, Camp David would have had the effect of endangering Saudi security. The Camp David Accords so violated the minimum acceptable Arab requirements for peace that it could have inevitably led to isolation of those powers accepting them from their own masses as well as from other Arabs. The Saudis are in no position to be isolated from their own masses, in view of the fragile nature of their regime. Third, Saudi Arabia perceives itself to be the center of the Arab and Islamic nation, and was compelled by the nature of this perception to reject Camp David.

Saudi Arabia, however, wants an accommodation. To this effect, the then Prince Fahd proposed a "peace plan" on August 6, 1981. This proposal called for Israeli withdrawal to its 1967 borders, the elimination of Israeli settlements in the Occupied Territories, Palestinian repatriation, and the establishment of a Palestinian state with Jerusalem as its capital. This Saudi plan has received Arab support, including that of the PLO at the Fez Summit. Therefore, while the Saudis want an accommodation, they are in no position to accept one that seems to violate the existing Arab consensus. The Saudis often seem to help create an Arab consensus for accommodation prior to their actually advocating it. Thus, during the Camp David talk, while they joined the anti-Sadat forces, they at the same time kept their contacts with Egypt open—at least secretly—and pressured other Arabs to moderate their positions. Because of the "power of their dollar," the Saudis have largely been successful. Their next move was to be a major Saudi attempt to bring about a U.S.-PLO dialogue in order to co-opt the PLO more fully into the peace process. The Israeli invasion of Lebanon, the departure of Arafat from Tripoli, Arafat's trip to Cairo, and the intifada worked in favor of Saudi objectives.

While internal differences within the PLO are considered harmful to the Palestinian cause of unity, they have also proven helpful to the moderate majority. Saudi Arabia, for example, feared the rejectionist Palestinians. Its government feared that radicalization of the Middle East would cause instability that would threaten the Saudi regime itself. Therefore, in order to contain the radicals, Saudi Arabia cooperated with Fateh and gave it a large dose of financial assistance. The assistance, however, has not prevented occasional discord between the two parties. PLO-Saudi relations have at times sunk very low, and seemed at their lowest during the Jordanian and Lebanese civil wars, when Saudi Arabia played a role that was supportive of anti-PLO forces. Similarly, the Iraqi invasion of Kuwait and the PLO's wavering response to it led to a deterioration of Saudi-Palestinian relations.

Other States

Unlike Saudi Arabia, Kuwait has not only given Fateh subsidies, but also supplied the PLO with diplomatic support when the organization was in crisis. This continuous support may be due, in part, to the influence of the large Palestinian community living in Kuwait. In late December 1970, for example, Kuwait suspended its subsidy to Jordan for its expulsion of the commandos. The PLO, on its part, responded in kind. "Arafat personally helped to settle the border dispute between Kuwait and Iraq in 1972..."[68] But the Iraqi invasion of Kuwait placed the PLO in a complex predicament and may contribute to a total breakdown of PLO relations with the Kuwaiti royal family.

The PLO proclaims a strategy of "non interference" in Arab affairs, and has attempted to do so even when the contradictions seemed impossible to reconcile. But, in the process, the PLO has come to mirror the divisions of the Arab world.

Just as the moderate and conservative Arab regimes have difficulties with the PLO, the more progressive states such as Libya and Algeria have quarrels with it, too. These regimes have also contributed to the tensions within the PLO. Iraq, for example, by creating its own guerrilla group, the Arab Liberation Front, in 1969, has contributed to the already existing divisions within the Resistance Movement. However, Iraq makes its own financial subsidies to the PLO and supports its stand on Arab-Israeli negotiations. But Iraq's invasion of Kuwait in 1990 put the

PLO in one of its most difficult positions in the Arab world since the PLO's creation.

Libyan relations with the Palestinians have passed through tense periods as well. But Qaddafi is the most outspoken among all Arab leaders in his support of the Palestinian revolution. Qaddafi first threw the Marxist Palestinian groups out of Libya as "godless," then changed his position after his quarrel with Sadat and rapprochment with the Soviet Union. However, his occasional support of the anti-Arafat factions of the Palestinian Resistance Movement also contributed to the divisions of that movement. Today, Qaddafi still fluctuates between support of and opposition to Arafat's leadership of the PLO.

Algeria may be the most popular among the Palestinians because of its own struggle for independence against a colonial settler regime. Its firm pro-PLO attitude also contributes to its popularity. However, Algeria's geographic location, distant from the battlefield, makes its support less significant than those of the confrontation states. In spite of that, Algeria has championed many political and diplomatic struggles to insure Arab and world recognition of the PLO as the sole legitimate representative of the Palestinian people. South Yemen was also supportive of the Palestinian organization, both at the political and military levels. Now, the Arab Republic of Yemen, the united Yemeni government, has excellent relations with the PLO.

Today, the polarization of Arabs into two groups—the moderates and the revolutionaries—is intensifying. The membership has shifted in favor of the moderates in terms of objectives—and numbers. Both regional and global events seem to have contributed to this shift. Regionally, the intifada has awakened the Arabs and reminded them of the centrality of the Palestinian dimension of the conflict and the Iraqi invasion of Kuwait has shifted their attention to new problems. Globally, the waning of the cold war and the sudden change in Eastern Europe and the Soviet Union have reminded the Arabs how easily their concerns could become very secondary. Even before such developments, during the summit meeting in Baghdad in December 1978, the Arab leaders had agreed for the first time on a common, multilateral formula for negotiating a Middle East peace. King Hussein, in briefing British reporters on December 19, 1978, raised several possible steps agreed upon at the summit and concluded that the "Arab countries generally were ready for all-party peace talks."[69] Therefore, Arab movement toward moderation has been evolving over time.

CONCLUSION

Over the past two decades, the Palestinian problem has become the focal question of the Middle East region. This is largely due to the rise of the Palestinian Resistance Movement. "The symbolic and material importance of this movement, both in terms of Arab-Israeli and inter-Arab relations, demonstrates the growing salience of non-state actors in world politics."[70]

The growth of the PLO over the past decades has led to official Arab reactions ranging from supporting it outright to warring against it. Understandably, the Arab regimes directly involved in the confrontation with Israel feared the guerrillas and attempted to control them lest they disrupt their governmental processes and lead them into an unwanted war with Israel. The guerrillas, on the other hand, realized their own limitations and attempted to appease these regimes by declaring a policy of "noninterference" in internal Arab affairs. This policy's failure often led the Arab regimes to crack down on the guerrillas. Such a policy has not only given justification to these regimes, but also antagonized the activist, antiregime elements within these countries. Clearly, it is such elements that the PLO needs during times of hardship and confrontation. By failing to challenge the regimes, the PLO has helped legitimize the state action taken against it. In the process, the PLO may have lost its most qualified potential supporters among the Arab masses and contributed to their alienation from the revolution.

Moreover, PLO emphasis on the Palestinian character of the revolution, while necessary for restoring the "Palestinian question" to public consciousness, has led to the "Palestinianization" of the revolution and the creation of unnecessary gaps between its cadres and the non-Palestinian masses where it exists. This has made it easier for some Arab regimes to crack down on the movement through the exploitation of such gaps.

Nevertheless, the PLO has been successful in restoring the Palestinian dimension to the Arab-Israeli conflict. Today, no Arab leader can ignore the Palestinians. The whole world has come to recognize that "the Palestinians must be represented in any conclusive peace talks with Israel."[71] PLO success in securing this recognition is, by itself, an outstanding achievement for a movement that has faced not only the Israeli enemy, which is dedicated to its annihilation, but also two civil wars in less than a decade. No future Middle East historian can study this era without references to the Palestinians and their role in regional affairs. Equally true is the fact that no future Palestinian historian can study the resistance movement without reference to its relationship to the Arab regimes and their influence on its policies and developments. It is this interrelationship that makes the PLO an outstanding case study of the role of nonstate actors in regional politics.

NOTES

1. *Free Palestine* (Washington, D.C.), August-September, 1970, p. 2.
2. Ibid.

3. Riad N. El-Rayyes and Dunia Nahhas, eds., *Guerrillas for Palestine: A Study of Palestinian Commando Organizations* (Beirut: An-Nahar Press, 1974), p. 14.
4. U.S., *Department of State Bulletin*, no. 57 (1969), p. 218.
5. Ibid.
6. John G. Stoessinger, *Why Nations Go to War* (New York: St. Martin's Press, 1974), p. 212.
7. Ibid.
8. Naseer Aruri, "The Antecedents of the Camp David Affair: Carter's Diplomatic Paradox," in Faith Zeidey, ed., *Camp David: A New Balfour Declaration* (Detroit: Association of Arab-American University Graduates, 1979), p. 3.
9. For details, see Edward Sheehan, "Step by Step in the Middle East," *Journal of Palestine Studies* 5, no. 3/4 (Spring/Summer 1976), p. 47.
10. Zbigniew Brzezinski et al., "Peace in an International Framework," *Foreign Policy*, Summer 1975, p. 10.
11. Anwar el-Sadat, *In Search of Identity: An Autobiography* (New York: Harper and Row, 1978), p. 306.
12. Ibid., p. 312.
13. Ibid.
14. Fayez A. Sayegh, "The Camp David Agreement and the Palestine Problem," *Journal of Palestine Studies* 8, no. 2 (Winter 1979), p. 39.
15. For an excellent discussion of Egyptian nationalism, see Wasif Abboushi, *Mashakel al-Tatawar wal-Tahdith Fil-Alam el-Arabi* (Problems of Development and Modernization in the Arab World) (Birzeit: Birzeit University Press, 1980), pp. 202–210.
16. Ibid., p. 204.
17. Fouad M. Moughrabi, "The Accommodationist Style in Contemporary Arab Politics," in Zeadey, *Camp David*, p. 11.
18. For the text of the Baghdad Summit proclamation, see Ibid., pp. 85–86.
19. Walter Lehn, *The Development of Palestinian Resistance* (Detroit: Association of Arab-American University Graduates, 1974), p. 45.
20. William B. Quandt et al., *Politics of Palestinian Nationalism* (Berkeley: University of California Press, 1973), p. 207.
21. *Falastine al-Thawra* (Beirut), 2 March 1975, p. 5.
22. Ibid.
23. *Al-Hadaf* (Beirut) 8, no. 36 (30 August 1975), p. 8.
24. *The New York Times*, 20 August 1975, p. 6.
25. Naseer Aruri, "Ittifakiyat Sina Kashakil min Ashkal Siyasat al-Ihtiwa' al-Amerikiyah" (The Sinai Accord as a Form of the American Policy of Containment) *Shu'un Filastiniyah* 56 (April 1976), pp. 31–36.
26. *Al-Hadaf* 8, no. 36 (30 August 1975), p. 8.
27. *Newsweek*, November 28, 1977, p. 37.
28. Ibid., December 5, 1977, p. 25.
29. Ibid., p. 33.
30. Ibid.
31. Ibid.
32. Ibid.
33. Ibid.
34. Lehn, *Development of Palestinian Resistance*, p. 23.
35. Chaliand, *Palestinian Resistance*, p. 19.

36. Edgar O'Ballance, *Arab Guerrilla Power 1967–1972* (London: Faber and Faber, 1973), p. 120.
37. Lehn, *Development of Palestinian Resistance*, p. 28. *Fateh* (Amman), 17 August 1970.
38. Lehn, *Development of Palestinian Resistance*, p. 28.
39. Ibid. p. 27.
40. *Fateh* (Amman), 17 September 1970.
41. *Life* 69, no. 14 (October 1970), pp. 28–33.
42. Interview with Murray Sayle in *The Sunday Times* (London) 27 September 1970, p. 5; reprinted in *The Middle East Newsletter* (Beirut), October/November 1970, pp. 7–8.
43. O'Ballance, *Arab Guerrilla Power*, p. 232.
44. Ibid., p. 158.
45. *Fateh* (Amman), 2 October 1970.
46. *Al-Hadaf* (Beirut) 3, no. 48 (13 November 1970).
47. Ibid., p. 5.
48. Ibid., p. 6.
49. El-Rayyes, *Guerrillas for Palestine*, S p. 116.
50. Ibid., p. 122.
51. *The Christian Science Monitor*, 13 December 1978, p. 11.
52. Michael Hudson, "Fedayeen Are Forcing Lebanon's Hand," *Mid East* 9, no. 4 (February 1970), p. 7.
53. Ibid.
54. Michael Hudson, "The Lebanese Crisis: The Limits of Consociational Democracy," *Journal of Palestine Studies* 5, no. 3/4 (Spring/Summer 1976), p. 114.
55. For full text of the agreement, see El-Rayyes, *Guerrillas for Palestine*, pp. 127–128.
56. Ibid., p. 132.
57. Leila Meo, "Syria and the Conflict in Lebanon," in Fouad Moughrabi and Naseer Aruri, eds., *Lebanon: Crisis and Challenge in the Arab World* (Detroit: Association of Arab-American University Graduates, 1977), p. 26.
58. Michael W. Suleiman, "Origins of the Lebanese Civil War," in Moughrabi and Aruri, *Lebanon*, p. 2.
59. Ibid., p. 27.
60. Ibid.
61. Tabitha Petran, *Syria* (New York: Praeger, 1972), p. 257.
62. John Bulloch, *The Making of War: The Middle East from 1967 to 1973* (London: Longman Group, 1974), pp. 87–88.
63. Ibid., p. 91.
64. Petran, *Syria*, p. 253.
65. *Swasia* 3, no. 22 (28 May 1976).
66. Meo, "Syria and the Conflict in Lebanon," p. 29.
67. Ibid., pp. 30–31.
68. El-Rayyes, *Guerrillas for Palestine*, p. 151.
69. *The Christian Science Monitor*, 21 December 1978, p. 3.
70. Richard W. Mansbach, Yale H. Ferguson, and Donald E. Lampert, *The Web of World Politics: Non-State Actors in the Global System* (Englewood Cliffs, N.J.: Printice-Hall, 1976), p. 104.
71. Ibid., p. 134.

6

The PLO and the International Community

"It is somewhat commonplace to say that if World War III were to break out, it would most likely be in the Middle East and its detonator would be the Arab-Israeli conflict. . . . An Arab-Israeli war could trigger nuclear holocaust."[1] The Middle East has been an important arena of world events from the beginning of written history. But at no time in modern history has the region been as significant as it is today. Contemporary world involvement in the Middle East is above all an involvement in the politics of oil. The Arab-Israeli conflict is related to these politics. The Palestinians are at the core of the Arab-Israeli conflict.

Since its inception in 1964, the PLO has recognized world interest in the region and has taken steps to establish the necessary links with the nations of the world. Today, it has developed complex relationships outside the Middle East. In the international diplomatic arena, the PLO may have scored greater success than on the local front. As noted in Chapter 2, the PLO is recognized by more than a hundred countries as well as by a number of significant international organizations, including the United Nations.

Having detailed U.N. recognition of the PLO in Chapter 2, there is no need at this point for further comments on this topic. It is enough to cite the Security Council's decision in January 1976 to invite the PLO under Rule 37 to participate in council debates. This rule allows the council to invite "any member of the United Nations" when its interests are affected. "The honor was first to be granted by the council to a national liberation movement . . ."[2] The General Assembly, as noted, has been even more forthcoming than the council in its support of the PLO.

Other U.N. organs and international groups have also recognized and supported the PLO. It is not an exaggeration to say that, of all the existing national liberation movements, the PLO may be the most recognized if not most supported by the world community of nations. Various analysts have attempted to determine the underlying reasons for this recognition and support. Many Israeli analysts have come to attribute this success to the rising significance of Arab oil. While oil may have influenced Western policies, its impact upon non-Western nations has not been the determining factor of their Middle East stands. Long before the use of oil as a diplomatic tool, the third-world and communist nations have supported the PLO and its struggle against Israel.

Other explanations of international support for the PLO include humanitarian considerations, reactions to Palestinian acts of terrorism, Israel's intransigence, and the rise of anticolonialist voices in the modern world. Many diplomats and students in the Middle East attribute PLO successes at the international level to the rise in world public interest in human rights. Mr. Alfred Atherton, former assistant secretary of state for Near Eastern and South Asian affairs, has reiterated this hypothesis when he said that "there is a great deal of sympathy in the United States for the Palestinians, for their plight over the years."[3] Mr. Atherton's assessment could be right; however, it is too simple to accept as a sole explanation of the overwhelming support the PLO receives. One is tempted to ask why didn't U.S. and world sympathies come prior to the rise of the Palestinian Resistance Movement?

An interesting explanation for this support for the PLO was advanced by radical guerrilla factions and later concurred in by Western journalists. This theory claims that Palestinian terrorism has focused international attention on the Palestinians and forced people everywhere to ask why such acts are being carried out. George Habash, leader of the PFLP asserted that such acts force people to learn about the plight of the Palestinians.[4] In a program on ABC television, an American reporter agreed with Habash and proclaimed that the media becomes the real "hostage" during acts of terrorism.[5]

A further contributing factor could be attributed to Israel itself. While its leaders claim peace to be the objective of their nation, their policies of raids on Palestinian camps, establishing settlements in the Occupied Territories, and publicly declaring these territories to be "liberated lands" contribute to anti-Israeli protests in the international community. Ze'ev Schiff, writing in *Ha'aretz*, the most prestigious Israeli daily, supports this notion. After asserting that "Likud policy will make another war inevitable," he concludes that this will only lead to improving the "Arabs' prospects of gathering international—even partial American—public acquiescence in a war against Israel. . . ."[6]

A more popular explanation ties the Palestinian struggle against Zionism to that of the third world struggle against colonialism and imperialism. One of the most remarkable developments of this century has been that colonialism, as a recognized principle of political interaction, is on its death bed. The popularity of people's struggles against colonialism and imperialism overwhelms the third-world. Even in the Western world, the concepts of colonialism and imperialism have become outmoded and disliked. The Palestinian Resistance Movement, as noted in Chapter 2, is seen by these countries as a popular movement struggling against colonialism and imperialism. Zionism is often equated with settler-colonialism.[7] Regardless of motives, it is clear that the PLO was able to win great support among most states of the world as it began to take a more moderate position on the issue of peace in the region. By toning down its emphasis on the armed struggle and commando activities, and stressing instead the possibility of a peace settlement, the PLO was able to gain more support. It is doubtful that the PLO would have the support it currently enjoys had it still been calling for the destruction of Israel rather than for an independent Palestinian state next to Israel. Therefore, PLO moderation, coupled with mounting a more effective public relations campaign, helped the PLO gain more support.

PLO diplomatic relations today spread to every continent and almost every nation. However, these relations are not without setbacks and failures. In the United States, for example, PLO successes have been minimal, if not on occasion negative. In order to evaluate these developments, a look at specific major relationships is in order.

THE PLO AND THE UNITED STATES

For more than four decades, the United States has served as Israel's benefactor. Initially, the U.S. position was dictated less by geopolitical considerations than by a religious as well as moral impulse—a desire to somehow compensate the Jewish people for the horrors they suffered during World War II. Internal politics, too, played a part, especially among elected officials who needed the so-called "urban Jewish vote." Only a few months after the emergence of the state of Israel, President Truman declared: "We are pledged to a state of Israel, large enough, free enough, and strong enough to make its people self-supporting and secure."[8]

Later U.S. presidents made good on Truman's pledge. Even American economic and strategic interests in the region have, on occasion, been subordinated to U.S. determination to safeguard Israel. As a result, the United States has lost a great deal of influence in the Arab world. U.S. interests in the region have also been jeopardized.

The catalogue of American interests in the Middle East is "well-known and hardly contested: the survival of Israel; access to oil and friendship to the Arabs; [and] the avoidance of confrontation with the Soviet Union ..."[9], according to former Senator J. W. Fulbright, who served as the chairman of the Senate Foreign Relations Committee. The U.S. interest in Israel, the senator stated, is "emotional and ideological: it is [in] our interest for Israel to survive because we wish Israel to survive."[10] U.S. interest in Arab oil is a matter of vital economic necessity—tangible and urgent. Until recently it was also uncontested that the U.S. wanted the Soviet Union out of the Middle East. Former U.S. Secretary of State John Foster Dulles warned against Soviet penetration of the area because it could "result in disastrous consequences for the West: it could cause a decisive shift in the world balance of power and a dangerous threat to Europe's economy."[11] This objective, however, has become insignificant in the aftermath of glasnost and perestroika.

Americans don't disagree about *what* their interests are but, rather, which will take priority. To the Israeli lobby—with its extraordinary influence on U.S. foreign policy—the security of Israel is the commanding objective.

In 1956, Israel (in the tripartite attack on Egypt) occupied the Gaza Strip and the Sinai. Only because of U.S. pressure (under President Eisenhower) did Israel withdraw from these areas. In contrast, it was the role of the Johnson Administration in the Security Council in 1967 that resulted in the formulation of Resolution 242 in the way it turned out to be: making Israeli withdrawal from the Occupied Territories dependent on Arab willingness to make peace. This weakens the U.N. Charter principle on "the inadmissibility of the acquisition of territory by war." Now (even though the U.N. principle is reiterated in Resolution 242), withdrawal is linked to peacemaking. In 1956, the U.S. dividend to Israel was the use of the Straits of Tiran. After 1967, the dividend became immeasurably larger—peace, trade, diplomatic relations with the Arab states, and limitation of Palestinian national aspirations as the U.N. resolution did not assert their right to self-determination.

"Until 1967, the official U.S. position on the Arab-Israeli conflict favored the status quo, as did the U.S. policy on Arab affairs."[12] The 1967 war, however, introduced new factors that forced a change on U.S. policymakers. That war transformed Israel from a state occupying a large part of Palestine into a state occupying all of Palestine and territories of other sovereign Arab states. American leaders, while occasionally mentioning the territorial integrity of all states in the region, did nothing to pressure Israel out of the Occupied Territories. Instead, they accepted the principle of negotiation. This principle became the cornerstone of the later U.S. peace initiatives. Palestinian guerrilla activities were seen by the U.S. as disruptive, at the least, to its efforts at negotiations.

The PLO, on its part, viewed the United States with even greater mistrust. As noted in Chapter 4, PLO literature often referred to the

U.S. as an "imperialist" power within the enemy camp. Their analysts assert that "the U.S. employs its capabilities in the services of Israel's short- and long-term objectives ... (because) it realizes that such actions guarantee its strategic aims."[13] Thus, the PLO ties American interests to those of Israel. The more radical factions of the PLO even go as far as to forecast a Palestinian-Arab military confrontation with the United States and Israel. The United States, on its part, contributed to the popularity of these notions. Occasionally, it has meddled in Arab affairs. In 1957, the American threat of intervention may have frustrated a nationalist attempt to overthrow Jordan's regime. In that year also, the Americans sent a task force to the Syrian coast, which is said to have frustrated communist plans to take over Syria. During the 1958 Lebanese civil war, American marines were dispatched on behalf of the conservative Lebanese regime. In 1970, American Sixth Fleet maneuvers and threats may have averted an all-out Syrian intervention on behalf of the Palestinians in Jordan. In 1976, American consent to the Syrian intervention in Lebanon allowed Assad's troops to reverse Palestinian advances. Moreover, U.S. aid to Israel, especially during the Arab-Israeli wars, adds to the credibility of the beliefs held by the Palestinians about the U.S.

Given such Palestinian perceptions as these, it is difficult for the American-PLO relations to blossom. Even the moderates among Palestinians do not openly advocate better relations with the United States. Any such ventures are viewed by the PLO mainstream and its radicals with suspicion. It is understandable then to hear Yahya Hammudeh, the former PLO chairman, saying that Palestinians want "nothing from the United States but that it refrain from making things worse."[14]

However, Palestinians generally differentiate between American policy and the American people. While attacking U.S. policy, Mr. Hammudeh asserts his "hope (that) the American people ... interest themselves in the (Palestine) problem and see to it that justice is carried out ..." and he attempts to create this interest by telling the American people: "I come from Jerusalem proper. Yet I am denied now even the right to be buried there."[15]

In spite of the public pronouncements on both sides, a dialogue between the PLO and the United States has occasionally existed. During the 1975–76 Lebanese war, PLO guerrillas assisted in the evacuation of 276 Americans and Europeans from Lebanon. Former Egyptian Foreign Minister Ismael Fahmi was reported to say that "direct contacts" took place between the United States and the PLO. Later, the Palestinian news agency "WAFA reported that the PLO leadership received a note of thanks from Dr. Kissinger for its role in the evacuation."[16] While denying that "direct contacts" had occurred, former Secretary of State Kissinger admitted that the United States has had contacts through "intermediaries." Similar contacts are reported to have taken place in 1980, as the PLO attempted to mediate between the United States and Iran over the American hostage crisis. *The Christian Science Monitor* reports that one channel through which the American government kept in touch with the PLO was "Zuhdi Tarazi, acting observer at the United Nations, and the Secretary General. Mr. Tarazi was understood to be passing on the PLO's ideas about developments in the Middle East to the Secretary General, who relays them to the State Department and may, on occasion, have made himself available for the return flow of thoughts."[17]

In addition, many senators and congressmen have met with Yasser Arafat and other PLO officials. In June, 1976, Mr. Shaftik El-Hout, head of the PLO's U.N. Security Council delegation, even attended a senatorial luncheon. Reportedly, the State Department approved the luncheon meeting.[18]

In 1976, it was also reported that the PLO had planned to open an office in Washington, D.C. *The New York Times* reported that the State Department saw no legal barrier to the PLO move.[19] A State Department spokesman, however, indicated that "this represents no change in our policy towards the PLO" and asserted that the United States would continue to prohibit "substantive contact" between the United States officials and the PLO so long as that organization continued its refusal to recognize Israel.[20] This pronouncement came to reinforce the various reports of a 1975 U.S. pledge "to stand firm in not recognizing the PLO, so long as that organization does not accept Resolution 242 and recognize the right of Israel to exist."[21] Wide reaction by the Israeli lobby to the proposed PLO Washington office forced the Department of Justice to deny the PLO request for the necessary permit. However, on March 15, 1978, U.S. nationals of Palestinian origin opened a Palestine Information Office in the U.S. capital. This office was financed by the PLO. By 1986, however, some circles began to call upon the government to close the office. In 1987, the office was ordered to close as a result of congressional action.

The above mentioned pledge was reported to be in return for Israeli consent to sign the second Sinai Disengagement Agreement. The United States has honored this pledge. Such a pledge may have forced the Carter administration into an impasse; while on the one hand, Mr. Carter recognized that Middle East "peace, to be durable, must also deal with the Palestinian issue" and spoke of the "need for a homeland for the Palestinians,"[22] he could not recognize or deal with the internationally recognized representative of the Palestinians, the PLO. In his final year in office, President Reagan finally started open and official contacts with the PLO after the organization's nineteenth PNC declarations. These contacts were later stopped because the PLO did not punish the perpetrators of a failed attack on Israel.

Since 1967, the U.S. has launched a number of attempts at securing a peaceful settlement of the Arab-Israeli conflict. These initiatives were based on U.N. Security Council Resolution 242. Because the PLO rejected this resolution and because of the vagueness of the wording of the resolution, all such attempts failed to bring about a comprehensive peaceful settlement. The resolution requires the "withdrawal of Israeli armed forces from territories occupied in the recent conflict (1967)"[23] in return for peace. While the Arabs interpret this clause to mean total Israeli withdrawal from the Occupied Territories, Israel reads it otherwise.

Professor Glenn Perry investigated this controversy and concluded that this provision must be read with other clauses affirming "territorial integrity" of all countries and "the inadmissibility of the acquisition of territory by war." Dr. Perry goes on to affirm that "the rules of international law applicable to the interpretation of treaties—and, by analogy, other documents—heavily confirm that the phrase "(withdrawal... from territories) cannot be construed as meaning anything other than withdrawal from all territories occupied in 1967."[24]

The Palestinians rejected Resolution 242 not because of this clause or its varied interpretations, but because it did not recognize the "legitimate rights" of the Palestinian people. In fact, the resolution fails even to mention the Palestinians. The only reference to the Palestinians is a call for a "just settlement of the refugee problem." The Palestinians came to look upon General Assembly Resolution 3236, passed in 1974, as superceding Security Council Resolution 242, passed in 1967. This is because Resolution 3236 affirms Palestinian national and individual rights. However, it is accepted in international law that a General Assembly resolution does not supersede a Security Council resolution.

The U.S. government accepts the resolution, but its interpretation of its disputed clause has shifted over the years. While welcoming President Sadat to the United States in February 1978, former President Carter is reported to have told the visitor that the United States does not agree with Egypt that Israel must return all of the Occupied Territories. The report goes on to add that the president told Mr. Sadat that the United States will not accept the concept of Palestinian "self-determination" if it means the establishment of a Palestinian state on Israel's borders.[25]

This rejection of Palestinian self-determination became the official policy of the United States with the coming of the Reagan administration. Perhaps, motivated more by a global (East/West) concern than a regional one, Mr. Reagan pursued a policy that was designed to intensify strategic cooperation with a number of countries in the region. In this context, Israel was seen as a strategic asset of considerable if not unique significance. In the process, the American administration came to view the Palestine question as a secondary matter that must not become an issue between a superpower and an important partner.

In the aftermath of the Israeli invasion of Lebanon, Mr. Reagan announced his peace plan. The Reagan Plan, besides ruling out Palestinian self-determination, also ruled out the possibility of PLO participation in negotiations. The plan supported Palestinian "self-government" in association with Jordan and called upon Israel to "freeze" further Jewish settlements in the Occupied Territories. Mr. Reagan further ruled out the possibility of a total Israeli pull-back from the Occupied Territories.

Rejected by both Israel and the PLO, the plan did not stand a chance, especially when the Reagan Administration got entangled in the Lebanese problems. Consequently, no serious efforts on the part of the American administration were made to put life into the Reagan Plan. However, after the intifada began, Secretary of State Schultz made a failed attempt at reviving the Reagan Plan.

As George Bush came to power, the dialogue with the PLO had been started. However, as the PLO moderated its position, the Israeli leadership became more adamant in its rejection of any PLO participation. But, while the American policymakers insisted that the PLO must recognize Israel's right to exist, they, at the same time, have continued to refuse to recognize the Palestinian right to self-determination. Under the Camp David formula, as well as the Reagan Plan, American recognition of Palestinian rights is clearly limited. While the U.S. recognized a Palestinian right to self-rule, this recognition encompasses only those Palestinians living in the Occupied Territories and entails local autonomy rather than independence.

THE PLO AND THE USSR

In spite of the considerable volume of material that has been written on the Soviet Union's policy toward the Arab world and the Arab-Israeli conflict, little has been written on its policy toward the PLO and the guerrilla movement during the formative years. Historically, there existed three principle trends in the analytical literature on Soviet policy in the Middle East.

One trend is concerned with Soviet interests as a state. Advocates of this *Realpolitik* approach argued that the Soviet Union's state interests dominated the Soviet outlook on the Middle East. Walter Laqueur and Oleg M. Smolanski, for example, concentrated on the Soviet Union's role as a superpower, and viewed the Soviet policy in the region within the framework of the cold war rivalry in the existing international balance of power system.[26]

The second trend was based on the old notion of anti-Semitism that existed under the Tsarist regimes. Writers expounding the "anti-Semitism" theme claimed that such a policy still existed in the Soviet Union. Soviet-Israeli relations are viewed as an extension of Soviet policy toward its Jewish minority.[27]

A third approach was largely based on theoretical-ideological interpretations of the Soviet decision-making process. Advocates of this approach asserted that "in a stable political and social system, ideology exerts a more lasting influence on policy than maneuvers based on short-term political realities."[28]

While Soviet policy may have ideological postulates in its long course, it also must have short-term and state-interest objectives. In fact, it would be difficult to discuss the ideological link in Soviet foreign policy with complete disregard of its leaders' perceptions of their interests. To base Soviet policy in the Middle East on notions of Russian "anti-Semitism," on the other hand, implies total Soviet irrationality. It would be foolhardy to accept this premise as the basis for an objective analysis of the foreign policy of a nation that has developed from a mere pawn in the international system to a superpower in less than fifty years. This is not to say that anti-Semitism does not exist in the Soviet Union nor that one should totally rule out the impact of anti-Semitic attitudes on Soviet foreign policy. To use anti-Semitism as the single determining factor of Soviet policy in the Middle East, on the other hand, would lead to a rather naive treatment of an important issue.

Inasmuch as ideology and political action have often been closely interwoven in the execution of Soviet foreign policy, one must pay attention to both in order to clarify some seemingly contradictory Soviet actions. If real contradictions occur, Soviet leaders seem to opt for what they perceive to be their national interests. If both ideology and national interest seem to be identical, ideology is normally emphasized.

Soviet interests in the Middle East can be traced back to the traditional Russian concern to protect its southern borders, and to insure secure naval passage to the Mediterranean. In the post-Stalin era, the primary Soviet interests in the region became entangled with military-strategic and global considerations. However, ideological and domestic factors have coincided with the Soviet global interests.

The ideological origins of the Soviet position on the Arab-Israeli conflict are rooted in Marxist interpretations of the "Jewish Problem." Karl Marx addressed this issue and argued that the Jews should liberate themselves from their religious beliefs and thus from the cause that prevented their social integration.[29]

Later Marxist thinkers and leaders rejected Zionism and the concept of Jewish nationalism. Lenin advocated total Jewish assimilation into their communities and believed that "the proletarian revolution would advance the process to its final stage by completely integrating Jews with their fellow workers."[30]

Therefore, it was ideologically consistent for Soviet leaders to oppose Zionism. If one adds the domestic factor to that of ideology, it becomes clear that the Soviet position on the question of Jewish nationality also reinforced their opposition of Zionism. As noted, a major tenet of Zionism is the belief that the Jews constitute a nation. When one considers the nationality problem within the Soviet Union in addition to their theoretical analysis of it, it is unavoidable to conclude that Soviet policy rejected the Zionist contention about Jewish nationality. Josef Stalin, himself coming from a minority group, wrote:

> It is impossible to conceive of people possessing a common "national character" who, nevertheless, cannot be said to constitute a single nation if they are economically disunited, inhabit different territories, speak different languages, and so forth. Such, for instance, are the Russian, Galician, Georgian and Caucasian Highland Jews, who in our opinion do not constitute a single nation.[31]

While current Soviet opposition to Israeli policies seem to conform to Marxist ideological beliefs, they also must be viewed from a *Realpolitik* perspective. The Middle East represents an area of multiple opportunities and serious concerns for Moscow. However, "the question of an advance or reverse in the Middle East, as compared with Soviet problems relating to [Eastern Europe], is not a matter of paramount importance."[32]

The emergence of Soviet influence in the Arab world began in Egypt in the mid–1950s. At that time, the primary Soviet interest in the region was to promote Third-World neutrality in order to eliminate Western influence and presence there. "In the 1960s, however, a more activist policy emerged, based primarily on military strategic considerations."[33] The primary Soviet goal became, according to Golan, "to secure bases and naval facilities."[34]

While Golan's interpretation may be correct, it cannot be accepted as the sole variable in explaining Arab-Soviet relations. Professor Lenczowski lists a number of issues that worked to strengthen these relations.[35] First, Arab neutralism, advocated by Egypt and other nationalist Arab regimes, converged with Khrushchev's division of the world into three camps rather than the rigid Stalinist two-camp dogma. The Arabs were viewed by Moscow to be in the "peace zone" rather than within one camp or another.

Second, Egypt and other Arabs needed Soviet arms, especially after the United States denied them to Arabs in the mid–1950s. By supplying arms to the Nasser regime and other Arab governments, the Soviet Union strengthened its position in the region and "cast itself as a friend who responded to the Arab search for dignity and strength."[36]

Third, in the Arab struggle for the liberation of Algeria and other parts of the Arab world, Arab and Soviet policies converged, both as a matter of principle and as a tactic. Western imperialism, whether real or imaginary, was seen as a common hostile target. The high point of this hostility occurred in 1956 when Egypt was invaded by England, France, and Israel in the wake of Nasser's nationalization of the Suez Canal Company.[37] The USSR promptly denounced the invasion and threatened to intervene. Moreover, Moscow replenished Egypt's arsenal after the attack.

Other sources of Arab admiration for the Soviet Union had been the Soviet role in the economic development of the nationalist Arab countries and its outspoken backing of the nationalist regimes in their struggle against the conservative and traditional elements in the Arab world.

The most significant factor contributing to better Arab-Soviet relations, however, has been the Soviet endorsement of the Arab view in regard to Israel's occupation of Arab lands. The Israeli occupation of Arab territories in 1967 is seen by the Soviet Union as an act of unprovoked aggression. Moscow has continued to demand that Israel evacuate the Occupied Territories. Therefore, the Soviet Union is seen by the Arabs as a close supporter of their rather recent position in the conflict with Israel.

This diplomatic support has been reinforced by military aid, especially during and after each Arab-Israeli war since 1956. Soviet arms and support of the nationalist Arab regimes has been very effective in linking Soviet-Arab interests, because it is tangible and directly related to vital issues of Arab territorial integrity.

In view of these linkages of Arab-Soviet interests and the Marxist outlook on Zionism, this question must be posed: Why did the Soviet Union support Israel in its formative years? In fact, Moscow voted in the U.N. General Assembly in favor of a Jewish state and recognized Israel soon after its formation. This support seems to undermine the premise of Soviet ideological consistency in its position on Zionism. Professor Lenczowski provides an answer to this question in *Realpolitik* terms:

It soon became evident to Moscow that the creation of Israel provided a built-in wedge, almost automatically guaranteeing a degree of tension in Arab-American relations. It was, therefore, not illogical for the Soviet government to take full advantage of these circumstances....[38]

Based on this interpretation, the creation of Israel was advantageous to the Soviet Union. Soviet calculations of the circumstances prior to the establishment of Israel may, therefore, have prompted the Soviet endorsement of Israel, only to have the Soviet Union reverse its stand in favor of the Arabs soon after Israel's adventure into Egypt in 1956 and especially after the 1967 War.

Soviet and Arab analysts reject this notion and provide their own interpretation:

The Soviet Union's vote in the UN General Assembly in favour of a Jewish state has to be seen in the light of Soviet policy vis-à-vis Western imperialism, notably its inherent opposition to British imperialism, rather than the endorsement of Zionism. The British mandate over Palestine began with, and was possible because of the British-Zionist alliance, an alliance vividly denounced by the Bolsheviks. Yet, towards the end of the mandate, the Zionists found themselves increasingly at odds with the British and by their very own intentions opposed to a continued British position in Palestine. In this situation, it was the anti-Soviet pro-British Arab regimes who were opposed to Stalin.[39]

Whatever the argument, it is possible to view the partition of Palestine as beneficial to the Soviet Union. It provided Moscow with a better opportunity to promote its own interests in the Middle East. Today, the USSR is a party in the Middle East. Moscow was a cochairman of the Geneva Peace Conference. The Soviet position on major Arab issues has not changed drastically since 1967 in spite of setbacks received in Egypt, Sudan, Yemen, and Somalia—and in spite of all the recent changes within their bloc. The Soviet Union accepts Resolution 242 as the basis of an Arab-Israeli peace accord, but their interpretations of the disputed clauses are closer to the Arab position, if not identical to it. Soviet support of national liberation extends to full recognition and aid to the PLO.

Soviet support of the PLO, while forthcoming now, did not originate with the birth of that organization. During the pre-1967 period, the USSR viewed the PLO as an extension of the Arab regimes. Their support of Nasser's position, which was pro-PLO, implied Soviet support of the PLO. After the 1967 War, the Soviet Union became "dissatisfied with what they saw as the adventurous trend of the resistance, and gave priority to progressive Arab regimes, notably Egypt, in the struggle against imperialism and Zionism."[40] It must be added that Moscow was also dissatisfied with the PLO's close relations with China. Moreover, the PLO and the Soviet Union disagreed on objectives. While Moscow advocated a peaceful resolution of the Arab-Israeli conflict, the PLO rejected all peace proposals and advocated total liberation of Palestine.

By 1968, the commandos had become a major force in the region's politics. At that time, Moscow began to soften its criticism and even welcomed Yasser Arafat on a secret visit to the Soviet capital in July, 1968.[41] A year later, the International Conference of Communist and Workers' Parties acknowledged the "legitimate rights" of the Palestinian people. By 1970, Soviet aid to the PLO had started. After the death of Nasser, Soviet-PLO relations were strengthened. It may be that Moscow's distrust of Sadat, Nasser's successor, had played a part in its shift of emphasis from total dependence on regimes to partial interest in regimes as well as in mass organization.

The task of converging the conflicting PLO-Arab state interests has not been easy for the Soviets. During the Jordanian Civil War, Moscow supported Nasser's initiatives at accommodation between Amman and the resistance movement. However, the Lebanese crisis proved to be beyond a compromise. While interested in maintaining their good relations with Syria and the PLO, the Soviet leaders were, at one point, faced with a situation where siding with either party would mean losing the other. Initially, they applauded the Syrian moves in Lebanon which, at first, aided the PLO. However, the Syrian switch to the conservative side frustrated Soviet policymakers and forced them to take on the role of quiet observers. Officially, the Soviet Union did not take any stand or issue any government pronouncement. However, by reading the Soviet press, one could discern the government's attitude toward the conflict.

The Soviet press often attempted to link the crisis in Lebanon with the outcome of the second Egyptian-Israeli Sinai Disengagement Agreement. This agreement, according to *Pravda*, created divisions in the Arab world and made the Arab countries suspicious of each other.[42]

Whenever possible, the Soviet press also attempted to link the conflict with Israel.[43]

When a cease-fire was reached in Lebanon, the Soviet Union enthusiastically supported it. Soon afterwards, Moscow offered its good offices to help bring about a rapprochment between Damascus and the PLO.

Soviet support of the PLO was, therefore, limited during the Lebanese crisis. However, at the diplomatic level Moscow has demonstrated its allegiance to the Palestinian struggle against Israel on many occasions. In 1973, for example, Brezhnev insisted in his summit with President Nixon on the inclusion of the clause "the legitimate interests of the Palestinian people" in their communiqué of June 25, 1973. "This was the first time that the United States had signed any document containing such a reference."[44] Another such document was signed by the Carter Administration in a joint statement by the two nations in 1977.

Today, the Soviet position is still close to that of the PLO, especially since the PLO has proclaimed its intention to accept a peaceful settlement of the Arab-Israeli conflict. The Soviet Union insists on PLO participation in any peace negotiations, Israeli withdrawal from all Occupied Arab Territories, and Palestinian self-determination as meaning a Palestinian state on the West Bank and the Gaza Strip. These objectives are clearly not far from those aimed at by the PLO at the current stage.

However, the recent developments in the Soviet Union and Eastern Europe are likely to have dramatic consequences on Soviet policies in general and their relations with the Palestinians in particular. Such tidal changes in the Soviet bloc are likely to lead to a restructuring of a world order that had been in place for nearly half a century. Consequent to these developments, the Palestine question has receded in prominence and priority for the Soviet Union. The new Soviet approach of openness to the West could potentially propel the Palestinian-Israeli conflict toward a relatively early settlement. Soviet openness to the United States could bring about a joint understanding on a solution and pressures on all sides in order to implement such a solution. On the other hand, should such a solution fail or should the Soviets and the Americans not work for it, then the conflict could become more complicated and Soviet-Palestinian relations could experience some strains. Already, Soviet-Israeli relations are warming up, in spite of the Soviet elevation of the status of the PLO diplomatic mission in Moscow to that of an embassy. Soviet Jews are now immigrating to Israel in large numbers. It is expected that many of these immigrants will be settled on the Occupied Territories, which could make a Palestinian-Israeli peaceful settlement harder to achieve.

THE PLO AND WESTERN EUROPE

The history of Western European-Arab relations is an old one. It was only a few decades ago that Western European powers were in control of the Middle East, and the Arab perception of Western Europe is influenced by that history. It is natural, therefore, for the Arabs to view the European countries as colonial powers. To the average Arab, it was England and France who arranged the Arab world into its current subdivisions, created Israel, and invaded Egypt in 1956.

While there are state variations in Western European policies in the Middle East, the overall approach is similar. In order that more accurate generalizations be drawn, Western European countries are defined as the current members of the European Economic Community. Since that body of nations has often discussed the Middle East and issued recommendations and policy guidelines for its members, it will be best to concentrate on these pronouncements. European policy on the Arab-Israeli conflict is based on the premise that "Israel must be recognized within secure boundaries."[45] Former French President Charles DeGaulle confirmed this premise when he said: "We did not let the Arabs ignore that, for us, the State of Israel was a fait accompli and that we would not allow it to be destroyed."[46] As a result, European-Israeli relations flourished during the first two decades of Israel's history. France provided Israel with weapons, including their most sophisticated war planes and tanks. West Germany struck a deal with Israel whereby Germany was to pay the Jewish state reparations for Nazi persecution of the Jews prior to and during World War II.[47] This deal, reached in 1952, implied German recognition of Israel not only as an independent state, but also as a representative of all the Jews in the world. The European Economic Community has also encouraged, since its founding in 1957, trade with Israel and even entertained Israel's admittance to the community. While the community did not admit Israel to its membership, it did sign a number of treaties with it to facilitate Israeli exports to European markets.

Like the United States, the Western European powers viewed the Palestinian people, prior to the 1967 War, as refugees in need of aid and resettlement. Even after that war, Europe maintained that the conflict was essentially between the Arab states and Israel as reflected in Resolution 242. In fact, that resolution itself was European in origin; it was the British who introduced it. European powers supported the resolution, and eventually viewed it as the basis for any future negotiations.

The growth of the Palestinian Resistance Movement and its operations in Europe led to a European awakening with regard to the people of Palestine. The French, in particular, familiar with their own resistance to Nazi occupation, began to see the Palestinians in a different light. President DeGaulle discussed Israel's occupation of Arab lands: "Now [Israel] is setting up, on the territories it has taken, the occupation that cannot take place without oppression, repression, and deportation, and there is springing up against it a resistance which in its turn qualifies as terrorism."[48] Also, France and other European powers "carefully distinguished between the military actions of a state (like Israel) and the terrorist activities and irregular bands of armed units representing no national state."[49] Therefore, they were able to join other nations at the United Nations in attacking Israeli reprisal raids against its neighboring countries.

While some European states do not diplomatically recognize the PLO, they have permitted its offices to operate from their capitals. In addition, most members of the European Economic Community have cast their vote in favor of U.N. General Assembly Resolution 3210 of October 14, 1974. That resolution recognized the PLO as the "representative of the Palestinian people" and invited its officials to participate in the assembly's deliberations. In fact, none of the European Economic Community's members voted against that resolution. Since then, the community has authored many resolutions of its own "expressing concern" about Israeli settlements in the Occupied Territories.[50] Most European countries have now officially recognized the PLO. These include, among others, France, Belgium, Italy, Sweden, and Austria.

Because of differing views within the EEC, the group has not explicitly defined its position on the conflict, beyond its acceptance of Resolution 242 as a framework for negotiations. Some members, led by France, interpret the resolution to mean Israeli withdrawal from all Occupied Territories. The French text of Resolution 242 speaks of "les territoires occupés," which translates as "*the* Occupied Territories," meaning all of them. Others, such as Germany and England, attempt to leave the door open for interpretations and may seem to favor "minor adjustments" in the borders.

However, despite Western European support of Resolution 242, these powers, prior to the 1973 war, had, like the U.S., become relaxed about continued Israeli occupation of Arab territory, and continued to aid and trade with Israel normally. It was only after the 1973 War that Western European governments began to actively urge Israel to withdraw from Arab lands.

The October 1973 Arab-Israeli War added a new dimension to European-Arab relations, namely, oil. The Arab oil embargo following that war hit the EEC members hardest. Consequently, European countries were seen to move closer to the Arab position. Oil was vividly proven effective as a diplomatic weapon. Another and perhaps more important European concern was the potential of a disastrous nuclear superpower confrontation over the Middle East. But if the Arab objective was to initiate a European-Israeli divorce, they failed. What they succeeded in doing was getting the European powers to play a more active role in seeking an Arab-Israeli settlement. European pressures on the United States grew rapidly, contributing to the pace of Dr. Kissinger's shuttle diplomacy. The avoidance of war, rather than peace, may have become Europe's most urgent need. Middle East wars are now feared in Europe because they could entail oil embargoes and Arab reprisal. Today, political analysts seem to agree that many European officials favor the inclusion of the PLO in any future peace negotiations.

While some European states are more receptive to accepting the PLO than others, all seem to be receptive to moderate Palestinian aspirations. Among the most outspoken supporters of European recognition of the PLO was the former Austrian Chancellor Kreisky. While some Western European states have not formally recognized the PLO, they seem to have accepted it as a partner in a Middle East peace process. At their meeting in Venice in 1980, for example, the nine members of the European Council issued the now famous Venice Declaration. This declaration, among other things, asserts the members' position that the PLO must be associated with peace negotiations.

The Palestinians, on their part, are suspicious of Western Europe. Their tragic plight is often blamed on European powers. However, their leaders realize the declining influence of Western Europe in the Middle East. PLO leaders also realize that, in the final analysis, Western Europe is committed to the State of Israel. They are, however, careful not to antagonize the Western powers because of their role in the U.N. Security Council and in peace negotiations. Since PLO leaders feel that if they were to commit Western Europe to a Palestinian state on the West Bank and Gaza, such a commitment would put enough pressure on the United States to influence the American outlook. In fact, such an attempt took place in January 1986, when Western European members of the U.N. Security Council voted for a resolution combining Resolution 242 and

Palestinian rights. The United States, however, vetoed the resolution. Also in 1986, the European Community began to provide support to the Palestinians under Israeli occupation and gave them preferential access to trade with the EEC.

Whether the Europeans are right or wrong, one conclusion is evident: while Western Europe remains committed to Israel's existence, it is opposed to its expansion. The European outlook on the Arab-Israeli conflict, while still pro-Israeli, has, since 1973, shifted slowly toward recognition of Arab claims and support for moderate Palestinian demands, including the right to self-determination.

THE PALESTINIANS AND CHINA

Ahmad Shukairy, the first chairman of the PLO, visited China in March 1965 to sign a military and diplomatic accord. Warmly receiving him, Mao Zedong told Shukairy:

Imperialism is afraid of China and the Arabs. Israel and Formosa are bases of imperialism in Asia. You are the front gate of the great continent, and we are the rear. Their goal is the same.... Asia is the biggest continent in the world, and they want to exploit it. The West does not like us, and we must understand this fact.[51]

Relations between the Palestinians and the People's Republic of China have always been close. Palestinian leaders have always visited China and praised the Chinese people and government. Palestinian ideologies are inspired by Chinese history and writings. While these are ingredients for better Chinese-Palestinian relations, the Chinese leadership has always urged the Palestinians to find their own path to liberation. Chairman Mao told a PLO delegation in 1965:

Do not tell me that you have read this or that opinion in my books. You have your war, and we have ours. You must create the principles and ideology on which your war stands. Books obstruct the view if piled up before the eyes. What is important is to begin action with faith. Faith in victory is the first element of victory—in fact, it may mean victory itself.[52]

Commando leaders visited China even prior to the initiation of their guerrilla activities. In 1964, Yasser Arafat, then only leader of Fateh, visited Beijing and received encouraging support from the Chinese leaders. In fact, "Chinese relations with the Palestinians are set apart from those of other non-Arab countries by the fact that China took no part in the creation of Israel and has never recognized its existence."[53] China was also the first communist country to publicly affirm the rights of the Palestinians as "a people," not merely as "refugees." The PLO was also recognized by China long before the Soviet Union paid attention to it and long before any other non-Arab state had recognized it.

Chinese support of the Palestinians was not limited to pronouncements and verbal declarations. Chinese arms aid was channelled to the PLO and other resistance groups since the mid-1960s. Since then, the Chinese also began military training of Palestinian commandos, both in China and in the Middle East.

In a study of Palestinian-Chinese relations, Lillian Craig Harris identified eight general features of these relations:

1. Beijing's aid to the Palestinians is more significant than is officially acknowledged. Prior to 1968, the Chinese were the only major power to support the Palestinian resistance movement.
2. While the Chinese advocate the total dezionization of Israel and liberation of Palestine, they would not object to a political compromise if accepted by the PLO.
3. China's support of the Palestinians does not entail its support of international terrorism. In fact, Beijing has always advised the Palestinians against such operations and viewed them as "impulsive acts" inconsistent with the objective of liberation.
4. China has always advocated Palestinian unity within the framework of the PLO. In spite of Fateh's lack of ideological commitment, China has consistently favored Fateh over the Marxist groups within the resistance movement.
5. Chinese support of the Palestinians is greater when the Palestinians are politically and militarily in a strong position. Therefore, China's policy as regards the Palestinians is pragmatic. Unsuccessful revolutionary movements in the Arab world, like the Popular Front for the Liberation of Oman, have been dropped by the Chinese. The Palestinians acknowledge this.
6. Sino-Palestinian relations were a facet of the Sino-Soviet conflict. The Chinese would have liked to undercut the Soviet Union where possible. However, China's support for the Palestinians was not conditioned on anti-Soviet attitudes or actions by the Palestinians. There have been no known Chinese attempts to amass anti-Soviet support among the Palestinians or to organize pro-China guerrilla groups.
7. While the Chinese provide the Palestinians with material and moral support, they do not interfere in Palestinian day-to-day activities. The Chinese principle may be the promotion of ideal goals of "unity" and "people's war" that may serve Beijing's posture in the Third World.
8. The Palestinians are inspired by the Chinese model for a popular war of liberation but not by its socialist model for a society. They have adopted Chinese revolutionary tactics, but not its ideological content. The mainstream of the PLO is not Maoist or communist.[54]

If these were the principle features of Sino-Palestinian relations, what are China's policy objectives? It is logical to conclude that, just as the

Soviets viewed Egypt as their gateway to the Middle East, China viewed the Palestinians as its bridge to that region. Chinese-Arab relations were never close. In the mid–1960s, Nasser openly criticized Beijing for its attempts to take over the Afro-Asian People's Solidarity Organization. Among all the Arab states, there was no Arab Albania or even a possibility of one. The creation of the PLO was a timely opportunity for China.

Another objective of Chinese Middle East policy can be detected by reading Mao, Lin Piao, and other Chinese texts. This objective is a doctrinal one. Chinese leaders view their presence in the Arab world as an aspect of their role in the world socialist revolution. Mao's theory, as later developed by Lin Piao, is based on a belief that the future of the world lies in the "countryside" among the oppressed masses.[55] Israel is seen as a "world city" and an outpost of imperialism. Therefore, the Chinese wanted to undermine the positions of all imperialists including the Soviet Union in the Middle East. They naturally gave their support to the revolutionary forces in the Middle Eastern "countryside" and opposed Israel as an "imperialist lackey."

By supporting the Palestinians, Beijing also wanted "to demonstrate to the world, and the Third World in particular, the viability and applicability of the Chinese revolutionary model."[56] Chinese leaders have always praised and even overplayed Palestinian successes. The Chinese saw the Palestinian revolution as the first national-democratic stage of revolution. They obviously hope that eventually it will be transformed into a socialist revolution.

John K. Cooley suggests a more pragmatic objective for Chinese policy toward the Palestinians; he writes:

I am convinced that there is another motive in Chinese support for the Palestinians and their revolutionary cousins along the shores of the Persian Gulf and the Arabian sea. All the evidence available to me suggests that this interest is oil.[57]

Mr. Cooley goes on to cite that China's expanding industrialization programs necessitate an outside source of oil. The Middle East could provide this source if the revolutionaries are to take power. But, given China's potential oil reserves, it is possible to argue that oil has played no significant part in its Mid-East policy. One can also argue that Chinese support of the Palestinians is mostly rhetorical and cost-free.

From a Palestinian perspective, China was the only major power that rejected a peaceful settlement that would have entailed recognition of Israel. Chinese political and military aid is seen as significant. The Palestinians also feel close to China because they agree on certain basic tactical and strategic matters. Some Palestinians add that their Chinese connections aids them in securing Soviet support and material aid. However, the Sino-Soviet conflict had put the Palestinians in a dilemma. If they appeared to align themselves with one party, they could have lost the other. Therefore, it was not unusual that high-level PLO visits to Moscow be followed by similar ones to Beijing. In addition, PLO spokesmen in both capitals usually stress their organization's priority of "defeating Israel rather than... ideological questions."[58]

While China may be faithful in its support of the Palestinians, its conflict with Moscow has influenced its Middle Eastern policy. At the time when Beijing rejected the notion of a Geneva Conference and peaceful settlement of the Palestine question, it found it proper to praise Sadat for ousting the Soviets from his country. Sadat has made it clear that he intended to solve the problem peacefully. Chinese support of Sadat extended to their praising him for his November 1977 trip to Jerusalem. It must be stressed that, while supporting the Sadat trip, China also made it clear that peace was not possible and that Sadat's trip and the Camp David Accords would only expose Israel to the world. Whether the Sino-Soviet conflict was behind this position or not is not clear at this point. But many Palestinians were aware of the implications of the Sino-Soviet conflict for their relations with the two powers and were careful not to get entangled in it. Such implications today have lessened, as Soviet-Chinese relations have improved. The Palestinians have, in any case, been successful in getting the support and the material aid of both.

THE THIRD-WORLD DIMENSION

Generally, third-world countries have been sympathetic to the Palestinians. The third world can be delineated as incorporating the countries of Africa, Asia, and Latin America, excluding Israel, China, Japan, and South Africa. Generally, third-world countries are members of one or more of the following groups: Conference of Non-Aligned Countries, Conference of Islamic Countries, the Organization of African Unity, the Afro-Asian People's Solidarity Organization, and the Organization of American States, with U.S. membership excepted. Therefore, a review of positions taken by these groups could indicate the general trend in the third world. Because this subject has been partially discussed in Chapter 2, this review must be limited to general positions only.

The principle of self-determination for the Palestinian people has had the endorsement of the Conference of Non-Aligned Countries since 1964. In their Cairo conference of October 1964, the heads of these states condemned "imperialistic policy pursued in the Middle East," and endorsed "the full restoration of all the rights of the Arab people of Palestine to their homeland and their inalienable right to self-determination."[59] This stand was further reaffirmed in 1970, 1972, 1973, and in later conferences. At these same meetings, conference members also declared "their full support to the Arab people of Palestine in their struggle for liberation from colonialism and racism."[60] In discussing peace in the Middle East, their resolutions did not fail to stress that "full respect for the inalienable rights of the Arab people of Palestine is a prerequisite to peace."[61] In their 1973 meeting, the leaders of the non-aligned states declared their "recognition of the Palestine Liberation Organization as the legitimate representative of the Palestinian people and of their just struggle."[62]

The Islamic Countries as well as the Organization of African Unity include many Arab states. However, the Arab countries do not compose the majority in either of the two groups. Like the Conference of Non-Aligned Countries, these two groups have continuously, and since their inception, affirmed the rights of Palestinians. Both also have recognized the PLO as "the sole legitimate representative of the Palestinian people wherever it is found."[63] In fact, of all non-Arab states of the world, the PLO receives most sympathy and support from the non-Arab Islamic states.

The Afro-Asian People's Solidarity Organization adopted similar resolutions at their conferences. At the fifth conference of this organization, held at Cairo in January 1972, the conferees resolved that "the PLO with its national council and executive committee is the sole representative of the Palestinian people, ... expresses ... people's will and aspirations, and it has the right to speak in their name."[64]

It is undisputed that the overwhelming majority of the countries of Asia and Africa support the Palestinians and recognize the PLO as their spokesman. In fact, there are more states in those two continents that recognize the PLO than there are that recognize Israel.

Unlike Asia and Africa, Latin American states have not been as outspoken on the Palestinian problem. Generally, these countries have, for a long time, remained aloof from the controversial issues pertaining to the Arab-Israeli conflict. However, Latin America has a long tradition of rejecting the acquisition of territory by force. Shortly after the 1967 War, Latin American states introduced a U.N. General Assembly resolution calling for complete Israeli withdrawal from the Occupied Territories. In general, however, prior to 1973, Latin American countries had no large political stake in the outcome of Middle Eastern controversies. However, the period since 1973 has witnessed many changes in the attitude of Latin American states toward the Palestine problem. "Confronted with the various economic and financial repercussions of the Arab oil embargo and the rise of the Palestine problem as a central issue in many international forums,"[65] these countries had to make some serious decisions.

Since the Organization of American States has not adopted any major resolutions in regard to the Palestinians and the PLO, it is imperative that an alternative to tapping Latin American attitudes be found. Noting the character of these countries participation at the United Nations provides such an alternative.

A review of the voting record of the Latin American states at the U.N. General Assembly indicates cohesive support for Israel during its formative years. However, toward the end of the 1960s, a shift began to occur. Since then, the majority of these states have moved toward neutrality or support of Arab positions.

Latin America, in fact, was the factor that tilted the balance in favor of Israel's establishment as an internationally recognized state.[66] The U.N. General Assembly vote to partition Palestine in 1947 was thirty-three in favor, thirteen against, and ten abstentions. The record shows that thirteen Latin American states had voted in favor of partition, one against it, and six abstained. The resolution to admit Israel to the United Nations received 18 favorable votes from Latin America and none against. During the 1950s and early 1960s, the Latin American states, with the exception of Cuba, supported Israel at the United Nations and other international forums.

In the late 1960s, fundamental changes occurred at the United Nations. The balance of power shifted with the admission of many newly independent states to the United Nations; Latin America was left with less than 16 percent rather than its previous 33 percent of the total General Assembly vote. The United States, then entangled in an unpopular war in Vietnam, lost its former domination over Latin American policies and its influence decreased on the continent. Accordingly, individual states began to align themselves in accordance to what they perceived to be their interests.

While the U.N. voting record remained a useful tool for detecting trends in policy positions, one must note that such votes are often symbolic and rhetorical, and therefore, may not give a definitive answer to all questions. However, such votes can be usefully employed here to point out latent policy changes.

A look at the voting record of Latin American states reveals changes at many levels regarding the Arab-Israeli conflict. Of these, the most relevant to this study are the ones that relate to the Palestinian people.

By the 1970s, most Latin American states had shifted to a position of neutrality or support for the Palestinians. The majority of Latin American states had by 1973 agreed on the principles of a Middle East settlement. These principles were outlined in the General Assembly Session XXVII, Resolution 3089-Section C as follows: (1) Acquisition of territory by force is inadmissible and (2) respect for the rights of the Palestinians is a prerequisite to the establishment of a permanent peace. Twelve Latin

American countries voted in favor of this resolution, only three voted against, and six abstained. In 1974, nine of these states voted in favor of recognition of the PLO as the legitimate representative of the Palestinians. By 1975, the majority of the Latin American countries recognized the PLO as such with a vote of thirteen in favor and three against with nine abstentions.[67]

As was suggested earlier, U.N. votes do not necessarily show what a state's policy toward the PLO is really like. Therefore, to complement the above generalizations and to detect underlying causes for the apparent shifts, a look at a selection of state-PLO relations at the bilateral level is necessary.

To begin with Mexico, one would find that the Mexican position at the United Nations represents a real policy. Former Mexican president Luis Echeverria visited various Middle Eastern countries in 1975. What was significant about his visit was his meeting with Yasser Arafat, chairman of the PLO. After that meeting, Mr. Echeverria announced Mexico's recognition of the PLO as the "sole legitimate representative of the people of Palestine."[68] The election of Jose Lopez Portilla to succeed Echeverria did not change the Mexican position nor did the election of Mr. Madrid or later leaders. In fact, the PLO has opened its offices in the Mexican capital with diplomatic privileges.

Brazil, on the other hand, has attempted to take a neutral position. However, it voted with the PLO in 1974 and against Israel on Resolution No. 3379 defining Zionism as a form of racism in 1975. This position has indicated a tilt in the Brazilian policy in favor of the Arabs. Analysts agree that Brazil's dependence on Arab oil was the major factor influencing the shift in policy.

At a time of economic problems in Brazil, the Brazilian government realized that "a good relationship with the Arabs cannot only prevent disaster, but can give Brazil positive advantages."[69] These advantages came in the form of an exploration concession to Petrobras, Brazil's national oil company, by Iraq, Egypt, Algeria, and Kuwait. Therefore, it is possible to argue that Brazil's pro-Arab stand is economically induced.

While Argentina's support of the Palestinians was evident in U.N. chambers, at the bilateral level the country has not publicly endorsed the PLO. This is in spite of Argentina's need for Arab oil and aid. Argentina's own domestic problems and its large Jewish community—nearly two-thirds of Latin American Jews—may be the factors contributing to this position. While struggling against internal leftist ideas and terrorism, it would be difficult for Argentina to recognize the PLO.

Cuba has consistently supported the Palestinians. Its officers have also been involved in training Palestinian commandos. Cuba's interest in the Palestinians stems from its revolutionary and ideological position.

Even during the Batista regime, Cuba voted against partition. Similarly, Allende's Chile identified itself closely with the Palestinian position. However, Allende's successor, Augusto Pinochet, reversed this position only to dramatically reverse it again in 1975. "Badly in need of economic transfusion, Pinochet came, like many others in the Third World, to regard Arab petrol money as his only savior."[70]

Venezuela's policy has also been supportive of the Palestinians. Venezuela is the least dependent on Arab oil of all Latin American countries. However, as a member of OPEC, Venezuela is interested in keeping good relations with other fellow members.

Peru's policy is influenced by the nonaligned bloc. Lima was the site of the 1975 Fifth Ministerial Conference of the bloc. Its policy is consistent with its role within that bloc of nations. As an oil producer itself and not a member of OPEC, Peru is under no economic pressures to support the Palestinians. Its support is, therefore, inspired by its ideological convictions.

Central American and Caribbean states, however, are most supportive of Israel in spite of their dire need for Arab oil. Costa Rica, Barbados, Haiti, and the Dominican Republic have maintained a traditional alignment with Israel. It may be that U.S. influence and Israel's generosity in aiding these countries technically contribute to their position. Nicaragua, on the other hand, has shifted toward a position supportive of the PLO. This recent shift was the result of revolutionary changes in the country. The Sandinista government recognized the PLO, closed Israel's embassy, and even refused to recognize their country's debts to Israel. Mrs. Chamoro's government has not reversed the new policy.

On the whole, it is clear that Latin America, like the rest of the third world, has increasingly shifted to a pro-Palestinian position. Oil may have been the most outstanding factor influencing this Latin American shift.

JAPAN AND THE PLO

Oil also has been a factor in influencing Japanese policy. Like Western Europe, Japan is dependent on Arab oil. Its policy had been one of noninvolvement prior to the 1973 War. Since then, Japan has begun to actively call upon Israel to withdraw from the Occupied Territories. By 1975, Japan welcomed a request by the PLO to open an office in Tokyo. The office was opened on December 19, 1976 with some diplomatic privileges (such as the right to meet with foreign ministry officials) but without the full diplomatic status granted PLO offices in many other countries. The Japanese position by now had come a long way toward supporting PLO aspirations for "self-determination," including the right for an "independent state." In October 1981, Mr. Suzuki, Japan's prime minister, welcomed Arafat in Tokyo, and since then Japan came even closer to the PLO's position, especially during and after the Israeli invasion of Lebanon.

It is possible to argue that the Middle East has changed the direction of Japan's foreign policy. Historically, Japan's foreign policy centered on a traditional position of support to U.S. diplomacy. The dependence on Persian Gulf oil has locked Japan into a network of regional concerns that differed from those forced by the United States. Consequently, Japan's responses were formulated in accord with its own interests, which were more similar to those of Western Europe.

THE PALESTINIANS AND OTHER REVOLUTIONARY GROUPS

"An understanding of the issue of alignment with the revolutionary forces of the world puts the Palestinian struggle in its proper place on the map of the international struggle against imperialism,"[71] a PFLP pamphlet declares. The pamphlet goes on to conclude that the Palestinian struggle is but one battle in the war against imperialism. Not only the PFLP but all Palestinian commando groups interact with other groups on the international scene struggling against imperialism. In fact, "the Palestinians see their struggle in its international context . . . and tie the liberation of Palestine to the international liberation struggle."[72]

Relations between the Palestinians and the communist revolutionary movements such as those of Vietnam, North Korea, China, and Cuba are strong and have been noted earlier. In this section, PLO relations with Western revolutionary (sometimes underground) movements will be discussed.

The U.S. leftist groups generally share a materialist conception of history and define themselves as Marxist. The practical result of this has been a common vision of the conflict in the Middle East. They all see that conflict "in terms of the imperialist penetration of the region for economic and strategic purposes."[73] Almost all approach Zionism as an outpost of imperialism in the region. These groups include the Communist Party of the United States (CPUSA), the Socialist Workers Party (SWP), the Workers World Party (WWP), the Revolutionary Communist Party (RCP), the Progressive Labor Party (PLP), and other splinter groups.

While these groups share a common perception of the Palestine problem, they disagree among themselves on ideological issues. Some are Soviet Marxists, others are Trotskyites, and others are Maoists. Their support of the PLO and the Palestinian revolution has been the most outspoken on behalf of Palestinian aspirations in the United States. Nevertheless, their contacts with the PLO and the Palestinians are almost nonexistent and limited to contacts with Palestinian students and supporters in U.S. colleges.

Analytically distinct from the Marxist groups are the leftist organizations of Blacks, Puerto Ricans, Indians, Chinese Americans, and Chicanos in the United States. These groups see themselves as oppressed minorities, and identify with other oppressed people around the world. Therefore, it was natural for them to develop anti-imperialist tendencies. Consequently, they came out in support of the Palestinian revolution and the PLO. Their views on Israel resemble those of the Marxist groups, which see Israel as an imperialist colony created to oppress the Palestinians and to safeguard certain economic and strategic imperialist interests in the region. The 1974 poll conducted by *Muhammad Speaks*, the organ of the Black Moslems, may be typical of sentiments among those minorities: "Polling some 3,200 Black people in Harlem, Bedford-Stuyvesant, and East Harlem (New York), the newspaper found that 71 percent support the Arabs while only 29 percent sided with Israel or had no view."[74]

Unlike Marxist groups, officials of some of these minority organizations have had direct contacts with the PLO. Many Black Moslem representatives have met with PLO officials on various occasions. In 1969, Eldridge Cleaver, a Black Panther leader, appeared at a public rally in Algiers with Yasser Arafat to condemn Israel and to proclaim his determined support of the Palestinian revolution. John K. Cooley reports that some Black Panthers visited Jordan prior to 1970 as guests of Fateh. Reports of Fateh training of the Panthers were denied. A Fateh spokesman is reported to have told a newspaper correspondent: "The revolutionary has to be trained by himself."[75]

Representatives of Black Panthers, Black Moslems, and other American groups have attended PLO Council meetings since 1969 as observers. In the wake of the resignation of Andrew Young (former U.S. Ambassador to the United Nations), representatives of the mainstream Black American organizations have also visited the Middle East and come out in support of the Palestinian right to self-determination. Most noted among outspoken Black American groups is Reverend Jesse Jackson's Operation Push. However, it must be remarked that Marxist and minority organizations in the United States are small in number and membership. Except for Operation Push, they have not drawn many people from the dominant U.S. liberal majority. They have, however, influenced leftist and minority intellectuals in general. The Palestine Solidarity Committee, however, includes a very active group of Palestinians as well as Jewish and gentile Americans, and has achieved some success.

European leftists are better organized and more powerful than those in the United States. Their support of the Palestinians is also more effective and direct. On occasion, European leftist volunteers have joined the Palestinian commando groups. Mr. Cooley reports that such volunteers were enlisted as early as 1968.[76]

In France, many intellectuals support the Palestinians. These include Maxime Rodinson, the late Jean-Paul Sartre, and other prominent figures. The French Communist Party follows the Moscow line in its support of the Palestinians. Other groups of socialists, orthodox Communists and non-Communist liberals also support the Palestinians. These groups have formed special committees devoted to supporting the Palestinian revolution.

A Palestine Committee was also formed in the Netherlands in 1969. One of its leaders, C. J. Comelbeek, is suspected to be a Trotskyite sympathizer. Italian leftists also organized a Palestine Committee for Solidarity with the People of Palestine in Rome. In London, anti-Zionist Jews publish an anti-Israel magazine, *Israel Imperial News*, and work with other pro-Palestinian groups. Mr. Cooley reports that the largest pro-Palestinian group, and the one most closely related to the British establishment, is the Council for the Advancement of Arab-British Understanding (CAABU). Also, a Friends of Palestine Committee of leftists was formed in London in 1968. Similar groups also exist in Ireland, former West Germany, Sweden, and other Western European countries. Press reports of Palestinian training of members of these groups are numerous. The most publicized, however, may be the 1969 group, which allegedly was trained in Palestinian camps in Jordan. This group is reported to have included thirty Britons, twenty Irish, twenty French, ten West Germans, eight Swedes, and sixty-two from the United States, Netherlands, Italy, and other countries.[77]

The most widely publicized contacts between the Palestinians and the European left have been the joint terrorist operations carried out by factions of the PFLP and the German Baader-Meinhof group. The West German government has documented such contacts and concluded that an international network of terrorism does exist. The West German government further reported that a Palestinian, the late Wadi Haddad, was heading this network.[78] The Japanese Red Army's operations on behalf of the Palestinians have also received wide publicity, in spite of PLO condemnation of such acts. Such acts carried out by non-Palestinians in the name of Palestine may have caused the Palestinians some loss of support at the international and Arab levels. Pro-Israeli journalists capitalized on them to depict the PLO as party to, if not the leader of, an international terror ring aimed at destroying world civilization.

In spite of the negative outcome of such acts, the PLO has become not only a major actor on the Middle Eastern scene, but also an actor on the international level. This development is a significant accomplishment for the PLO. More significant, however, are Israeli reactions to the PLO, to which this research will now turn.

NOTES

1. Hisham Sharabi, *Palestine and Israel: The Lethal Dilemma* (New York: Pegasus, 1969), p. ix.
2. Leila Meo, "Al-Filastiniyun Fil-Umam al-Mutahida" (Palestinians at the United Nations), *Al-Iktissad al-Arabi* (Arab Economics) 10 (April 1977), p. 31.
3. U.S. Department of State, Bureau of Public Affairs, *U.S. Policy in the Middle East: December 1973–November 1974*, Special Report (Washington, D.C.: Department of State Publications, 1975), p. 7.
4. See, for example, the statement quoted in Oriana Fallaci, "A Leader of the Fedayeen: We Want War Like the Vietnam War," *Life* 48, no. 12 (22 June 1970), p. 18.
5. "Hostage," ABC, Special Report, 30 January 1978.
6. *Swasia* 4, no. 20, 5 August 1977, p. 1.
7. See Maxime Rodinson, *Israel: A Settler Colonial State?* Trans. David Thorstand (New York: Monad Press, 1973), for example.
8. John Snetsinger, *Truman, the Jewish Vote and the Creation of Israel* (Stanford: Hoover Institute Press, 1974), p. 131.
9. J. W. Fulbright, *Beyond the Interim Agreement* (New York: Americans for Middle East Understanding, 1975), p. 5.
10. Ibid.
11. Sharabi, *Palestine and Israel*, p. 49.
12. W. F. Abboushi, *The Angry Arabs* (Philadelphia: Westminster Press, 1974), p. 251.
13. Clovis Maksoud, "Al-Abaad al-Amrikiyah al-Israeliyah Limashro' al-Malek Hussein Wa Kayfiyat Ihbatoh" (Long-Term American-Israeli Objectives to King Hussein's Plan and the Means to Its Defeat) *Shu'un Filastiniyah* 9 (May 1972), p. 5.
14. From an interview with Andrea Brunais, *The Tampa Times*, 17 September 1977, p. 3D.
15. Ibid.
16. *Swasia* 3, no. 26 (18 June 1976), p. 6.
17. *The Christian Science Monitor*, 23 June 1976, p. 3.
18. *The Washington Post*, 27 June 1976, p. 12.
19. *The New York Times*, 20 November 1976, p. 6.
20. *The Washington Post*, 23 November 1976, p. 10.
21. Yehoshiyahu Leibowitz, "Rights, Justice, and Reality," *Ha'aretz* (Jerusalem), 5 August 1977, reprinted in *Swasia* 4, no. 23 (16 September 1977), pp. 5–7.
22. *The New York Times*, 28 June 1977, p. 6.
23. For further discussion of the PLO position on Resolution 242, see Chapter 7.
24. Glenn Perry, "Security Council Resolution 242: The Withdrawal Clause," *The Middle East Journal* 31, no. 4 (Autumn 1977), p. 431.
25. *The Cincinnati Enquirer*, 5 February 1978, p. 1.
26. See Walter Laqueur, *The Struggle for the Middle East: The Soviet Union in the Mediterranean 1958–1968* (London: Routledge and Kegan Paul, 1969); and Oleg

M. Smolanski, *The Soviet Union and the Arab East under Khrushchev* (Lewisburg, Pa.: Bucknell University Press, 1974).

27. See, for example, Ben Ami, *Between Hammer and Sickle* (Philadelphia: Jewish Publication Society of America, 1967).

28. Walid Sharif, "Soviet Marxism and Zionism," *Journal of Palestine Studies* 6, no. 3 (Spring 1977), p. 78.

29. T. B. Bottomore, ed., *Karl Marx: Early Writings* (New York: McGraw Hill, 1963), p. 34.

30. Regina Sharif, "Latin America and the Arab-Israeli Conflict," *Journal of Palestine Studies* 7 (Autumn 1977), p. 85.

31. Joseph Stalin, *Works* Vol. 2, (Moscow: Foreign Languages Publishing House, 1953), p. 307.

32. Ivo J. Lederer and Wayne S. Vucinich, eds., *The Soviet Union and the Middle East: The Post-World War II Era* (Stanford: Hoover Institution Press, 1974), p. 1.

33. Galia Golan, *The Soviet Union and the Arab-Israeli War of October, 1973* (Jerusalem: Hebrew University, 1974), p. 5.

34. Ibid., p. 6.

35. George Lenczowski, "Socialism in Syria," in Helen DesFosses and Jacques Levesque, eds., *Socialism in the Third World* (New York: Praeger, 1975), p. 78.

36. Ibid., p. 79.

37. The invasion took place for various reasons. Nationalization of the canal may have been only an excuse for Israel, Britain, and France in their attempt to destroy Nasser.

38. Lenczowski, "Socialism in Syria," p. 58.

39. Sharif, "Latin America," p. 97.

40. Riad N. El-Rayyes and Dunia Nahas, eds., *Guerrillas for Palestine: A Study of the Palestinian Commando Organizations* (Beirut: An-Nahar Press, 1974), p. 165.

41. Ibid.

42. *Pravda*, 16 July 1976, p. 4, in *Current Digest of the Soviet Press*, 16 August 1976, pp. 10–11.

43. Ibid.

44. El-Rayyes and Nahas, *Guerrillas for Palestine*, p. 167.

45. Hussein Abu el-Namel, "Uropa al-Gharbiyeh wal-Arab wa-Israel" (Western Europe, the Arabs, and Israel) *Shu'un Filastiniyah* 48 (August 1975), pp. 63–64.

46. Quoted in *The Middle East Newsletter* 4, no. 1 (December 1971/February 1972), p. 6.

47. Aqeel Hashem and Said El-Azm, *Israel fi Uropa al-Gharbiyeh* (Israel in Western Europe) (Beirut: PLO Research Center, 1967), p. 146.

48. Quoted in *The Middle East Newsletter* 4, no. 1 (December 1971/February 1972), p. 7.

49. Edward A. Kolodzeij, *French International Policy under DeGaulle and Pompidou* (London: Cornell University Press, 1974), p. 496.

50. *Arab Report and Records* 16, 31 August 1977, p. 707.

51. *Al-Anwar* (Beirut), 6 April 1965, quoted in John K. Cooley, "China and the Palestinians," *Journal of Palestine Studies* 1, no. 2 (Winter 1972), p. 21.

52. Ibid., p. 25.

53. El-Rayyes and Nahas, *Guerrillas for Palestine*, p. 161.

54. Lillian Craig Harris, "China's Relations with the PLO," *Journal of Palestine Studies* 7, no. 1 (Autumn 1977), pp. 123–154.

55. Lin Piao, "Long Live the Victory of People's War: Mao Tse-tung's Theory of Peoples War," in William Lutz and Harry Brent, eds., *On Revolution* (Cambridge, Mass.: Winthrop, 1971), pp. 127–146.

56. Harris, "China's Relations," p. 125.

57. John K. Cooley, *Green March, Black September: The Story of the Palestinian Arabs* (London: Frank Cass, 1973), p. 123.

58. Harris, "China's Relations," p. 125.

59. In Free Palestine, *International Declarations on the Rights of the Palestinians* (Washington, D.C.: Free Palestine Press, 1977), pp. 4–5.

60. Ibid., pp. 6–7.

61. Ibid., p. 9.

62. Ibid., p. 12.

63. Ibid., p. 13.

64. Ibid., p. 12.

65. Regina Sharif, "Latin America and the Arab-Israeli Conflict," *Journal of Palestine Studies* 7, no. 1 (Autumn 1977), p. 98.

66. See Richard P. Stevens, *American Zionism and U.S. Foreign Policy: 1942–1947* (New York: Praeger, 1962).

67. General Assembly Resolution No. 3375 (XXX), November 10, 1975.

68. *Jerusalem Post*, 7 August 1975.

69. *Middle East Economic Digest* (Beirut) 19, No. 4, (4 April 1975), p. 18.

70. Sharif, "Latin America," p. 117.

71. PFLP, *Muhimat al-Marhalah al-Jadidah* (Requirements of the New Stage) (Beirut: PFLP Publications, 1972), p. 142.

72. Hisham Sharabi, "Tahrir Filastin wal-Taharur al-Watani" (Palestinian Liberation and National Liberation), *Shu'un Filastiniyah* 3 (July 1971), p. 113.

73. Karen Farsoun, Samih Farsoun, and Alex Ajay, "Middle East Perspectives from the American Left," in Baha Abu-Laban and Faith T. Zeady, eds., *Arabs in America: Myths and Realities* (Wilmette, Ill.: Medina University Press, 1975), p. 55.

74. Quoted in Ibid., p. 74.

75. John K. Cooley, *Green March Black September*, p. 185.

76. Ibid., p. 187.

77. Ibid., p. 188.

78. The West German government reported these linkages in a bulletin issued in April 1978. For further details, see *The Christian Science Monitor*, 30 June 1978.

7

The Palestinians and Israel

"If the Middle East is ever to know peace, there will have to be a settlement between Israel and the Palestinians. The deeds and propaganda of the fedayeen have underscored this truth and emphasized the basic dilemma of the two people in conflict over the same land."[1] In the final analysis, it is not international recognition or relations with foreign powers that will bring about "lasting peace," but mutual understanding and recognition between the Palestinians and the Israelis. Perhaps this mutual understanding will come about, but the events of the day offer little hope for peace and many indications that there will be more bloodshed in the future.

The Palestinians interact with the Israelis at three levels: (1) as citizens of Israel; (2) as subjects in the Occupied Territories; and (3) as hostile diplomats, commandos, and diaspora refugees in the surrounding countries. At all three levels, relations between the Palestinians and the Israeli establishment are poor. Fear, resentment, and even outright hatred exist between the two peoples. Each party has committed acts that neither is willing to forgive or forget. Both people have come to be guided by their passions and regard their rights as self-evident and firmly based on logic and law. After decades of wars, passions replaced reason and irrationality becomes commonplace. Today, it is no longer a simple task for the two people to distinguish between passion and reason.

THE PALESTINIANS OF ISRAEL

In his book, *The Arabs in Israel: 1948–1966*, Sabri Jiryis describes the living conditions of the Palestinians who remained in the territory on which Israel was proclaimed in 1948.² This book is perhaps the most comprehensive study available in any language on the Arab minority in Israel. Published first in Hebrew then translated into Arabic by the author himself, it is primarily based on Hebrew sources, including Israeli Parliamentary debates, official Gazette court cases, and other governmental publications. This book was updated and published in 1976 by the Monthly Review Press.

The author, himself a former Israeli citizen, describes how the Israeli laws deprive the Palestinians of Israel of their fundamental human rights. He further demonstrates that Israeli policies toward the Arab minority are colonial in nature at all levels of education, agriculture, labor, and services.

One needs to recall that Israel was created on territory comprising close to 80 percent of the total land area of Palestine (although the U.N. partition scheme allocated only 54–55 percent of the land to the Jewish state). The remaining 25 percent of land taken (originally earmarked for the Palestinian Arab state) included heavy concentrations of Arab population. The policies and actions of the Jewish-state-in-the-making during 1947–48 are significant to clarifying Israel's relations with its Arab inhabitants.

In his 1940 diary, Joseph Weitze, former head of the Jewish Agency's Colonization Department, wrote:

Between ourselves it must be clear that there is no room for both Arabs and Jews in this country.... We shall not achieve our goal of being independent people with the Arabs.... And there is but to transfer all of them: not one village, not one tribe should be left.... There is no other way out.³

Mr. Weitze's dream came close to becoming true in 1948. Of all the Palestinians, only about 120,000 individuals remained in Israel. However, the remaining Palestinians realized what Israel's intentions were. One of their slogans under Israeli sovereignty became, "We lost to Israel at war but we will defeat it in our bedrooms." Their numbers multiplied fast, and today they number 750,000 out of a total population of about four million—or about 18 percent. In spite of this Arab "victory," Mr. Weitze's remarks are consistent with the type of settler colonialism out of which Israel was born. Unlike the British settlers in Rhodesia, the French colons in Algeria, and the Belgian colonizers in the Congo, who appropriated vast tracts of land and depended for their cultivation upon underpaid labor, the Zionists almost totally expropriated the Palestinian population.

Israeli hopes of ridding their country of all its Arab inhabitants failed. Consequently, the government "began a procedure of separating it [the Arab minority] from the main body of the Palestinian Arab people."⁴ Israeli authorities have always referred to their Arabs not as a national minority but as a conglomeration of various religious and ethnic communities. It is not surprising, therefore, that official statistics and announcements do not mention "Arabs," but only "Jews" and "non-Jews."

The Arabs of Israel are located in 104 distinctly Arab villages and in six towns with large Jewish majorities. Generally, these towns are clustered in three regions: the Galilee, with 60 percent of Israel's Arab population, the Little Triangle bordering the West Bank, with 20 percent, and the Negev, with 7 percent. Common among these towns and villages is their proximity to border areas adjoining the Arab states. Also common among them is their economic structure and performance, which "contrasts sharply with the more advanced and the more rapidly expanding Jewish region."[5]

After the establishment of the State of Israel, Israeli leaders were anxious to preserve their country as a state for all the Jews of the world. This is consistent with Zionist doctrines. Consequently, the Israeli government has enacted a body of laws that can be regarded as discriminatory. Less than two years after its establishment, Israel enacted the Law of Return, "which allows every Jew, just because he is a Jew, the right to immigrate to Israel (thereby giving him rights superior even to those of the indigenous inhabitants)."[6] In 1952, the Israeli Nationality Law was enacted. This law grants Israeli nationality automatically to all Jews, whereas Palestinians must meet many conditions prior to receiving it. The Absentee Property Law of 1950 and the Land Requisition Law of 1953 had the effect "of confiscating Arab land alone."[7]

The Israeli League for Human and Civil Rights conducted an extensive study of Israel's land confiscation policies, and published their findings in 1973. The report covers the areas occupied in 1967 as well as the territory within the borders of Israel in 1948. What is shocking about the report is that it reveals from inside Israel itself that whole villages were destroyed to make room for Israeli settlers and immigrants. In fact, a close look at their figures shows that a total of 385 villages were destroyed by Israel. This was reported by Israel Shahak of the Israeli League for Human and Civil Rights.[8]

Shahak's figures do not conform with those reported by Jiryis. The reason here may be due to the nature of Shahak's report, dealing with selective districts where destruction of Arab villages was massive. The Israeli government defends this massive destruction of Arab villages as necessary because they are fundamentally related to the objectives of Zionism. The leaders claim that they were "compelled" to confiscate Arab lands in order to settle Jews on them. Others, including former Prime Minister Begin, feel that the land is Jewish because of Biblical and historical connections and justify its confiscation on such grounds. The Palestinians obviously reject such claims.

Another form of legal discrimination took shape immediately after the formation of Israel. On December 12, 1948, Israel imposed de facto military rule on the Arab villages and cities. On March 20, 1950, this rule was converted into an established law. According to this law, the military ruler of the Arab inhabited areas had the right to take any measures against anybody within his jurisdiction without judicial considerations. These measures ranged from house arrest, banishment, and administrative arrest to forbidding the movement of the person outside his residential zone.[9] In fact, every Arab was forbidden to leave his residence and go anywhere outside his village, including his place of work, without a permit from the military governor. These regulations went on for eighteen years until 1966, when they were technically abolished only to be imposed a year later on the Occupied Territories. However, it must be noted that, to this very day, hundreds of Arab political activists are still required to carry permits to move from one place to another. In fact, in 1966 martial law was taken out of the hands of military governors only to be put in the hands of the Israeli police. Blanket restrictions were lifted, but individual restrictions continued, making life more difficult for those Arabs who had been earmarked for special police control.

Discriminatory governmental policies are also evident at the educational level. Soon after the establishment of Israel, the Ministry of Education regulated the educational programs in the schools. As a result, Arab students were forbidden from studying the history of their homeland except through the eyes of the Israelis. Programs on the Old Testament and Jewish history far exceeded in number those on Arab history. Even the Arab language was, and is, taught through lectures in Hebrew.

While the Arabs of Israel make up almost 18 percent of the country's population, their proportionate share in its educational system is far below that. The highest Arab enrollment is at the elementary level, due to their high natural increase. At that level of education, Arab youngsters form 20 percent of all students enrolled. However, a look at higher levels of education indicates a different reality. In the secondary schools, Arabs make up only 7.7 percent of the total student enrollment. At the sub-university level, they make up only 2 percent. In the universities, the participation drops to 1.7 percent. While the factors behind this situation could be seen by some observers as part of normal democratic procedures, they still indicate certain discriminatory practices.

"According to Israeli statistics for the year 1969, for every 100 Jewish students at schools, 9.6 were at the universities, while the percentage among Arabs was 0.9. The Arab countries, taken altogether, whether developed or backward, have a percentage of 2.7, which is three times the percentage among Arabs in Israel."[10] Even if an Arab student makes it to an Israeli university, he is prohibited from joining many programs.

Arab schools are not suitable for education and lack rooms and other necessary facilities. This prompted the mayor of Nazareth to say: "The vast majority of the existing (Arab) school buildings should be called stables, because they are more suitable for animals than for human beings."[11] In fact, many Arab youngsters start their school not in classrooms but outside under trees. Also, the schools lack adequate numbers of qualified teachers.

While these forms of governmental discrimination have created severe difficulties for the Arabs of Israel, the most disturbing area of discrimination has been in the area of social relations. A Louis Harris poll on April 1, 1972, exposed negative Israeli racial attitudes toward their Arab minority. According to this poll, between 60 and 85 percent of those adult Israelis interviewed felt Arabs to be "intellectually inferior," "more inclined to irrationality," "lazier," etc., than Jews.[12] Another study done by an Israeli researcher, Yochanan Peres, found similar evidence of ingrained negative racial attitudes. Eighty-four percent of Israelis interviewed felt that "Arabs will not reach the level of progress of Jews." A higher number, 87 percent, felt that "Arabs understand only force," 82 percent opposed intermarriage with Arabs and 66 percent opposed "living next door to an Arab." A shocking 92 percent of those interviewed felt that "there should be fewer Arabs in Israel."[13]

Politically, the Arabs of Israel have joined the Rakah faction of the Communist party. Few have joined the socialist Matzpen or other parties. Rakah advocates full equality for Israel's Arabs and peace with the Arab countries that incorporates a Palestinian state in the West Bank and the Gaza Strip. With a majority of Arab members, Rakah became the forum for Arab demands. On March 30, 1976, Rakah's Arab leadership called for the famous "Land Day Strike." The strike "was complete and total."[14] All Arab economic activities stopped to protest Israel's confiscation of Arab lands. The strike began peacefully but was soon interrupted by Israel's armed security forces, leading to seven Arab deaths and a number of injuries.

Prior to the "Land Day Strike," Israel Koenig, the northern district commissioner of the Ministry of the Interior, had submitted a memorandum to the prime minister analyzing the situation of the Arabs of Israel. His analysis and subsequent suggestions, known as the "Koenig Report," caused an uproar in Arab and some Israeli circles. According to the Hebrew language daily, *Al-Hamishmar*, the report "includes dangerous evaluations and statements that, if accepted as authorized positions, would cause conflict between the Jewish majority and the Arab minority."[15] Koenig's report was claimed to be Koenig's private opinions, and the Ministry of Interior refused to dismiss him from his responsibility over the major Arab populated areas of Israel. His report advocated the de-Arabization of Arab areas of Israel by force,[16] the imposition of rigid law enforcement measures in the Arab sectors, the isolation of Rakah, the establishment of a loyal Arab party, and various other oppressive measures to keep the Arab population under governmental control.[17] Therefore, a major objective of the Koenig plan was to de-Arabize and Judaize the northern Galilee. Originally included in the U.N. partition scheme as part of the projected Palestinian state, Galilee is heavily populated by Arabs. The Arabs in this part of Israel are almost 50 percent of the population, but because of their high birth rate, Koenig saw them as threatening to become a majority in the area in a few years time. Koenig's plan proposed a "thinning out" of the Arabs by various means of subterfuge.

This report by the official in charge of 60 percent of the Arabs of Israel serves to indicate, along with the previous discussion, that the Palestinian-Israeli interaction at this direct and basic level is not a pleasant one. Israel's policies toward its Arab minority led Dr. A. C. Forrest, the late editor of the Canadian *United Church Observer*, to write in 1971:

Twice I have been in South Africa within a few days of being in Israel. I know no two countries in the world with so much in common, unless it is Rhodesia and Israel. But the Israelis make the South Africans look like babes in the wood when it comes to practicing apartheid and keeping another race in its place and misleading the world about it.[18]

Dr. Forrest's remarks may seem shocking to his Canadian and American readers, because Israel is generally perceived as a democratic state. While this study is not concerned with Israel's democracy for its Jewish citizens, evidence points out that democracy for the Arab citizens of Israel is still a dream. Similarities between Israel's discriminatory practices against its Arab minority and those of South Africa against its Black population have been recognized by many countries, as well as by the U.N. General Assembly, as evidenced in Resolution No. 3379 of November 10, 1975 defining Zionism as a form of racism.

THE OCCUPIED TERRITORIES

Israel's victory over its Arab neighbors in 1967 and the subsequent Israeli occupation of new territories provided Israel with an opportunity to achieve a lasting peace in the area. Instead, the Israeli government chose to establish its control of the West Bank and the Gaza Strip.* These territories were not regarded by Israel as occupied but as "liberated." Therefore, it is natural to read Israeli government publications asserting that, "In the course of the six-day war new territories to the north, center,

*Although this study does not deal with the Israeli occupation of the Golan, it is important to note that about 100,000 Syrians were displaced as a result of Israel's occupation of this area.

and south of the former boundaries of the State of Israel were liberated."[19] Consequently, Israel initiated a process of "creeping annexation" over the territories.

While Israel's establishment led to an almost total Palestinian evacuation of the conquered areas, its 1967 victory did not. A minority of 200,000 Palestinians left the Occupied Territories in 1967, leaving 657,000 individuals behind in the West Bank and 540,000 in the Gaza Strip.[20] However, this did not prevent Israel from annexing Arab Jerusalem, including the Old City soon after its occupation, and proclaiming the whole city to be its capital. The Palestinians of these territories viewed Israel as an occupying power, but feared its schemes of annexation. Israel's annexation of Arab Jerusalem, however, has not been recognized by the world community. In fact, with U.S. support, the United Nations has censured this annexation.

These schemes have materialized as Jewish settlements in those areas. Jewish settlements were established in the Occupied Territories as early as 1967 and continue to be established there until this very day. Yehuda Harel, an Israeli settlement leader, told a *New York Times* correspondent:

Israel is a country without borders. No two people in Israel or abroad agree on the borders of Israel. What we have is where Jewish people have settled. The only solid thing is that, in the last eighty years, the Jewish people have never willingly given up a settlement. The people feel that by coming here (to the Occupied Territories), they have made the border.[21]

Early Jewish settlements in Palestine formed the backbone of the Jewish state. In fact, Israel began with Jewish settlements. Before the end of 1977, Israel had established on Arab expropriated lands in the Occupied Territories a total of ninety-five Jewish settlements. Of these, forty-eight were established in the West Bank, eighteen in the Gaza Strip, and twenty-five in the Golan Heights.[22] This trend continues to the present day and the Israeli government continues its construction of even more settlements. By 1986, Israel had constructed 104 settlements in the West Bank alone, housing 52,000 settlers. In response to a question on new settlements in the West Bank, Menahem Begin, Israel's former Prime Minister, responded: "The term 'the West Bank' means nothing. It is Judea-Samaria. It is Israeli land, belonging to the Jewish people."[23]

Two phases may be distinguished in Israel's settlement policies. Phase 1 extends from 1968 to 1977, when the Labor Alignment dominated government. During this phase the average annual increment was about 770 settlers. During the second phase, which extends from 1977 to 1984, during which time the Likud dominated the government, the average annual increment was 5,400 settlers. In 1984, for the first time, the growth reached 15,000 settlers a year. In 1985, the number of settlers grew by

9,165. Subsequently, a slowdown has continued under the national coalition governments that ruled until 1990 when the Likud returned to dominate the government.

An independent Israeli research group headed by Dr. Meron Benvenisti maintains a continuously updated and computerized data base on Israeli settlements. According to this West Bank Data Base Project, the number of Jewish settlers in the West Bank alone now exceeds 60,000.

An impressive growth in numbers between 1980 and 1985 (almost 40,000) is related to Likud's strategy of shifting emphasis from the subsidized rural settlements to the demand forces pushing for the suburban settlements. Consequently, during this period, more than 80 percent of total investment was directed to the West Bank metropolitan areas near Jerusalem and Tel Aviv. The new settlers became the urban dwellers who saw in the settlements a more economical way to live. The old rural settler, on the other hand, was the ideologue who believed in his/her "right" to inhabit what is called "Judea and Samaria."

Of more significance to the Palestinians in the Occupied Territories than the settlements are the restrictions imposed on them by the occupying power. The laws applied by the Israeli authorities in these territories are the Defense (Emergency) Regulations that were applied to the Arabs of Israel between 1949 and 1966. The application of these regulations constitutes a violation of international law. The Geneva Convention of August 12, 1949, regarding the protection of civilians in wartime, to which Israel is a signatory, forbids the enactment or introduction of new laws in the Occupied Territories.[24]

These regulations were originally written and applied by the British in 1945. Mr. Jacov Shimshon Shapira, who later became Israel's attorney general and minister of justice, attacked these same regulations (which he came to apply) as "uncivilized." In 1946, Mr. Shapira said:

The system established in Palestine since the issue of the Defense Laws is unparalleled in any civilized country; there were no such laws even in Nazi Germany. It is our duty to tell the whole world that the Defense Laws passed by the British mandatory government of Palestine destroy the very foundation of justice in this land.[25]

Justice, however, became less relevant to the Israeli minister of justice when the subjects were Arabs. Consequently, Israeli violations of human rights in the Occupied Territories go unquestioned by Israeli officials. A few Israelis, however, have come to speak out against their government's repressive policies. Ms. Felicia Langer spoke for these well-intentioned Israelis:

The progressive forces in Israel are struggling against the occupation and are striving for peace. They are fighting the oppression in the occupied Arab territories, and the trampling of human rights, and the violation of the UN Charter and the Geneva Convention.[26]

Israel's violations of human rights are multifaceted and extend to a number of areas. One of these is the right to leave and return to one's country. This right is recognized in the Universal Declaration of Human Rights, the International Covenant on Civil and Political Rights, and other international documents. Soon after the occupation, the U.N. General Assembly adopted Resolution 2443 of December 19, 1968 calling upon Israel to allow those who became refugees in 1967 to return. Israel's attitude to repatriation was given by Moshe Dayan, its former minister of foreign affairs, when he said that "Israel will not permit the return of the hundreds of thousands of West Bank residents who left the country before and during the Six Day War."[27]

Another area of Israeli violations of the human rights of the Palestinians of the Occupied Territories is that of expulsion and deportation. "Article 49 of the Fourth Geneva Convention was drafted in response to the mass deportation of Jews which occurred in World War II."[28] It prohibits an occupying power from expelling, deporting or transferring civilians outside the area under occupation. Israel, however, has continued to employ a policy of systematic expulsion of Arabs from the Occupied Territories. While in office, former Israeli Prime Minister Golda Meir defended the policy of expulsion on a security basis.[29] Mass expulsion has been ordered by Israel on several occasions. A U.N. Special Committee has confirmed that the population of some West Bank and Golan Heights villages were forcibly expelled and driven out of the borders.[30] Other deportations also occur. Many of those deported include doctors, judges, lawyers, educators, and even mayors of towns.[31] Deportation of Palestinians usually takes place without prior notice or a court order. Israeli expulsion of Palestinian professionals is seen as a deliberate policy to deprive the Palestinian people under occupation of their effective leaders.

Many Palestinians are detained in Israeli prisons without trial. The military governors of the Occupied Territories have the right, according to the Emergency Regulations, to put under administrative detention any individual within their jurisdiction. The detainee remains imprisoned without charges for as long as the military governor deems necessary. The number of administrative detainees reached 1,311 in May of 1970 and was increased after the 1973 October War. *Ha'aretz* reported that in less than two months in 1974, 150 persons had been placed under administrative detention.[32] But when the intifada started, the numbers of administrative detainees grew into the thousands.

Another Israeli violation of human rights in the Occupied Territories is the practice of collective punishment. The Fourth Geneva Convention explicitly prohibits "collective penalties."[33] A usual method of collective punishment much used by Israeli authorities is the punitive curfew, whereby a whole city or village is put under total curfew for a number of days as a punishment for some offense carried out by individuals within the area. Examples of these punitive curfews are many, and they now occur on a regular basis. Since the intifada began, not a single day has passed without the imposition of some curfews. Such curfews were reported as early as 1967, such as that at the Shati refugee camp in Gaza Strip. A British reporter described it as follows:

> For the first 28 hours no one was allowed on any pretext to leave his house—which in a refugee camp means one or two small rooms without a latrine.... The reason given for the five-day curfew at Shati was the explosion of a tiny homemade petard (the official Israeli account said it consisted of half a pound of TNT in a Pepsi-Cola bottle) near a Gaza fish market, causing no casualties. The culprit was said to have run along the beach in the direction of the refugee camp. Failing to identify him, the Israelis, besides imposing the curfew, blew up nine fishermen's storehouses in which they kept their nets and tackle, and destroyed a number of fishing boats.[34]

In fact, destruction of houses is a common Israeli punitive measure. Within ten years of the occupation, "upwards of 15,000 houses have been destroyed (in the Occupied Territories) since June 1967."[35] The practice has become almost a daily routine now. Any person committing a security offense is liable to have his home destroyed. Other residents of the house have to evacuate it prior to the destruction. Often adjacent homes are affected as well.

One of the most troubling of the Israeli violations of Palestinian human rights is that of torture and physical abuse of Arab detainees. One need not quote Arab sources on this issue. Israeli and Western observers provide a long list of such atrocities. Even the U.S. Department of State has written about these violations. In its annual human rights report to Congress, the State Department cited such Israeli abuses.[36] A more detailed report in *The Sunday Times* of London concluded that "torture of Arab prisoners is so widespread and systematic that it cannot be dismissed as 'rogue cops' exceeding orders. It appears to be sanctioned as deliberate policy."[37] The most comprehensive report on Israeli torture of Palestinian detainees in the Occupied Territories was written by an Israeli attorney, Felicia Langer, who defended some of those detainees. In her book, *With My Own Eyes*, Ms. Langer details a number of specific cases, and concludes that torture of detainees is "characteristic of Israeli rule in the Occupied Territories."[38]

Israel, understandably, denies all allegations of violations of Palestinian human rights, and claims that its occupation is liberal and humane. The Israelis report that their occupation has "improved standards of living" and granted the inhabitants true "freedom of the spirit."[39] The Palestinians reject these Israeli claims and assert that "Israeli policy in the West Bank and Gaza Strip was geared, right from the start, toward turning these areas into a colony with some unique features specific to Zionist settler-colonialism."[40]

A review of the economic development of the Gaza Strip and the West Bank indicates an improvement in the standard of living as well as features of Israeli "colonial" behavior. Israeli figures indicate an annual GNP growth rate of 15 percent in the West Bank during the early years of occupation. This growth, however, is attributed to the Israeli absorption of West Bank labor in its market and the migration of professionals to the Gulf region. These Gulf Palestinians send large sums of money home to their families. Moreover, Israel clearly benefited from its occupation. The economy of the Occupied Territories became dependent on the dominant Israeli economy. Prior to the intifada, the Occupied Territories were a significant market for Israeli goods. Between 1970 and 1986, the West Bank and Gaza acquired between 83 and 92 percent of all their imports from Israel. Their exports to Israel, likewise, ranged between 46 and 75 percent.

Israeli industries and business enterprises found a huge reserve of cheap labor in the Occupied Territories. As might be expected, they exploited the situation and employed a growing number of Palestinians. It is estimated that by the time the intifada started, about 120,000 Palestinians worked in Israel.

What is disturbing about this phenomenon is not the high number of employees, but the degree to which they have been exploited. On average, a Palestinian worker earns half the wages of an Israeli doing the same work.

More disturbing is the fact that the Palestinian workers are prohibited from either joining the Histadrut or forming a union of their own. They are thus without the protection and benefits of unionism, and are compelled to remain at the mercy of their employers. Moreover, automatic deductions are taken from the salaries of West Bank and Gaza Strip workers employed in Israel for taxes and charges for social services, the benefits of which they never receive.[41]

The Israeli government's water and land policies in the Occupied Territories are crucial to Israeli-Palestinian relations in these areas. By 1985, Israeli settlers in the West Bank—making up less than 3 percent of the population—used more than 20 percent of the total water consumed in the region. Israel has instituted measures that gave it control of West Bank and Gaza water resources. Consequently, levels of water in Arab wells have become lower and, in some instances, dried up. Given that a third of the water reaching Israel originates in the West Bank, it is possible to argue that Israel's policies in regard to this occupied region are motivated, in part, by its concern over its own water resources. Thus, besides its interest in defensible borders, or for some, historic borders, Israel may also have an interest in hydraulic borders.

Another issue that disturbs experts is the Israeli practice of land acquisition. Figures on this practice are disputed. However, experts on the West Bank put Israel's land confiscation at anywhere from 27 to 64 percent of the total land area of the West Bank. The Israeli West Bank Data Base Project, perhaps the most authoritative source, concluded that "by April, 1985, the Israeli authorities had ensured control over 52 percent of the West Bank land mass."[42] In the process, many Palestinians effectively lost the means for their livelihood.

The Israeli economy, especially the agricultural sector, has also gained an outlet to Arab markets through the "open bridges" to Jordan. While Arab countries do not permit trade with Israel, they encourage trade with the Occupied Territories. However, Israeli products have been found floating in Arab markets. It is not unusual for Israeli products, especially unmarked fruits and vegetables and other unidentified manufactured items, to be sold to Arab markets through West Bank middlemen. However, while reports of such transactions may be accurate, it is almost impossible to estimate their value.

Tourism is another area in which Israel has gained economically because of the occupation. While Israel has been known to be a viable tourist attraction, the Occupied Territories have added significantly to its tourist industry. These territories included the Old City of Jerusalem, Bethlehem, Jericho, the Jordanian Dead Sea resorts, Hebron, and many other attractions for pilgrims and tourists. This has contributed significantly to Israel's tourist industry and provided for a larger flow of hard currency into Israel.

Politically, Palestinians of the Occupied Territories are denied the rights to self-determination or even to self-rule. Decisions affecting their lives are made by Israel. The only representatives they ever elected were those for their own municipalities. Even then, the municipalities are subject to the dictates of the Israeli military governors, and elected officials are often dismissed or even expelled.

In response to Sadat's visit to Israel, the Israeli government announced on December 27, 1977 a plan of "self-rule" for the West Bank and Gaza. Known as the Begin Plan, this proposal represented little change from the usual Israeli military rule over the Occupied Territories. A *New York Times* editorial pointed out that the plan "does not take an Arab eye to read into it much rule but little self."[43] *The Washington Post* quoted Israeli Prime Minister Begin as saying that his plan is meant to provide a final settlement for the Palestinian problems.[44]

According to the Begin Plan, the Arabs of the West Bank (referred to as Judea and Samaria) and the Gaza Strip will elect an eleven-member administrative council to govern their affairs. Jewish residents will be subject only to Israeli jurisdiction. The administrative council will have jurisdiction over local education, religious affairs, commerce, agriculture, tourism, health, and policing.

A tripartite committee of Israel, Jordan, and the administrative council will be established to review existing legislation and abolish what may be unnecessary regulations and decide on "the competence of the administrative council to promulgate regulations." Since the committee's rulings must be unanimous, Israel will have a veto power over legislation of the administrative council even in the limited areas of education, religion, etc. Therefore, it appears that West Bank and Gaza Palestinians will be no better off than before; Israel will simply replace her military rule with a veto power. Israeli authorities will remain in charge of "security and public order." The Palestinians of these areas will have a choice of either Israeli or Jordanian citizenship, and Israelis will continue to settle in the West Bank and Gaza. Palestinian refugees from outside the areas will be allowed back in "reasonable numbers." Jerusalem, presumably, will remain under total Israeli jurisdiction.[45]

Egypt rejected the Begin Plan, the PLO ridiculed it, and the Palestinians of the West Bank and Gaza discarded it in favor of the PLO objective of self-determination. The Palestinians of the Occupied Territories, in fact, have always refused local self-rule as a substitute for total Palestinian self-determination. The Camp David framework, as discussed in Chapter 5, is seen in a similar fashion.

Having reported the sentiments of the West Bank and Gaza Palestinians in Chapter 2, there is no need to cover this subject here. It is sufficient to say that those Palestinians reject Israeli occupation and regard the PLO as their only spokesman. These sentiments were confirmed in September 1986 when the U.S. daily, *Newsday*, the Australian Broadcasting Corporation, and the Jerusalem daily *Al-Fajr* conducted a joint poll of Palestinians in the West Bank. That poll showed an almost universal (93.5 percent) support for the PLO. Arafat received strong, but not universal support (71.2 percent). Most significantly, the poll indicated a very strong hostility toward King Hussein of Jordan, as his support was limited to 3.5 percent. West Bank Palestinians perceived violence as a justified and effective means of struggle (83 percent) and a large segment of them (73.9 percent) felt that peace is not possible under present (1986) conditions.[46]

It is proper to state that interaction between Israel and the Palestinians at this level is not in the least a pleasant and cordial one. Those Palestinians see Israel as an occupying enemy force with intent to subjugate them and suppress their national and individual political rights. While this may be true of some Israeli circles, there are also many Israelis who have come to question their own government's policies toward the Occupied Territories. This polarization of Israel's society over the occupation has been heightened with the advent of the Palestinian intifada in 1987.

THE INTIFADA

On December 9, 1987, the Palestinians under occupation rebelled. That rebellion, the intifada, shows Palestinian readiness to suffer and to die just as the Algerians did for eight bloody years. In the process, they have crossed the barrier of fear. Once that barrier has been crossed, the other side can kill and maim, but it cannot win. As a result, the Palestinians have come to occupy Israel psychologically as Israel occupies them militarily. Finally, the Israeli occupation is facing a moment of truth. Either they continue to react as an imperial power and face the grave consequences imperial powers have faced, or they make peace—which certainly means the end of the occupation.

It is clear today that analysts cannot study the politics of the Arab-Israeli conflict, and in particular the Palestinian question, without coming to grips with the Palestinian uprising. This uprising represents the acceleration of an ongoing process of resistance. As such, the uprising represents not the interruption of an order as it does the culmination of an order. It is the natural reaction to an unnatural occupation. Far away from the events, people reacted with surprise, or shock; but there is nothing surprising or shocking about the refusal of a new generation to inherit pain and powerlessness, or an older generation to resist subjugation and oppression.

More than three years of sustained resistance revealed the futility of attributing the intifada to a specific incident. The uprising was not a response to a casual episode but an inevitable rekindling of mass resistance to Israel's repressive occupation. The occupation has in some way or another touched the life of every Palestinian living in the West Bank and the Gaza Strip. Political suppression, economic colonization, ideological and cultural strangulation have been the main denominators of Israel's occupation. The civil and human rights of the Palestinian population have been denied, as have their national rights and even their identity. Such practices as annexation, confiscation of land, construction of settlements, expulsion and imprisonment of activists, torture in prisons, censorship of the media, requirements of carrying identity cards, displaying different color license plates, harassment at checkpoints, limitations on domestic and international travel, and a host of measures limiting personal and civil freedom have contributed to Israel's attempts at strangling the Palestinians political expression and frustrating their national aspirations.

Israeli designs, however, were doomed to failure. In early December

1987, Israel learned that it is not beyond the reach of history. The Palestinians rebelled. Their rebellion has sent Israel a clear and a strong message: the colonial era has ended. When the rebellion started, however, it began spontaneously. The forces behind it had been preparing the stage for it since Israel's occupation began. If the political forces at work gave the intifada its organizational and political content, the Israeli behavior over the previous twenty years gave it its very birth and made its outbreak inevitable.

Within days of the start of the December 9, 1987 intifada, the political forces formed a joint command known as the Unified National Leadership of the Uprising (UNLU) and began to issue directives. The UNLU, made up of the pro-PLO representatives from Fateh, the PFLP, the DFLP, and the Communist Party coordinated in Gaza with the newer Islamic Jihad. Their leaflets, distributed clandestinely every other week or so, directed the masses and the support groups and put forth their message and demands. The leaflet, which has often been employed by the underground political forces, became the most powerful form of written political expression of the Palestinians under occupation. To those Palestinians, the leaflet was transformed into a sort of a biweekly governmental directive. Signed by the UNLU/PLO, it told people when to go to work and when to strike, when to demonstrate, break curfews, go to schools, visit families of those killed, wounded or imprisoned, and a host of other activities. The leaflet also directed the support groups and the masses to organize neighborhood committees for education, welfare, health, agriculture, and to guard their neighborhoods. The mass support the leadership received made the Palestinian intifada a remarkable phenomenon in the history of the Palestinians and foiled Israel's attempts at crushing it.

The leaflets have continuously asserted Palestinian demands to end the occupation and their right to self-determination. The link between the Palestinians under occupation and the PLO is emphasized in every leaflet and by the fact that the leaflets themselves are signed by the UNLU of the PLO. The so-called Jordanian option, whereby Israel negotiates the future of the territories with Jordan, was also condemned in the leaflets. The Palestinians clearly want nothing less than their independence. The Jordanian king got the message and subsequently severed Jordan's administrative ties with the West Bank. By that time, however, the new administration had been in place. Popular committees were already running the new and clandestine apparatus of the Palestinians under occupation.

By then, the Palestinians in the Occupied Territories were, at the instruction of the UNLU, building self-sufficiency. Popular committees ran towns, villages, and refugee camps. Schools sprung up in homes, churches, and mosques. Yards and vacant lots were being tilled, planted, and cultivated. Potential blood donors were classified by blood type to prepare for emergencies. Makeshift clinics were created in camps, neighborhoods, and villages. Water wells were tested and treated as emergency water resources in case of Israeli cut-off of water. Landlords were forgiving rent payments. Security patrols armed with whistles and flashlights were set up to watch out for attacks by settlers and the army. Food supplies were also stored in almost every neighborhood. In sum, the intifada is a clear manifestation of the revolutionary transformation of the entire Palestinian body politic under occupation.

The Israelis were caught by surprise. Their leaders predicted the end of the intifada in a matter of days. Defense Minister Rabin even refused to interrupt a visit to the United States at the start of the intifada, while assuring reporters that the uprising would die out in a matter of days. But the intifada intensified, and so did Israel's repressive measures. Consequently, Israel became polarized between those who argued for expulsion of the Palestinians and those who advocated the end of the occupation. But almost all Israelis, as evidenced by the statements of their leaders and the media, came to the conclusion that a return to the pre-intifada status quo was impossible. Thus, as a form of political expression, the intifada sent the Palestinian message to Israel, and to the world as well.

But the Unified National Leadership, and the nationalist political forces behind it, would not have been able to accomplish this historic feat if it was not for the popular support they received and the persistent and active role of many grassroot institutions that have worked for many years to institutionalize the resistance to the occupation. The grassroot institutions include a host of student, women's, workers', and professional committees and unions. It is these groups that have broadened the arena of participatory politics among the Palestinian masses. To them, the phenomenon of intifada is not new. They have spearheaded many uprisings since 1967. Many of their members have spent years in Israeli jails, where they earned the respect of their fellow Palestinians.

It is obvious that the intifada long ago reached the point of no return. Israel must now act either in favor of accommodation or confrontation. The status quo is simply a thing of the past. If one can learn only one thing from the intifada's first three years, it is that the route of confrontation will lead Israel to disaster without achieving any return to the status quo. In sum, Israeli options have been limited.

ISRAEL AND THE DIASPORA PALESTINIANS

About three million Palestinians live outside Palestine today. Many of them are refugees. Almost all of them feel that they were unjustly deprived of their right to live on the land of their forefathers. When former Israeli Prime Minister Golda Meir was asked if Israel admits a measure of responsibility toward the Palestinian refugees, she summed up Israel's position in the following manner: "No, no responsibility whatsoever. If you say, is Israel prepared to cooperate in the solution of their plight, the answer is yes. But we are not responsible for their plight."[47]

While many Israelis have come to assume a measure of responsibility for the plight of the Palestinians and show a willingness to help relieve it, the official Israeli position remains uncompromising. Israeli officials claim that it was the Arab states who created the refugee problem when they invaded Palestine in 1948. Having discussed such claims and the Zionist planning in Chapter 1, there is no need to repeat it at this point. It is sufficient to say that, without Zionism, there would have been no Palestine problem.

Israel continues its hard-line position that the Palestinian refugees must be integrated and settled in the host Arab countries. In support of this policy, the Israeli leaders cite other refugee problems that have been "solved by integration and resettlement," such as in India and Pakistan.[48] The Palestinians, for their part, reject assimilation and maintain a strong attachment to their homeland. Almost all the Palestinians see the PLO, the commando groups affiliated with it, and the intifada as the means for their return to their homeland, as was noted in Chapter 2.

On its part, the PLO advocated political and armed struggle against Israel. Whether PLO and commando activities or their diplomatic efforts form a viable means for the achievement of Palestinian objectives is in doubt. Probably the achievement of such goals requires more than commando operations or Palestinian diplomacy. Arab military and economic capabilities and international political and economic support will most probably prove necessary to supplement Palestinian activities in order that the Palestinians achieve their objectives. This, however, is for future historians to study. Without more meaningful Arab and international support, the Palestinians must pin their hopes on a protracted long-term struggle. Such a struggle has started with the intifada. But the PLO was faced with the issue of objectives. Are they aiming at total return to former homes or a West Bank/Gaza Strip state? This issue they have now clarified with the Declaration of Independence. The other problem they were faced with was whether to drop or continue commando operations.

Regardless of potentialities, Palestinian armed operations against Israel have achieved a number of specific goals. First, they have brought to light their grievances. Palestinians today are considered by the international community to be at the crux of the Arab-Israeli conflict. There is now a worldwide awareness that any solution must deal with the

Palestinian problem. Even in Israel, the question of the Palestinians has evolved into a major topic of concern and debate. Mr. Ohad Zmora, the managing editor of the Israeli daily *Davar*, explained the essence of the debate in these terms:

Everybody agrees that without a solution of the Palestinian problem there will not be a solution of the conflict in the Middle East. This is a consensus. The difference of opinion is about what kind of pragmatic, political solution is desirable, not about how central the Palestinian problem is.[49]

Second, Palestinian commando operations have influenced the rate of Israeli immigration and emigration. For Israel, immigration is a vital matter of concern. In fact, the creation of Israel would have been impossible without immigration. Guerrilla activities may contribute to a decline in immigration and an increase of cases of emigration.

In 1975, and for the first time in Israel's history, emigration exceeded immigration. While it is hard to credit this trend solely to Palestinian commando operations, it is possible to conclude that those operations contributed to such a development. In her study of the West Bank, Elizabeth Monroe concluded that the decline in immigration was due to "the growing volume of eyewitness accounts of Jewish colonization and consequent Arab resistance."[50] Of course, changes in the Soviet policies have reversed the declining trend of immigration. In fact, recent Soviet immigration has been alarmingly massive. Many Palestinians fear that the new immigrants will be settled on the Occupied Territories.

A third consequence of Palestinian armed activities is the high cost Israel is paying for preventive measures. While the total financial cost is hard to assess, it is reasonable to conclude that Israel's attempts to seal its borders, especially the northern one, and to establish security measures at schools, factories, kibbutzim, and all places where Israelis are found are fairly expensive and constitute an added burden to the state's already burdened economy. In addition, such Palestinian activities undoubtedly influence Israel's tourist industry and limit its expansion. Israeli foreign trade may have also suffered.

Palestinian armed operations also have domestic implications for Israel. In a country of coalition governments, political stability is often related to the government's ability to rule. Palestinian operations contribute to instability, and a government which shows laxity in dealing with guerrilla activities is considered weak and therefore susceptible to harsh criticism. Israel's response to these activities has been to retaliate against the commandos by bombing Palestinian refugee camps and other military and civilian targets. Israeli retaliation, by itself, creates a new problem for Israel. Such massive retaliation usually provokes loud protests and condemnations by the world community. The U.N. Security

Council has often criticized Israel for such actions. In fact, Israel's isolation in the international community cannot but be related to its inflexibility toward the Palestinians.

While Palestinian armed operations against Israel achieve some limited and short-term Palestinian objectives, they have been on the decline. Whatever the reason, the trend of decline is evident. It may be related to Palestinian-Arab relations, to Israel's improved preventive measures, and to the weakening of Palestinian bases in Lebanon after Israel's invasion. An examination of some of the resistance communiqués and Israeli reports indicate a significant gap between Palestinian claims and Israeli acknowledgments of the number of operations, and both may be inaccurate. Reports of casualties and incidents gathered from both Israeli and Palestinian sources are inadequate. Exaggerated claims of victory by various Palestinian groups may often be introduced to serve their own purposes. Israeli reports, on the other hand, are not specific and tend to minimize the role of the commandos. For instance, on July 24, 1969, the *Jerusalem Post* reported that an Israeli from Haifa was found dead after he ate a poisoned watermelon. The report then went on to state that a "bomb was planted in the watermelon" but "the detonator of the bomb was disconnected." *Fateh* was reported as insisting that "death was caused by the bomb."[51]

Therefore, reliable figures on casualties from both sides are difficult to obtain. One can, however, attempt to determine the numbers of operations that have been carried out by the commandos by examining Western as well as Palestinian and Israeli sources and to judge the trend in commando activities.

Statistics on the number of commando operations are highly disputed. The Palestinian figures exceed those of Israel. In 1969, for example, Palestinian sources reported 3,400 such attacks. Israeli sources reported only 2,500 for the same year. Even when using Palestinian figures, one can detect a rapid decline in commando operations. This decline must be attributed in part to events in the region. In fact, the trend of decline started in 1970, the year when the Jordanian civil war occurred. Further drastic declines occurred in 1975–1976, when the guerrillas were fighting a war for survival in Lebanon. This decline continued beyond 1976. For example, Israeli figures put such activities at 203 in 1982 and at 173 in the following year. Even PLO figures indicate only 863 such activities in 1985, including those carried out in southern Lebanon. Clearly, Israel's invasion of Lebanon, and subsequent divisions within the Resistance Movement contributed to such a decline. The intifada also helped in this regard as the Palestinians adopted a new approach to resistance.

It is also possible to argue that the decrease in the number of the commando operations is due to the new international recognition given the Palestinians and the PLO. Accordingly, the Palestinians began to emphasize the role of diplomacy and political compromise in their struggle.

Some analysts, however, credit Israeli counterinsurgency measures alone for the decline. In his book *Revolutionary Warfare in the Middle East*, Dr. Bard O'Neill discusses the Palestinian commandos as an insurgent force and concludes that Israel's counterinsurgency measures have been rather successful.[52] While this writer may disagree with O'Neill's treatment of the commandos purely as an insurgency group, some of his conclusions may be valid. Israel's counter-commando activities have undoubtedly achieved some success. Aside from the preventive and punitive measures in the Occupied Territories, Israel's successes in containing Palestinian guerrilla power reached the Arab countries. Israel's cross-border attacks have, as noted earlier, contributed to the circumstances leading to civil wars in Jordan and Lebanon. Moreover, Israel's invasion of Lebanon contributed to a shift in the targeted areas of attack, as it set back Palestinian infrastructures.

While Israel's counter-guerrilla activities may have achieved some success, it is doubtful that one can explain the decline of commando operations on this basis only. If one is to accept this explanation, why then did such Israeli activities not succeed as well in the period between 1968 and 1970? Other explanations must be taken into consideration. It is possible to argue that a major cause for the decline is the shift within the PLO regarding immediate objectives and means. In order to detect such shifts, one needs to examine the changes in the position of the PLO regarding Israel's existence.

The National Covenant, as adopted in 1964 and amended in 1968, represented the basic position of the PLO on the Palestine question. Four points sum up the relevant clauses regarding Israel. The first is that Palestine is an integrated and undivided whole belonging to the Palestinian Arabs. The second point is that Israel's existence is illegal and represents a threat to the Arab cause and to humanity. The third point emphasizes that the objective of the PLO is to liberate Palestine and to eliminate the "Zionist entity" through armed struggle only. Compromise was not seen as possible. The final point maintains that the Jews constitute a religious community and not a nation. As such, they do not have a right to political or national self-determination, but will be allowed to continue to live in Palestine only as a religious minority in an Arab state. This was the Palestinian position since the British Mandate over Palestine, and takes root in Palestinian Arab nationalism.

An important change in the position of the PLO since has been the idea of a democratic secular state in Palestine. Theoretically, this idea has changed the clause in the National Covenant that regarded as Palestinians only those Jews who lived in Palestine prior to the "Zionist invasion." Now, all Jews living in Palestine are seen to have a right to continue living in Palestine as equal citizens in a democratic state. This idea has been expressed since 1969 by various Palestinian groups and takes root in the new revolutionary ideologies adopted by the commandos. When he addressed the U.N. General Assembly in 1974, Yasser Arafat reiterated this position:

I proclaim before you that when we speak of our common hopes for the Palestine of tomorrow we include in our perspective all Jews now living in Palestine who choose to live with us there in peace and without discrimination.[53]

This change has resulted in a new and a significant development, namely Palestinian-Israeli contacts. The PLO, which rejected such contacts in its formative years, began to encourage exploratory contacts with progressive elements in Israeli society in 1976. PLO representatives even met with a number of Rakah representatives at various occasions in 1976 and 1977. These meetings were not limited to Rakah but were extended to include Zionist elements in Israel.[54] Abu Mazen, a PLO leader, spoke on the issue during the thirteenth session of the Palestine National Council in 1977. He defended the contacts as a means to "intensify the contradictions within Israeli society," and to obtain "some Israeli support for the national rights of the Palestinian people."[55] Yasser Arafat explained the contacts in a different way. Dr. Abu-Lughod reported Arafat's explanation in the following manner:

[Arafat] stated that the Palestinian objective is to establish a democratic nonsectarian state in which all those who wish to live in Palestine would have to live as equal citizens. To bring about that State, armed struggle is necessary. But that does not preclude other forms of struggle—political, diplomatic, and personal. If Palestinian Moslems and Christians are prepared to live with Jews in Palestine, then they must be able to talk to them and persuade them by deed that they mean it.[56]

Arafat's explanation seemed to be in accordance with the modified PLO objective of a democratic-secular state. Abu Mazen's expectations, however, are far from being achieved. While there are voices in Israel supporting the Palestinians, the predominant sentiments in Israeli society are anti-PLO. The leftists and the progressive elements in Israel have come to support recognition and negotiation with the PLO, but those are few. Arieh Eliav, former secretary-general of the Labor Party, has, on occasion, even defended the Palestinian commandos as "fighters for a just cause."[57] Others also defended the Palestinians. A review of Israel's public opinion polls indicates a growing support among the Israelis for Palestinian rights. The participants in the dialogue reported in Fabian and Ze'ev's books, *Israelis Speak*, attest to this growth. One of the participants, who is himself anti-Palestinian, remarked: "In my own home, my daughter speaks about the right of the Palestinians."[58]

A third and dramatic change in the PLO's objectives has been its acceptance of the idea of a Palestinian state adjoining Israel. This change came in the wake of the October 1973 War. While the democratic-secular notion entails the end of Israel as a Zionist state, the new Palestinian state objective indicated acceptance of Zionist Israel, at least as a stage prior to the achievement of the secular state. The political program issued by the twelfth session of the Palestine National Council of June 1974 indicates this shift:

The Liberation Organization will employ all means, and first and foremost armed struggle, to liberate Palestinian territory and to establish the independent combatant national authority for the people over every part of the Palestinian territory that is liberated.[59]

Since then, there have been many declarations by Palestinian leaders on the possibility of establishing a Palestinian state side by side with Israel. Nayef Hawathmeh, the PDFLP leader, explained this position in more detail when he discussed what he called the "Interim Program." He said that in order that Palestinians "do not catch fish in the desert," they need a pragmatic program. This program must "guarantee the right of the Palestinian refugees to return to their country from which they were exiled," and "the right to self-determination and the building of an independent Palestinian state in the West Bank, Jerusalem, and Gaza."[60] This state, according to Hawatmeh, "will open the road to a series of developments" that will lead "to a democratic solution . . . in the form of a united and democratic state in Palestine."[61]

Yasser Arafat and other PLO leaders have also discussed this modified Palestinian objective. In January 1978, Arafat is reported to have told visiting U.S. congressmen that the PLO is willing to take part in Arab-Israeli negotiations. He is also reported to have proposed that a U.N. peacekeeping force be stationed on the border between Israel and any possible Palestinian state in the West Bank and Gaza.[62] When asked the reason why the PLO does not recognize Security Council Resolution 242, Arafat responded that the resolution was the PLO's "last card," and went on to explain:

I cannot play it (the last card) and get nothing in return but the right of a dialogue with the Americans. That is all I have been offered up to now. The Americans want me to accept the right of Israel to exist as a state in the Middle East, but the Americans and the Israelis are not prepared to say that we Palestinians have the right to exist as a state.[63]

The PLO, however, played its "last card" and accepted U.N. Security Council Resolution 242 in November 1988. In fact, even earlier, when Arafat signed the February 11, 1985 accord with King Hussein of Jordan, he also came to accept the notion of direct negotiations with Israel on the basis of that U.N. resolution, as interpreted by the Arabs. This represents a dramatic and major shift of the earlier PLO position regarding Israel's existence. It must be noted that some Palestinians resisted this shift. The PFLP, for example, attacked the notion of a Palestinian state as "counter-revolutionary," and insisted on a continuous struggle for the total liberation of Palestine and the establishment of the democratic-secular state.[64] This group, however, has in time come to accept the notion of an independent state. The political program approved by the thirteenth session of the Palestine National Council attests to this fact. The program clearly called upon the leadership "to pursue the struggle to... exercise self-determination and to establish their (Palestinian) independent national state on their soil."[65] By November 1988, all doubt about PLO objectives were dispelled as the Organization officially called for Palestinian-Israeli negotiations. The Declaration of Independence has become the clearest statement of Palestinian objectives to date.

What led the PLO to accept this notion of a diplomatic solution and a Palestinian state in the West Bank and Gaza? First, the PLO may have feared that its rejection of the idea may lead to its isolation from any settlement that may be reached. This isolation could lead to the return of the West Bank to Jordan, something the PLO rejected. By accepting a state, the PLO would strengthen its position as the spokesman for the Palestinians, and eventually weaken Israel and bring pressure on it to end the occupation.

If, on the other hand, Israel rejects the notion of a Palestinian state, then the PLO would have achieved another objective, namely, exposing Israel's "expansionist" schemes to the world. As noted, Israel has rejected the idea and vehemently objected to a Palestinian state on its borders. There is evidence to indicate that the Palestinians have gained ground in the public opinion war. World public opinion has shifted to support this Palestinian demand, and Israel today finds itself isolated in its rejection of this proposal. Even in the United States and Israel many citizens are beginning to question the wisdom of Israel's rejection, especially after the start of the intifada.

Second, PLO acceptance of a Palestinian state is also related to the positions of the Arab countries. The PLO leaders realize that they alone cannot hope to achieve a total victory over Israel. The assistance of the Arab states, especially Egypt, Syria, Jordan, and Saudi Arabia, is needed. The Arab states concerned are interested in a political solution based on Israel's return to the 1967 boundaries and the establishment of a Palestinian state. It is, therefore, imperative for the PLO to conform to Arab objectives, at least as a tactical maneuver.

Third, the point of view of the Soviet Union and the United States has influenced the PLO's shift toward the acceptance of a Palestinian state. Both countries accept U.N. Security Council Resolution 242 as the basis for a negotiated settlement. By accepting a Palestinian state, the PLO hoped to bring superpower pressure on Israel to evacuate the Occupied Territories.

Fourth, internal Palestinian pressures to accept a Palestinian state have been building up within the PLO. Many Palestinian intellectuals and many of those living in the Occupied Territories favor an end to Israel's occupation as an urgent objective and a pragmatic goal. This Palestinian dimension has had its impact upon the PLO's decision to accept a Palestinian state in only part of the original homeland. The intifada made this demand clear in its UNLU directives.

This new PLO attitude toward a political solution has influenced its behavior. The number of commando operations has declined significantly, and the PLO diplomatic activities have intensified. A political solution calls for diplomatic activities and restraint at the military level. In its hope to achieve a political solution, the PLO has had to show restraint. In the process, the PLO has evolved to emphasize political over military action.

But the response from Israel's government has been disappointing. Israel has continued to maintain the posture of neither recognizing the PLO nor conceding the right of Palestinians to self-determination. In fact, recent Israeli governments have shown signs of hardening their attitude. Not only does Israel refuse to recognize the PLO, but it has also rejected the idea of a Palestinian state and has reinterpreted the U.N. Security Council Resolution 242 in a way that would exclude the return of any West Bank territory to the Arabs.[66] In doing so, Israel could be blocking the best chance there has yet been for peace. Israel also seems to be pushing the PLO away from diplomacy and back to violence. Columnist Joseph C. Harsch commented on this hard line and its implications for peace in the days of the Begin government as follows:

Mr. Begin has painted himself into a corner. He is obviously sincere in his desire to have a "greater Israel," so sincere and so deeply devoted to that cause that it seems unlikely that he himself will be able to change. But then, Mr. Begin will not be Prime Minister of Israel for all time. A fresh start with him in office seems unlikely but, with someone else, always possible.[67]

Whether a future Israeli government could display the courage and wisdom needed to achieve peace depends not only on that government itself but also on the circumstances of the time. For the day, the current government under Shamir is not likely to achieve a comprehensive settlement of the problem. A golden opportunity for peace seems to be slipping away and its return cannot be guaranteed.

On the other hand, one would be mistaken to assume that a change in Israeli leadership is all that is needed to achieve peace. Peace is complicated and requires mutual recognition and understanding. In addition, a final settlement must include the PLO. Without the PLO, which is considered by the world at large and the Palestinians themselves to be the sole legitimate representative of the Palestinian people, the seeds of more violence will remain. To end the violence, one needs to eliminate its causes, not only treat its symptoms. Therefore, the rights of the Palestinians, as seen by the PLO, need to be guaranteed and safeguarded if the Middle East is to have a durable peace.

With its recent shift of objectives and acceptance of a Palestinian state in the West Bank and Gaza, the PLO has offered Israel a real chance for a political solution. In doing so, the PLO has recognized Israel's right to exist. Israel now needs to recognize a Palestinian right to exist. The contradictions between Zionism and Palestinian national aspirations would not be an obstacle to peace provided that Zionism modifies its objectives in the same way the PLO has. The idea of a "greater Israel" may seem appealing to romantic Zionists. But is it realistically possible if one desires peace? The answer is bound to be no. Israeli leaders must now choose between peace and territorial expansion. Both simply cannot be achieved at the same time.

NOTES

1. Zeev Schiff and Raphael Rothstein, *Fedayeen: Guerrillas against Israel* (New York: David McKay, 1972), p. 242.

2. Sabri Jiryis, *The Arabs in Israel: 1948–1966* (New York: Monthly Review Press, 1969).

3. Quoted in Johan Galtung, "Conflict Theory and the Palestine Problem," *Journal of Palestine Studies* 2, no. 1 (Autumn 1972), p. 43.

4. Tawfiq Zayyad, "The Fate of the Arabs in Israel," *Journal of Palestine Studies* 6, no. 1 (Autumn 1976), p. 93.

5. Fred M. Gottheil, "On the Economic Development of the Arab Region in Israel," in Michael Curtis and Mordercai Chertoff, eds., *Israel: Social Structure and Change* (New Brunswick, N.J.: Dutton, 1973), p. 238.

6. Sabri Jiryis, "Recent Knesset Legislation and the Arabs in Israel," *Journal of Palestine Studies* 1, no. 1 (Autumn 1971), p. 53.

7. Ibid.

8. Israel Shahak, *Document of the Israeli League for Human and Civil Rights: Destruction of Villages* (Tel Aviv: Israeli League for Human and Civil Rights, 1973), p. 10.

9. Tawfiq Zayyad, "The Arab in Israel," in James J. Zogby, ed., *Perspectives on Palestinian Arabs and Israeli Jews* (Wilmette, Ill.: Medina Press, 1977), p. 49.

10. Ibid., p. 54.

11. Ibid., p. 55.

12. *Time* Magazine, 1 April 1972.

13. Yochanan Peres, "Ethnic Relations in Israel," in Michael Curtis, eds., *People and Politics in the Middle East* (New Brunswick, N.J.: Dutton, 1971), p. 45.

14. *Al-Hamishmar* (Tel Aviv), 7 September 1976, quoted in *Swasia* 3, 43 (15 October 1976), p. 6.

15. Ibid., p. 1.

16. Hussein Abul-Namel, "Wathikat Koenig wal-Ma'azak al-Sahyuni" (The Koenig Document and the Zionist Problem), *Shu'un Filastiniyah* 61 (December 1976), pp. 189–204.

17. Text of the report is translated and published in English in the *Journal of Palestine Studies* 6, no. 1 (Autumn 1976), pp. 190–200.

18. A. C. Forrest, *The Unholy Land* (Toronto: McClelland and Stewart, 1971), pp. 120–121.

19. Elisha Efrat, *Judea and Samaria: Guidelines for Regional and Physical Planning* (Jerusalem: Ministry of Interior, Planning Department, 1970), p. 1.

20. Brian Van Arkadi, *Benefits and Burdens: A Report on the West Bank and Gaza Strip Economies since 1967* (New York: Carnegie Endowment for International Peace, 1977), pp. 53–54.

21. *The New York Times*, 31 August 1975.

22. Ann Mosely Lesch, "Israeli Settlements in the Occupied Territories, 1967–1977," *Journal of Palestine Studies* 7, no. 1 (Autumn 1977), pp. 26–47.

23. *L'Express* (Paris), 23–29 May 1977, p. 55; translated from the French transcripts as *Who Is Menahem Begin?* (Beirut: Institute of Palestine Studies, 1977), p. 60.

24. Felicia Langer, "Israeli Violations of Human Rights in the Occupied Arab Territories," in Zogby, *Perspectives*, p. 60.

25. Quoted in ibid., p. 61.

26. Felicia Langer, *With My Own Eyes* (London: Ithaca Press, 1975), p. 164.

27. *Jerusalem Post*, 13 June 1972.

28. Abdeen Jabara, *Israel's Violation of Human Rights in Arab Territories Occupied in June, 1967* (Detroit: Association of Arab American University Graduates, 1976), p. 13.

29. International Covenant of the Red Cross, *Annual Report for 1971* (Geneva, 1972), p. 49.

30. *The Christian Science Monitor*, 31 December 1973, p. 2.

31. For further details see Naseer Aruri, *Occupation: Israel over Palestine* (Belmont, Mass.: Association of Arab-American University Graduates, 1989).

32. *Ha'aretz* (Tel Aviv), 19 June 1974, cited in Jabara, *Israel's Violation of Human Rights*, p. 20.

33. Jabara, *Israel's Violation of Human Rights*, p. 20.

34. *The Guardian* (London), 26 January 1968, p. 11, cited in Ibid., p. 21.

35. Michael Adams, "Israel's Treatment of the Arabs in the Occupied Territories," *Journal of Palestine Studies* 6, no. 2 (Winter 1977), p. 37.

36. *The Christian Science Monitor*, 14 February 1978. Another good source on

Israel's violations of human rights in the West Bank is the hearings before the Subcommittee on Immigration and Naturalization of the Committee on the Judiciary, U.S. Senate, *The Colonization of the West Bank Territories by Israel*, Ninety-Fifth Congress, Fifth Session, 17–18 October 1977.

37. *The Sunday Times* (London), 1 June 1977, p. 1.
38. Langer, *With My Own Eyes*, p. 1.
39. Gideon Weigert, *Arabs and Israelis: Life Together* (Jerusalem: Jerusalem Post Press, 1973).
40. Jamil Hilal, *The Palestinians of the West Bank and Gaza Strip: Social and Economic Conditions under Israeli Occupation* (Beirut: PLO Department of Information and National Guidance, 1976), p. 8.
41. For more details see U.S. Senate, *Colonization of the West Bank*, pp. 166–170.
42. Meron Benvenisti, *1986 Report: Demographic, Economic, Legal, Social and Political Developments in the West Bank* (Jerusalem: Jerusalem Post Press, 1986), p. 25.
43. *The New York Times*, 2 January 1978, p. 10.
44. *The Washington Post*, 4 January 1978, p. 1.
45. The full text of the Begin Plan can be found in *The New York Times*, 29 December 1977.
46. For full details of the poll, see *Al-Fajr* (Jerusalem), 12 September 1986.
47. An interview in *The Sunday Times* (London), 15 June 1969, quoted in Larry L. Fabian and Ze'ev Schiff, eds., *Israelis Speak* (New York: Carnegie Endowment for International Peace, 1977), p. 15.
48. Julian J. Landau, *Israel and the Arabs* (Jerusalem: Israel Communications, 1971), p. 134.
49. Fabian and Schiff, *Israelis Speak*, p. 25.
50. Elizabeth Monroe, "The West Bank: Palestinian or Israeli?" *Middle East Journal* 31, no. 4 (Autumn 1977), p. 408.
51. *Jerusalem Post*, 24 July 1969, p. 2.
52. Bard O'Neill, *Revolutionary Warfare in the Middle East* (Boulder: Paladin Press, 1974).
53. Yasser Arafat, *Falastin Tahya* (Palestine Lives) (Washington, D.C.: Free Palestine, 1974), p. 22. This is a printed version of Arafat's address to the U.N. General Assembly, 13 November 1974.
54. See *Swasia* 4, no. 5, (4 February 1977).
55. Ibrahim Abu-Lughod, *Arab World Issues* (Detroit) 4 (1977), p. 5.
56. Ibid., p. 7.
57. Quoted in Hamdan Bader, "Ara' Harkabi wa-Mawkefuh min-al-Sha'ab al-Falastini wa-Kadiyatuh" (Harakabi's Views and his Stand on the Palestinian People and Their Problem), *Shu'un Filastiniyah* 48 (August 1975), p. 85.
58. Fabian and Schiff, *Israelis Speak*, p. 46.
59. Text of the Program issued by the 12th Session of the PNC appear in ibid., pp. 226–227.
60. Nayef Hawatmeh, *Al-Thawra Wahaq Takrir al-Masir wal-Dawlah al-Mustaqele* (The Revolution and the Right to Self-Determination and the Independent State) (Beirut: PDFLP, 1977), p. 51.
61. Ibid., pp. 51–52.

62. *The New York Times*, 14 January 1978, p. 1.

63. *Arab Press Service Recorder*, 18 October 1977.

64. PFLP, *Al-Badil al-Thawri Limashru' al-Dawla al-Falastiniyah al-Tasfawi* (The Revolutionary Alternative to the Liquidatory Palestinian State Project) (Beirut, 1974).

65. Fateh, *Al-Ilan al-Siyassi wal-Bayan al-Khitami* (The Political Program and the Final Communiqué) (Kuwait: PLO Department of National Guidance and Information, 1977), p. 11.

66. For more details see *The Christian Science Monitor*, 9 March 1978, p. 1.

67. Joseph C. Harsch, "Mr. Begin's Fallacy," *The Christian Science Monitor*, 7 March 1978, p. 23.

8

Conclusion: Problems and Prospects

People suffering from foreign occupation and oppression have resorted to guerrilla warfare throughout recorded history. But only in modern times has guerrilla warfare become the acknowledged weapon of the weak in their struggle against the strong. Guerrilla warfare has achieved many successes and setbacks in the twentieth century. The popularity of guerrilla warfare in the last few decades is unprecedented in all of recorded history. The U.S. Department of Defense reported twenty-eight guerrilla insurgencies in 1958, forty-two in 1965, and fifty in 1969.[1]

The activities of the guerrillas have influenced the domestic and foreign policies of the countries concerned. While the PLO is not a classic example of a guerrilla insurgency agent, its presence in the Middle East scene has significant implications for the countries of the region as well as for international relations. Over the past two decades, the PLO has proven to be a major actor in the region and no less significant than a number of sovereign states.

The PLO seems to embody Palestinian sentiments and aspirations. These people have suffered grave injustices as a result of the advent of Zionism. Subsequent to the establishment of Israel in 1948, the Palestinian people were scattered throughout the Arab World. Few remained in Israel. Whether in Israel or outside in refugee camps, the Palestinians feel that they were unjustly deprived of their national and human rights by an invading foreign community. To them, Zionism was seen as an extension of Western colonialism and imperialism.

During the first decade after Israel's establishment, the Palestinians had hoped that the Arab countries would face Israel and liberate their homeland. The Arabs, of course, could not match Israel's superiority in arms, technology, and organization and, perhaps, unwilling to sacrifice their own status on behalf of the Palestinians. Consequently, in the late 1950s some Palestinian intellectuals began to organize themselves in preparation for long-term guerrilla warfare.

Fearing that the guerrillas might force upon them an unwanted war with Israel and in order to insure that the Palestinian struggle remained manageable to Arab governments, some Arab leaders advocated the establishment of the PLO. Ahmad Shukairy was empowered during an Arab summit meeting to establish the PLO. Once established in 1964, the PLO was correctly seen by the guerrillas and some Palestinian intellectuals as a tool of the Arab states for containing Palestinian armed activities.

As a result of the overwhelming Arab defeat in the 1967 War with Israel and the guerrillas' success at Karameh, Arab and Palestinian masses began to support the guerrillas. Consequently, the guerrilla groups grew in numbers and power and were able to dominate the PLO. The influence of Arab governments within the organization declined. Since then, the PLO has become a major actor in Middle Eastern politics. The international community has become once more aware of the Palestinian dimension of the Arab-Israeli conflict. At the United Nations and elsewhere, the Palestinian struggle for self-determination is now seen as a legitimate movement, and the PLO has been acknowledged as the sole legitimate representative of the Palestinians and accorded a legal status at the United Nations and elsewhere.

While the PLO includes many guerrilla groups and other nonmilitary Palestinian entities, it has multi-functional structures comparable to those of modern governments. The PLO's supreme body is the National Council, which is formed of representatives of all Palestinians, including the guerrilla groups. This body draws the major guidelines for the organization and elects an Executive Committee which handles the day-to-day functions.

With the ascendance of the guerrillas in the PLO and their penetration of its various organs, the organization began to reflect their views. The revised covenant of the PLO clearly shifted to emphasize armed struggle and the role of mass mobilization. Even the PLO's long-term objectives were modified to conform to those of the guerrillas. These objectives, however, have in recent years become strikingly more moderate than formerly. Instead of advocating the total liberation of Palestine, the PLO today is willing to settle for a Palestinian state in the West Bank and the Gaza Strip.

The guerrillas have multiplied into a number of groups. Some are genuinely Palestinian, others were formed by Arab governments, and few were so secretive that their identities or programs could not be clarified. Not all the groups agree on strategy and tactics. But the dominant one, Fateh, rejects ideological commitments as counterproductive at this stage of the struggle. While most guerrilla groups dissociate themselves from armed attacks outside Israel, some advocate them as a weapon for focusing international attention on the plight of the Palestinians and for striking at Israel's economic interests. Without exception, all groups viewed violent armed struggle as a means for the achievement of their objectives. Palestinian violence can best be explained as a reaction to perceived Israeli settler-colonialism.

At the same time that Palestinian strategy has proven successful in forcing the world to become conscious of Palestinian rights, it has failed to liberate any Palestinian territory. Palestinian strategy is, therefore, limited at this stage. In fact, the Palestinians face a number of internal and external problems regarding their strategy and tactics. Occasional disunity of the commando groups was one of the severe problems that the PLO had to overcome. Other problems include the lack of a sanctuary, insufficient mobilization of the Palestinian masses, the often strained relations with Arab regimes, the visibility of commandos in urban centers, and, of course, Israel's power and its willingness to use force at any time and place.

It is the relationship of the PLO to Arab regimes that has been most problematic. If Palestinian guerrilla power failed to become an effective instrument of liberation, it is mostly because of failures in dealing with Arab regimes rather than with Israel. Practically every Arab country that had guerrillas on its soil had attempted to limit their power and control their strategy. In Jordan as in Lebanon, Palestinian guerrillas were faced with Arab armies dedicated to forcing them into submission. Therefore, the Palestinian ability to engage the Israelis at will has been hampered by their uneasy relations with other Arabs. In addition, Israel is a formidable enemy that seems to refuse to give an inch of Palestine to the Palestinians.

Palestinian military difficulties have not been paralleled by political ones. In fact, the opposite is true; even while the Palestinians were being stymied militarily, they were achieving significant political successes. At the United Nations and other international forums, the PLO has been acknowledged as a national liberation movement and the representative of the Palestinian people. Major powers have had to take a stand on the PLO. Today, PLO support in the international community is large. The Soviet Union, China, the Afro-Asian nations and many European and Latin American countries support the PLO. While the United States dialogue with the PLO is limited, it has nevertheless changed to include an acceptance of the notion of the "legitimate rights" of the Palestinian people.

This international support has proven to be of great importance to the Palestinians. It has a significant psychological and diplomatic value. In a war of attrition, there can be no decisive military victory over a strong enemy. At best, one hopes to inflict heavy losses, tire the enemy out, and through international pressure force it to negotiate withdrawal. Today, the Israelis may be able to defeat the Palestinians militarily, but they cannot destroy them politically. At some point or another, Israel will have to negotiate with them.

In Israel and the Occupied Territories, Israel faces a resisting Palestinian population that it has conquered but cannot rule. The intifada has put Israel into a defensive posture. Israel fights the PLO, but the latter continues to illegitimize Israel's occupation by focusing international attention on it. In its reaction to the Palestinian struggle, Israel is clearly "grappling with the effect rather than the cause of the problem."[2] The cause will not disappear until a settlement eliminates the basic motivation for hostility among the Palestinians.

Perhaps the most striking characteristic of the PLO in the past two decades has been its ability to survive and develop in the face of massive Israeli and Arab attacks upon it. Had the PLO been simply a military movement with a limited number of supporters, its elimination would have been possible. Its strong roots among the Palestinian masses, the support of the Arab masses, and the international recognition and aid it receives have made it virtually impossible for any country or regime to annihilate it. Today, and in spite of massive Israeli retaliations, the PLO has shown it can muster a level of resistance "too high for Israel to shrug off as unimportant."[3] The result of this, writes Michael Hudson, "has been the resurrection of a Palestinian political identity on a modern base."[4]

The PLO, however, still faces a number of problems that can threaten its viability. The first is the problem of multiplicity of guerrilla groups. By accommodating the divergencies among all groups within the PLO for the sake of unity, the organization has provided itself with a national platform and become more representative of all trends among the Palestinian population. In the process, the PLO may have "suffered the possible disadvantage of being a loosely rather than tightly controlled organization."[5] Its loose unity has proven shaky, to say the least. Within the ranks of the guerrilla groups, unity seems to be stronger when they face a common enemy, but becomes more tenuous when the threat from the enemy subsides. When faced with the Jordanian crisis, the commando groups hurried to join the PLO Central Committee and, later, its Joint Command, but when the crisis was over, the PLO groups reverted to independent decision making and action. Similar developments occurred after the second Sinai Disengagement Agreement, the Lebanese crisis, after President Sadat's trip to Jerusalem, during the Israeli invasion of Lebanon and, now, during the intifada. During the Lebanese crisis, however, Syria attempted unsuccessfully to take over the PLO through its own sponsored and supported guerrilla groups. This was an important test case for the PLO vis-à-vis various plans to destroy it or control it. It means that the PLO can be expected to continue to play a role in the peace-and-war politics of the Middle East. However, agreement on doctrine and ideology among all Palestinian commando groups seems impossible, and any consideration of total unity must be ruled out. It may be assumed, however, that so long as the Palestinians face common enemies and have common aspirations, cooperation rather than confrontation will be the mode of the guerrilla groups' behavior. In addition, Fateh is by far the largest and most powerful guerrilla group. It is the dominant group within the PLO. It is possible to assume that the contradictions among the various groups will be contained because of the major role played by Fateh. But contradictions within Fateh itself can become a more serious problem for the PLO. In fact, such contradictions have led to the post-Lebanon divisions within the organization.

Second, the need for an active sanctuary inside the occupied homeland should not be underestimated.[6] The 1982 Israeli invasion of Lebanon has, in effect, robbed the Palestinian commandos of their last sanctuary adjoining Israel's borders. As noted, a sanctuary is an important element in guerrilla warfare. The loss of their Lebanese sanctuary did not halt Palestinian commando activities against Israel. In fact, some guerrilla leaders predicted more operations and the "Vietnamization of the Middle East."[7] While this predicted Vietnamization is unlikely without an "Arab Hanoi," Palestinian commando operations are still expected to rise if Israel's response to the intifada remains limited to punishment and reprisals. Sanctuaries are important, but not essential to guerrilla success. In Cuba, Yugoslavia, and China, the revolutionaries did not have active sanctuaries on foreign soil, although they did enjoy relatively safe havens at home. In Burma and, to a lesser extent, in Greece, outside sanctuaries proved of limited value. The Palestinian guerrillas have proven to be self-sustaining commandos who can go on fighting indefinitely. Israel's assault on Lebanon leaves no doubt about that development. The PLO commandos fought a classic guerrilla war of attrition against a superior invading force. The commandos retreated when outnumbered and attacked when the enemy relaxed or attempted to reinforce its position. When one considers the technological and numerical Israeli superiority, PLO losses cannot but be seen as very minimal in terms of numbers. The length of the war and the inability of the Israelis to take Beirut also says something about PLO active resistance, especially when one recalls Israel's "six-day" victory over Egypt, Syria, and Jordan in 1967. It is also expected that the Palestinians will eventually be able to reestablish some sanctuary in Lebanon. But most important, the intifada has saved the PLO from its dilemma after Lebanon. Now, the sanctuary is at home and the fighters live there.

Third, the potential contradictions between the interests of the Palestinians and those of the host Arab states still threaten the viability of the PLO. In the final analysis, the PLO and its revolutionary guerrillas represent a destabilizing threat to the entire Arab world. The radical revolutionary groups make no secret of their intention to radicalize the Arab masses. A PFLP leader asserted to his American interviewer that when the guerrillas achieve their victory, "not only would Palestine be liberated, but all of Arab society. I can assure you," the leader continued, "that before we put down the gun, we will have assisted at the birth of a new man in the Arab world."[8] The threat of armed Palestinian revolutionaries has already been felt by Jordan and Lebanon. The official policy, but not necessarily the practice, of the PLO has been not to interfere in the internal affairs of the host countries. This strategy has obviously proven its ineffectiveness. To interfere in such affairs, on the other hand, may lead to more serious and devastating consequences. This represents a dilemma for the PLO. If it chooses not to interfere in Arab affairs, it stands to lose its freedom of action; if, on the other hand, it decides to confront the Arab regimes, it risks complete annihilation. In either case, the PLO cannot win. Only a strong and mobilized mass movement in the Arab countries can safeguard the interests and freedom of the PLO. This, however, is yet to be achieved.[9] In the meantime, the PLO has chosen to minimize these contradictions and to deal with them within the framework of Arab diplomacy. It would seem that this choice is the only one available to the PLO so long as it rejects the temptation to go underground, which would deprive it of its representational role.

Fourth, counter-guerrilla measures carried by Israel have been reasonably effective. The fact that Israel is such a formidable foe has significant implications for the PLO. The PLO so far is able to survive Israel's strength and the poor environment for guerrilla warfare. "Possibly there was a time when Israel could have carried out a successful surgical operation against the nascent guerrilla movement."[10] Today, such a possibility seems rather remote unless radically new factors arise to alter the power of the PLO. Despite all of its might, therefore, Israel is unable to put an end to the PLO and the guerrillas. Israel's invasion of Lebanon in 1982 has given yet another proof of that. However, Israel can and does limit the actions of the PLO. Penetration into Israel, mobilization of the Palestinians under Israeli control, and participation of the PLO in peace negotiations have all been limited as a result of Israeli actions and policies.[11] Consequently, while Israel does not threaten the survival of the PLO, its actions hinder the growth of that organization and can weaken it.

Fifth, the greatest threat to the PLO comes not from violent Israeli retaliations, but rather from the possibility of an Israeli acquiescence to a peaceful settlement that does not include the PLO. While the viability of such a settlement would be in doubt, it nevertheless remains a possibility. Such a settlement, if it occurs, would tranquilize the situation and bring about the creation of an environment inimical to the growth and legitimacy of the organization. Certain elements that now support the PLO would then be inclined to terminate their support. Many Arab governments that favor a political settlement may become actively hostile to the PLO. Palestinian and Arab mass support of the PLO may also be jeopardized if the PLO continues its struggle against Israel. Of course, this possibility presupposes Israel's acquiescence to a political settlement also acceptable to the Arabs and the major powers. This would constitute a major shift in Israel's policy and is not likely to happen so long as Israeli leaders insist on basing peace negotiations on their own interpretation of the Camp David framework. Perhaps, only strong and persistent U.S. pressure can influence Israeli leaders to make the concessions needed for peace.

In the meantime, tensions are expected to continue. The intifada will inevitably continue, so long as Palestinian aspirations are being rejected by Israel. But the intifada is limited and the PLO, if it hopes for a military defeat of Israel, would have to rely upon the Arab armies. The Arab armies are still far too weak to defeat Israel. Moreover, the Arab states are far too divided to fight Israel effectively. The limitations of waging guerrilla warfare against Israel can be summed up by stating four essential differences between the conditions in Palestine and those in areas like Vietnam and Algeria, where the guerrillas eventually succeeded.

1. The ratio of Palestinian Arabs to Israeli Jews in Israel/Palestine is small compared with population ratios that favor resistance movements. For example, Vietnam had about 40 million Vietnamese and only about half a million Americans. Even if one is to include the South Vietnamese with the Americans, the ratio still remained in favor of the Viet Cong and the North Vietnamese. Similarly, Algeria had about 10 million Arabs and less than half a million French. In Israel and the Occupied Territories, the Arabs number little more than 2 million and the Israelis more than 4 million.

2. The nature of Palestine's geography is different from that of Vietnam or Algeria. Vietnam has thick forests suitable for guerrilla hideouts and ambushes. Algeria, like Vietnam, has a terrain favorable to guerrilla warfare. The rugged mountains of Algeria served as a natural sanctuary for the commandos, whereas in Palestine the plains and even the hills are exposed to the enemy and offer small hope for effective guerrilla warfare.

3. Israel's "long arm" and its ability to strike anywhere in the Arab countries—and beyond—deprive the guerrillas of a secure shelter outside the enemy's reach. In both Vietnam and Algeria, such shelters were readily available. China and North Vietnam served as havens for the Vietnamese guerrillas, while Morocco and Tunisia provided shelters for Algerians. The Palestinians

often have to face the enemy in their own training camps and recruiting centers.
4. Palestinian attacks against Israel normally united that country. Such attacks can weaken the moderate elements within Israel's society and strengthen the radical conservative ones. The recently formed peace movement, which advocates a peaceful settlement with the Arabs, can be weakened by commando operations. Therefore, while Vietnamese guerrilla activities split American society, and the Algerian war split French society, Palestinian attacks strengthen rather than weaken Israel's society.

In spite of all the hindrances that limit the PLO and its guerrilla arm, the organization has achieved many successes and proven its viability on the battlefield as well as in diplomatic chambers. There is no question today that the PLO has a veto power on political accommodations between the Arabs and Israel on the Palestine question. This fact has accounted for the shift of most of those involved in the process of Arab-Israeli negotiations to accept the principle of Palestinian participation. The involved parties, with the exception of the U.S. and Israel, would like to see PLO representation in any talks. The U.S. position under the Reagan Administration accepted the need for representatives of the Palestinian people in negotiations, but still rejected the PLO. The Bush Administration has talked to the PLO. Israel, for its part, rejects any form of PLO participation. Israel's rejection serves only to weaken the position of the moderates in the PLO and to strengthen that of the hardliners. Whether the PLO will ever join other Arabs in peace negotiations with Israel cannot be foretold. One thing is certain, however; if peace in the area is to be durable, the PLO must consent to it.

Its recent change of objectives has made the PLO more versatile and allowed its leadership to participate in peace negotiations aimed at establishing a Palestinian state over the West Bank and Gaza. Today, the PLO can be an instrument of either peace or war. However, so long as Israel refuses to talk to the PLO, the conflict is likely to continue. If, on the other hand, Israel decides to negotiate with the PLO, as did the Americans with the Vietnamese guerrillas or the French with the Algerian resistance movement, then the PLO could be transformed into a tool for peace and a responsible sponsor of the emergent Palestinian polity.

NOTES

1. Samuel P. Huntington, *Political Order in Changing Societies* (New Haven: Yale University Press, 1968), p. 4. See also N. I. Klonis, *Guerrilla Warfare* (New York: Robert Speller, 1972); and David Wilkinson, *Revolutionary Civil War: The Elements of Victory and Defeat* (Palo Alto, Ca.: Page Franklin Publications, 1975).

2. Joseph Churba, *Fedayeen and the Middle East Crisis* (Maxwell Air Force Base, Ala.: Air University, 1969), p. 42.

3. Michael Hudson, "The Palestinian Arab Resistance Movement: Its Significance in the Middle East Crisis," *Middle East Journal* 23, no. 3 (Summer 1969), p. 291.

4. Ibid., p. 307.

5. Rashid Hameed, "What is the PLO?" *Journal of Palestine Studies* 4, no. 4 (Summer 1975), p. 108.

6. "Active sanctuary" may be defined as a secure base across the border from the occupied homeland, providing the commandos with logistics, support, and material for the successful prosecution of guerrilla warfare.

7. *The Christian Science Monitor*, 20 March 1978, p. 2.

8. Hisham Sharabi, *Palestinian Guerrillas: Their Credibility and Effectiveness* (Washington, D.C.: Georgetown University, 1970).

9. Beginnings of PLO-Arab mass contacts can be seen in the 1975–76 Lebanese civil war. The Lebanese National Alliance also supported the PLO in the Israeli invasion of Lebanon.

10. Sharabi, *Palestine Guerrillas*, p. 46.

11. U.S. support has enabled Israel to limit the PLO role in peace negotiations.

Appendix 1

The Balfour Declaration

On November 2, 1917, Arthur James Balfour, British Foreign Minister, addressed the following written communication to Lord Rothschild*:

> Foreign Office
> November 2nd, 1917.

Dear Lord Rothschild,

I have much pleasure in conveying to you, on behalf of His Majesty's Government, the following declaration of sympathy with Jewish Zionist aspirations which has been submitted to, and approved by, the Cabinet

"His Majesty's Government view with favour the establishment in Palestine of a national home for the Jewish people, and will use their best endeavours to facilitate the achievement of this object, it being clearly understood that nothing shall be done which may prejudice the civil and religious rights of existing non-Jewish communities in Palestine, or the rights and political status enjoyed by Jews in any other country."

I should be grateful if you would bring this declaration to the knowledge of the Zionist Federation.

[Signed] Arthur James Balfour

---

*Lord Lionel Walter Rothschild.

Appendix 2

The Palestine National Covenant

Article 1—Palestine is the homeland of the Palestinian people. It is an inseparable part of the bigger Arab nation, and its people are an integral part of the Arab people.

Article 2—Palestine, with the borders that existed during the British Mandate, is an indivisible geographical unit.

Article 3—The Palestinian people have a legitimate right to their homeland. They are the ones to determine their destiny after the liberation of their lands as they will and choose.

Article 4—The Palestinian identity is a permanent and enduring trait that passes from father to son. The Israeli occupation, and the dispersion of the Palestinian people, resulting from the ill fortunes that befell them, cannot deprive the Palestinian people of its Palestinian personality and identity.

Article 5—The Palestinians are those Arab citizens who under normal conditions used to live in Palestine until 1947; they include those who remained there as well as those who were evicted. The offsprings of an Arab Palestinian parent, since that date, whether born in Palestine or outside, are regarded as Palestinians.

Article 6—The Jews who used to live under normal conditions in Palestine until the Zionist invasion of the country are to be considered Palestinians.

Article 7—Identification with, and spiritual, material, and historic attachment to, Palestine are irrefutable truths. It is a national duty to bring up the Palestinian individual as a revolutionary Arab, and to employ all the means of enlightenment and education to acquaint him with his native land—spiritually and materially—and to prepare him for the armed struggle in order to recover his homeland.

Article 8—The Palestinians now live in a stage of national struggle for the liberation of Palestine; therefore, the contradictions between the national forces

Official English translation.

are secondary and must disappear for the sake of basic conflict between Zionism and imperialism on the one hand and the Arab Palestinian people on the other. On this basis, the Palestinians, whether inside or outside it, form one national front whose task is the liberation of Palestine through armed struggle.

Article 9—The armed struggle is the only way to liberate Palestine; it is, therefore, a strategy and not a tactic. The Palestinian people confirm their absolute determination and undeniable will to continue the armed struggle and march toward the armed popular revolution for the liberation, and the return to, their homeland, as well as for their right to a normal life and in determining their destiny with sovereignty over their land.

Article 10—The commando action is the nucleus of the Palestinian popular liberation war, and this requires escalation, protection, and mobilization of all the Palestinian massive and scientific resources which should be organized and deployed in the Palestinian revolution. What is also required is to achieve the merger of the national struggle by all classes of the Palestinian people and the solidarity between the masses in order to guarantee the continuity, escalation and victory of the revolution.

Article 11—The Palestinians shall have three slogans: National Unity, National Mobilization and Liberation.

Article 12—The Arab Palestinian people believe in Arab unity, and in order to participate in its fulfillment, they must preserve their Palestinian personality, seek to assert its presence and resist all plans that may seek to obliterate or weaken it.

Article 13—Arab unity and the liberation of Palestine are two complementary objectives in the sense that one prepares the ground for the fulfillment of the other. Arab unity leads to the liberation of Palestine, and the liberation of Palestine leads to Arab unity; work to achieve either of them goes side by side with work to achieve the other.

Article 14—The fate of the Arab nation, or even Arab existence itself, is dependent on the fate of the Palestine case. From this attachment between the two spring the effort and pursuit of the Arab nation to liberate Palestine; the Palestinian people shall play the leading role in the fulfillment of this nationalist and sacred aim.

Article 15—The liberation of Palestine from the pan-Arab point of view is a nationalist duty to repel the Zionist-imperialist invasion of the bigger Arab nation and to liquidate the Zionist presence in Palestine. The full responsibility of this rests on the Arab nation, peoples and governments, and in particular on the Palestinian people. For that, the Arab nation must mobilize all its military, material, spiritual, and human potentials for effectively participating with the Palestinian people in the liberation of Palestine. The Arab nation, especially at this stage of the Palestinian revolution, must fully support and assist the people of Palestine, materially and morally, and to provide them with all the means that would enable them to continue with their leading role in the armed revolution until the liberation of their homeland.

Article 16—The liberation of Palestine, from the spiritual point of view, provides the holy land with an atmosphere of security and peace whereby all the religious sanctities will be protected and religious freedom guaranteed. All people will be allowed to visit their holy places with no discrimination as to color, language, creed, or race. For this reason, the people of Palestine look forward to the support of all the spiritual forces in the world.

Article 17—The liberation of Palestine from the human point of view would bring back to the Palestinian his freedom, integrity, and pride. Therefore, the Arab Palestinian people aspire for the support of all those who believe in the dignity and freedom of man in the world.

Article 18—The liberation of Palestine from the international point of view is a defensive act made imperative by the necessity of self-defense. Therefore, the Palestinian people, who seek the friendship of all nations, aspire to the support of all peace-loving and freedom-loving peoples for the restoration of legitimate conditions in Palestine, the establishment of peace and security....

Article 19—The partition of Palestine in 1947 and the creation of Israel are both null and void, no matter how long ago that had taken place; because they were against the will of the Palestinian people and in contradiction with their natural right to their country as well as with the principle of self-determination.

Article 20—Balfour's Declaration, the mandate pact and all their consequences are also null and void. The claim of historic and spiritual connection between the Jews and Palestine contradict with the facts of history as well as with the conditions that would normally make up a State. Since Judaism is a heavenly religion with no independent national entity, the Jews cannot consider themselves as one nation with an independent national personality, but rather citizens in the countries in which they live.

Article 21—The Arab Palestinian people, who express themselves by the armed Palestinian revolution, reject all solutions that may stand as alternatives to the full liberation of Palestine; they also reject all proposals that seek to liquidate the Palestinian cause....

Article 22—Zionism is a political movement, a part of world imperialism, and is against all liberation movements in the world. It is a fanatic racialist movement in its nature, antagonistic and expansionist in its aims, and fascist Nazist in its means. Israel is a tool for the Zionist movement and a human and geographic base for world imperialism, and a center inside the Arab world for imperialism to counter the Arab nation and prevent it from progress, unity and liberation. Israel is a constant threat to peace in the Middle East as well as in the whole world. Since the liberation of Palestine obliterates Zionism and imperialism in Palestine, and leads to peace in the Middle East, the Palestinian people, therefore, look forward to the support of all liberals in the world, as well as the support of those who love peace, progress and goodness. They beseech all these elements, regardless of their tendencies and inclinations to assist and support the Palestinians in their just strife for the liberation of their homeland.

Article 23—Peace, security, and justice require of all nations—for the purpose of preserving good relations among them, and strengthening the allegiance of the citizens to their nations—consider the Zionist movement as illegal and to ban it.

Article 24—The Arab Palestinian people believe in the principles of freedom, justice, sovereignty, self-determination, human integrity, and the right of all nations to practice each of them.

Article 25—For the purpose of fulfilling the aims and principles of the Charter, the Palestine Liberation Organization shall undertake its complete role in the liberation of Palestine.

Article 26—The Palestine Liberation Organization, which represents all the forces of the Palestinian revolution, is responsible for the activities of the Arab Palestinian people in their struggle to liberate their land and return to it to practice their right of self-determination. This applies to all military, political and financial matters, as well as anything related to the Palestinian problem on the Arab and international levels.

Article 27—The Palestine Liberation Organization cooperates with all Arab States, each according to its potentials, and it adheres to a neutral policy in its relations with these States in the light of the requirements of the liberation battle. On the basis of this, it does not interfere in the internal affairs of any Arab State.

Article 28—The Arab Palestinian people affirm the originality of their national revolution and its independence; they reject all kinds of interference, tutelage and subservience.

Article 29—The Palestinian people have the first right to the liberation and recovery of their land, and they determine their stand towards the various nations and powers on the basis of the latter's stand on the Palestinian case, and the degree of support they offer to the revolution for the fulfillment of its aims.

Article 30—The fighters and bearers of arms in the battle of liberation are the nucleus of the popular army which will be the protective shield for the gains of the Arab Palestinian people.

Article 31—The Organization will have a flag, an oath, and an anthem, all this will be decided upon by a special resolution.

Article 32—To this Charter will be attached a document to be called the constitution of the Palestine Liberation Organization. The constitution would determine the way of forming the Organization, its committees and establishments, and the prerogatives of each as well as the duties assigned to each in accordance with the Charter.

Article 33—This Charter is not to be modified except with a majority of ⅔rds of the National Council of the Palestine Liberation Organization in a special session to be convened for that purpose.

Appendix 3

The Palestinian Declaration of Independence

Palestine, the Land of the three monotheistic faiths, is where the Palestinian Arab people was born, on which it grew, developed and excelled. The Palestinian people was never separated from or diminished in its integral bonds with Palestine. Thus the Palestinian Arab people ensured for itself an everlasting union between itself, its Land and its history.

Resolute throughout that history, the Palestinian Arab people forged its national identity, rising even to unimagined levels in its defense, as invasion, the design of others, and the appeal special to Palestine's ancient and luminous place on that eminence where powers and civilization are joined... All this intervened thereby to deprive the people of its political independence. Yet the undying connection between Palestine and its people secured for the Land its character, and for the people its national genius. Nourished by an unfolding series of civilizations and cultures, inspired by a heritage rich in variety and kind, the Palestinian Arab people added to its stature by consolidating a union between itself and its patrimonial Land. The call went out from Temple, Church and Mosque that to praise the Creator, to celebrate the compassion and peace was indeed the message of Palestine. And in generation after generation, the Palestinian Arab people gave of itself unsparingly in the valiant battle for liberation and homeland. For what has been the unbroken chain of our people's rebellions but the heroic embodiment of our will for national independence? And so the people was sustained in the struggle to stay and to prevail.

When in the course of modern times a new order of values was declared with norms and values fair for all, it was the Palestinian Arab people that had been excluded from the destiny of all other peoples by a hostile array of local and foreign powers. Yet again had unaided justice been revealed as insufficient to drive the world's history along its preferred course.

Official English translation.

And it was the Palestinian people, already wounded in its body, that was submitted to yet another type of occupation over which floated the falsehood that "Palestine was a land without people." This notion was foisted upon some in the world, whereas in Article 22 of the Covenant of the League of Nations (1919) and in the Treaty of Lausanne (1923), the community of nations had recognized that all the Arab territories, including Palestine, of the formerly Ottoman provinces, were to have granted to them their freedom as provisionally independent nations.

Despite the historical injustice inflicted on the Palestinian Arab people resulting in their dispersion and depriving them of their right to self-determination, following upon U.N. General Assembly Resolution 181 (1947), which partitioned Palestine into two states, one Arab, one Jewish, yet it is this Resolution that still provides those conditions of international legitimacy that ensure the right of the Palestinian Arab people to sovereignty.

By stages, the occupation of Palestine and parts of other Arab territories by Israeli forces, the willing dispossession and expulsion from their ancestral homes of the majority of Palestine's civilian inhabitants, was achieved by organized terror; those Palestinians who remained, as a vestige subjugated in its homeland, were persecuted and forced to endure the destruction of their national life.

Thus were principles of international legitimacy violated. Thus were the Charter of the United Nations and its resolutions disfigured, for they had recognized the Palestinian Arab people's national rights, including the right of Return, the right of independence, the right to sovereignty over territory and homeland.

In Palestine and on its perimeters, in exile distant and near, the Palestinian Arab people never faltered and never abandoned its conviction in its rights of Return and independence. Occupation, massacres and dispersion achieved no gain in the unabated Palestinian consciousness of self and political identity, as Palestinians went forward with their destiny, undeterred and unbowed. And from out of the long years of trial in evermounting struggle, and Palestinian political identity emerged further consolidated and confirmed. And the collective Palestinian national will forged for itself a political embodiment, the Palestine Liberation Organization, its sole, legitimate representative recognized by the world community as a whole, as well as by related regional and international institutions. Standing on the very rock of conviction in the Palestinian people's inalienable rights, and on the ground of the Arab national consensus and of international legitimacy, the PLO led the campaigns of its great people, molded into unity and powerful resolve, one and indivisible in its triumphs, even as it suffered massacres and confinement within and without its home. And so Palestinian resistance was clarified and raised to the forefront of Arab and world awareness, as the struggle of the Palestinian Arab people achieved unique prominence among the world's liberation movements in the modern era.

The massive national uprising, the intifada, now intensifying in cumulative scope and power on occupied Palestinian territories, as well as the unflinching resistance of the refugee camps outside the homeland, have elevated awareness of the Palestinian truth and right into still higher realms of comprehension and actuality. Now at last the curtain has been dropped around a whole epoch of prevarication and negation. The intifada has set siege to the mind of official

Israel, which has for too long relied exclusively upon myth and terror to deny Palestinian existence altogether. Because of the intifada and its revolutionary irreversible impulse, the history of Palestine has therefore arrived at a decisive juncture.

Whereas the Palestinian people reaffirms most definitively its inalienable rights in the Land of its patrimony:

Now by virtue of natural, historical and legal rights, and the sacrifices of successive generations who gave of themselves in defense of the freedom and independence of their homeland;
In pursuance of Resolutions adopted by Arab Summit Conferences and relying on the authority bestowed by international legitimacy as embodied in the Resolution of the United Nations Organization since 1947;
And in exercise by the Palestinian Arab people of its rights to self-determination, political independence and sovereignty over its territory;
The Palestine National Council, in the name of God, and in the name of the Palestinian Arab people, hereby proclaims the establishment of the State of Palestine on our Palestinian territory with its capital Holy Jerusalem (Al-Quds Ash-Sharif).

The State of Palestine is the state of Palestinians wherever they may be. The state is for them to enjoy in it their collective national and cultural identity, theirs to pursue in it a complete equality of rights. In it will be safeguarded their political and religious convictions and their human dignity by means of a parliamentary democratic system of governance, itself based on freedom of expression and the freedom to form parties. The rights of minorities will duly be respected by the majority as minorities must abide by decisions of the majority. Governance will be based on principles of social justice, equality and non-discrimination in public rights of men or women, on grounds of race, religion, color or sex, under the aegis of a constitution which ensures the rule of law and an independent judiciary. Thus shall these principles allow no departure from Palestine's age-old spiritual and civilizational heritage of tolerance and religious coexistence.

The State of Palestine is an Arab state, an integral and indivisible part of the Arab nation, at one with that nation in heritage and civilization, with it also in its aspiration for liberation, progress, democracy and unity. The State of Palestine affirms its obligation to abide by the Charter of the League of Arab States, whereby the coordination of the Arab states with each other shall be strengthened. It calls upon Arab compatriots to consolidate and enhance the emergence in reality of our state, to mobilize potential, and to intensify efforts whose goal is to end Israeli occupation.

The State of Palestine proclaims its commitment to the principles and purposes of the United Nations, and to the Universal Declaration of Human Rights. It proclaims its commitment as well to the principles and policies of the Non-Aligned Movement.

It further announces itself to be a peace-loving State, in adherence to the principles of peaceful coexistence. It will join with all states and peoples in order to assure a permanent peace based upon justice and the respect of rights so that humanity's potential for well-being may be assured, an earnest competition for excellence may be maintained, and in which confidence in the future will eliminate fear for those who are just and for whom justice is the only recourse.

In the context of its struggle for peace in the Land of Love and Peace, the State of Palestine calls upon the United Nations to bear special responsibility for the Palestinian Arab people and its homeland. It calls upon all peace- and freedom-loving peoples and states to assist in the attainment of its objectives, to provide it with security, to alleviate the tragedy of its people, and to help it terminate Israel's occupation of the Palestinian territories.

The State of Palestine herewith declares that it believes in the settlement of regional and international disputes by peaceful means, in accordance with the U.N. Charter and resolutions. Without prejudice to its natural right to defend its territorial integrity and independence, it therefore rejects the threat or use of force, violence and terrorism against its territorial integrity or political independence, as it also rejects their use against the territorial integrity of other states.

Therefore, on this day unlike all others, November 15, 1988, as we stand at the threshold of a new dawn, in all honor and modesty we humbly bow to the sacred spirits of our fallen ones, Palestinian and Arab, by the purity of whose sacrifice for the homeland our sky has been illuminated and our Land given life. Our hearts are lifted up and irradiated by the light emanating from the much blessed intifada, from those who have endured and have fought the fight of the camps, of dispersion, of exile, from those who have borne the standard for freedom, our children, our aged, our youth, our prisoners, detainees and wounded, all those whose ties to our sacred soil are confirmed in camp, village and town. We render special tribute to the brave Palestinian Woman, guardian and sustenance and Life, Keeper of our people's perennial flame. To the souls of our sainted martyrs, to the whole of our Palestinian Arab people, to all free and honorable peoples everywhere, we pledge that our struggle shall be continued until the occupation ends, and the foundation of our sovereignty and independence shall be fortified accordingly.

Therefore, we call upon our great people to rally to the banner of Palestine, to cherish and defend it, so that it may forever be the symbol of our freedom and dignity in that homeland, which is the homeland for the free, now and always.

In the name of God, the Compassionate, the Merciful, say:

"O God, Master of the Kingdom,
Thou givest the Kingdom to whom Thou wilt,
and seizest the Kingdom from whom Thou wilt,
Thou exaltest whom Thou wilt, and
Thou abaseth whom Thou wilt,
in Thy hands is the good;
Thou art powerful over everything."

Selected Bibliography

BOOKS

Abboushi, W. F. *The Angry Arabs*. Philadelphia: Westminster Press, 1974.

Abu-Lughod, Ibrahim. *The Thirteenth Session of the Palestine National Council*. Detroit: Association of Arab-American University Graduates, 1977.

———, ed. *The Transformation of Palestine*. Evanston, Ill.: Northwestern University Press, 1971.

———, ed. *Palestinian Rights: Affirmation and Denial*. Wilmette, Ill.: Medina, 1982.

Al-Azm, Sadek Jalal. *Dirasah Nakdiyah Lifikr al-Mukawamah al-Falastiniyah* (A Critical Study of Palestinian Resistance Thought). Beirut: Dar al-Tali'ah, 1973.

Aloush, Naji. *Debates on the Palestinian Revolution*. Beirut: n.p., 1970.

Al-Qasim, Anis. *Al-I'dad al-Thawri li-Marhalat al-Tahrir* (Revolutionary Preparations for the Liberation Stage). Beirut: PLO Research Center, 1967.

Ami, Ben. *Between Hammer and Sickle*. Philadelphia: Jewish Publications Society of America, 1967.

Amos, John W., II. *Palestinian Resistance: Organization of a Nationalist Movement*. New York: Pergamon Press, 1980.

Antonius, George. *The Arab Awakening: The Study of the Arab National Movement*. Philadelphia: Lippincott, 1965.

Arafat, Yasser. *Falastin Tahya* (Palestine Lives). Washington, D.C.: Free Palestine Press, 1974.

Aruri, Naseer. *The Sinai Accord as a Phase of the U.S. Containment Policy*. Detroit: Association of Arab-American University Graduates, 1976.

———, ed. *The Palestinian Resistance to Israeli Occupation*. Wilmette, Ill.: Medina University Press.

———, ed. *Occupation: Israel over Palestine*. Belmont, Mass.: Association of Arab-American University Graduates, 1989.

Becker, Jillian. *The PLO: The Rise and Fall of the Palestine Liberation Organization*. London: Weidenfeld and Nicolson, 1984.

Begin, Menachem. *The Revolt: Story of the Irgun.* New York: Henry Schuman, 1951.
Benvenisti, Meron. *The West Bank Handbook: A Political Lexicon.* Jerusalem: Jerusalem Post Press, 1987.
Bulloch, John. *The Making of a War: The Middle East from 1967 to 1973.* London: Longman Group, 1974.
Chaliand, Gerard. *The Palestinian Resistance.* Middlesex, England: Penguin Books, 1972.
Churba, Joseph. *Fedayeen and the Middle East Crisis.* Maxwell Air Force Base, Ala.: Air University, 1969.
Cobban, Alfred. *National Self-Determination.* London: Oxford University Press, 1945.
Cobban, Helena. *The PLO: People, Power and Politics.* London: Cambridge University Press, 1984.
Cooley, John K. *Green March. Black September: The Story of the Palestinian Arabs.* London: Frank Cass, 1973.
Curtis, Michael, and Mordercai Chertoff, eds. *Israel: Social Structure and Change.* New Brunswick, N.J.: Dutton, 1973.
Dhaher, Ahmad Jamal. *Palestine Liberation Organization.* Morgantown: West Virginia University, 1975. Unpublished Ph.D. Dissertation.
Efrat, Elizha. *Judea and Samaria: Guidelines for Regional and Physical Planning.* Jerusalem: Ministry of Interior, Planning Department, 1970.
El-Rayyes, Riad N., and Dunia Nahas, eds. *Guerrillas for Palestine: A Study of the Palestinian Commando Organizations.* Beirut: An-Nahar Press, 1974.
Epp, Frank H. *The Palestinians: Portrait of a People in Conflict.* Scottdale, Pa.: Herald Press, 1976.
Esco Foundation for Palestine. *Palestine: A Study of Jewish, Arab and British Policies.* New Haven, Conn.: Yale University Press, 1947.
Fabian, Larry L., and Ze'ev Schiff, eds. *Israelis Speak.* New York: Carnegie Endowment for International Peace, 1977.
Forrest, A. C. *The Unholy Land.* Toronto: McClelland and Stewart, 1971.
Fulbright, J. W. *Beyond the Interim Agreement.* New York: Americans for Middle East Understanding, 1975.
Glubb, Sir John Bagot. *A Soldier with the Arabs.* New York: Harper and Row, 1957.
Golan, Galia. *The Soviet Union and the Arab-Israeli War of October, 1973.* Jerusalem: Hebrew University Press, 1974.
Gresh, Alain. *The PLO: The Struggle Within.* London: Zed Press, 1988.
Hadawi, Sami. *The Arab-Israeli Conflict.* Beirut: Institute for Palestine Studies, 1969.
Harkabi, Y. *Palestinians and Israel.* Jerusalem: Israel Universities Press, 1974.
Hart, Alan. *Arafat: Terrorist or Peacemaker?* London: Sidgwick and Jackson, 1985.
Hashem, Aqeel, and Said El-Azm. *Israel fi Uropa al-Gharbiyah* (Israel in Western Europe). Beirut: PLO Research Center, 1967.
Hashshad, Adli. *The Palestinian People and Their Repatriation.* Cairo: n.p., 1964.
Hawathmeh, Nayef. *Al-Thawra Wahaq Takrir al-Masir wal-Dawlah al-Mustaqela* (The Revolution and the Right to Self-Determination and the Independent State). Beirut: DFLP, 1977.

———. *Munazzamat al-Tahrir al-Filastiniyah Bayn al-Karar al-Watani wat-Tanazulat al-Yaminiyah* (The Palestine Liberation Organization Between the National Decision and the Rightist Compromises). Beirut: Democratic Front for the Liberation of Palestine, 1977.
Hertzberg, Arthur, ed. *The Zionist Idea: A Historical Analysis and Reader*. New York: Python Press, 1959.
Herzl, Theodor. *The Complete Diaries of Theodor Herzl*. New York: Theodor Herzl Foundation, 1960.
———. *The Jewish State*. New York: Scopus, 1943.
Hilal, Jamil. *The Palestinians of the West Bank and Gaza Strip: Social and Economic Conditions under Israeli Occupation*. Beirut: PLO Department of Information and National Guidance, 1976.
Hunter, Shireen, ed. *The PLO after Tripoli*. Washington, D.C.: Center for Strategic and International Studies, 1984.
Hussain, Mehmood. *The Palestine Liberation Organization*. Delhi, India: University Publishers, 1975.
Jabara, Abdeen. *Israel's Violation of Human Rights in Arab Territories Occupied in June, 1967*. Detroit: Association of Arab-American University Graduates, 1976.
Jabber, Fuad A., ed. *International Documents on Palestine*. Beirut: Institute for Palestine Studies, 1972.
Jiryis, Sabri. *The Arabs in Israel: 1948–1966*. New York: Monthly Review Press, 1976.
Kadi, Leila. *Arab Summit Conferences and the Palestine Problem*. Beirut: PLO Research Center, 1966.
Kahn, Arthur, and Thomas F. Murray. *The Palestinians: A Political Masquerade*. New York: Americans for a Safe Israel, 1977.
Kerr, Malcolm H. *The Arab Cold War: Gamal Abdel Nasser and His Rivals*. New York: Oxford University Press, 1970.
Khalidi, Rashid. *Under Siege: PLO Decision Making During the 1982 War*. New York: Cambridge University Press, 1986.
Khouri, Fred J. *The Arab-Israeli Dilemma*. Syracuse: Syracuse University Press, 1976.
Khurshid, Ghazi. *Dalil Harakat al-Mukawamah al-Falastiniyah* (A Handbook of the Palestinian Resistance Movement). Beirut: PLO Research Center, 1971.
Landau, Julian J. *Israel and the Arabs*. Jerusalem: Israel Communications, 1971.
Langer, Felicia. *With My Own Eyes*. London: Ithaca Press, 1975.
Laqueur, Walter. *The Struggle for the Middle East: The Soviet Union in the Mediterranean 1958–1968*. London: Routledge and Kegan Paul, 1969.
Lederer, Ivo J., and Wayne S. Vicinich, eds. *The Soviet Union and the Middle East: The Post WW II Era*. Stanford: Hoover Institute Press, 1974.
Lehn, Walter. *The Development of Palestinian Resistance*. Detroit: Association of Arab-American University Graduates, 1974.
Lockman, Zachary, and Joel Beinin. *Intifada: The Palestinian Uprising against Israeli Occupation*. Boston: South End Press, 1989.
Mallison, W. T., Jr. *The Balfour Declaration: An Appraisal in International Law*. North Dartmouth: Association of Arab-American University Graduates, 1971.
Mansbach, Richard W., Yale H. Ferguson, and Donald E. Lampert. *The Web of*

World Politics: Non-State Actors in the Global System. Englewood Cliffs, N.J.: Prentice-Hall, 1976.
McDowall, David. *Palestine and Israel: The Uprising and Beyond*. Berkeley: University of California Press, 1990.
Meir, Golda. *My Life*. New York: Putnam's, 1975.
Manuhim, Moshe. *Jewish Critics of Zionism*. Detroit: Association of Arab-American University Graduates, 1976.
Meo, Leila. *Lebanon: Improbable Nation*. Bloomington: Indiana University Press, 1965.
———, Audrey Shabbas, and Fuad K. Suleiman. *The Arab Boycott of Israel*. Detroit: Association of Arab-American University Graduates, 1976.
Migdal, Joel S., ed. *Palestinian Society and Politics*. Princeton, N.J.: Princeton University Press, 1980.
Moore, John Norton, ed. *The Arab-Israeli Conflict: Documents*. 3 vols. Princeton, N.J.: Princeton University Press, 1974.
Moughrabi, Fouad, and Naseer Aruri, eds. *Lebanon: Crisis and Challenge in the Arab World*. Detroit: Association of Arab-American University Graduates, 1977.
Nassar, Jamal R., and Roger Heacock. *Intifada: Palestine at the Crossroads*. New York: Praeger, 1990.
Norton, Augustus Richard, and Martin H. Greenberg. *The International Relations of the Palestine Liberation Organization*. Carbondale, Ill.: Southern Illinois University Press, 1989.
O'Ballance, Edgar. *The Arab-Israeli War, 1948*. New York: Praeger, 1957.
———. *Arab Guerrilla Power 1967–1972*. London: Faber and Faber, 1973.
Odeh, Odeh P. *Masra' Falastin* (The Death of Palestine). Jerusalem: Sandukah Brothers, 1950.
O'Neill, Bard. *Revolutionary Warfare in the Middle East*. Boulder: Paladin Press, 1974.
———. *Armed Struggle in Palestine*. Boulder: Westview Press, 1978.
Peretz, Don, Evan Wilson, and Richard Ward. *A Palestine Entity?* Washington, D.C.: The Middle East Institute, 1970.
———. *The West Bank*. Boulder, Westview Press, 1986.
Petran, Tabitha. *Syria*. New York: Praeger, 1972.
Quandt, William B., Fuad Jabber, and Ann Lesch. *The Politics of Palestinian Nationalism*. Berkeley: University of California Press, 1973.
Rodinson, Maxime. *Israel: A Settler Colonial State?* Trans. David Thorstand. New York: Monad Press, 1973.
Sahliyeh, Emile. *In Search of Leadership: West Bank Politics since 1967*. Washington, D.C.: Brookings Institution, 1988.
Said, Edward. *The Question of Palestine*. London: Routledge and Kegan Paul, 1980.
Sakhnini, Isam. *PLO: The Representative of the Palestinians*. Beirut: Palestine Research Center, 1974.
Sayegh, Fayez A. *A Palestinian View*. Amman: General Union of Palestine Students, 1970.
Sayegh, Rosemary. *Palestinians: From Peasants to Revolutionaries*. London: Zed Press, 1979.

Schiff, Zeev, and Raphael Rothstein. *Fedayeen: Guerrillas against Israel*. New York: David Mckay, 1972.
Schmidt, Dana. *Armageddon in the Middle East*. New York: John Day Co., 1974.
Shafiq, Munir. *Al-Thawra Bayn al-Naqd wal-Tahtim* (The Revolution between Criticism and Destruction). Beirut: Dar al-Tali'ah, 1973.
Sharabi, Hisham. *Palestine Guerrillas: Their Credibility and Effectiveness*. Washington, D.C.: Georgetown University Press, 1970.
———. *Palestine and Israel: The Lethal Dilemma*. New York: Pegasus, 1969.
Shukairy, Ahmad al-. *From Summit to Defeat*. Beirut: PLO Research Center, 1971.
Smith, Charles D. *Palestine and the Arab-Israeli Conflict*. New York: St. Martin's Press, 1988.
Smolansky, Oleg M. *The Soviet Union and the Arab East under Khrushchev*. Lewisbourg, Pa.: Bucknell University Press, 1974.
Snetsinger, John. *Truman, the Jewish Vote and the Creation of Israel*. Stanford, Ca.: Hoover Institute Press, 1974.
Speiser, E. A. *The United States and the Near East*. Cambridge, Ma.: Harvard University Press, 1947.
Stein, Leonard. *Weizmann and England*. London: W. H. Allen, 1964.
———. *The Balfour Declaration*. New York: Simon and Schuster, 1961.
Truman, Harry S. *Memoirs: Trial and Hope*. Garden City, N.Y.: Doubleday, 1956.
Van Arkadi, Brian. *Benefits and Burdens: A Report on the West Bank and Gaza Strip Economies since 1967*. New York: Carnegie Endowment for International Peace, 1977.
Weigert, Gideon. *Arabs and Israelis: Life Together*. Jerusalem: Jerusalem Post Press, 1973.
Weizmann, Chaim. *Trial and Error: The Autobiography of Chaim Weizmann*. New York: Harper, 1949.
———. *The Jewish People and Palestine*. Jerusalem: Palestine Publishing, 1936.
Yaniv, A. *P.L.O.: A Profile*. Jerusalem: Israel Universities Study Group for Middle Eastern Affairs, 1974.
Yodfat, A. Y., and Y. Arnon-Ohanna. *PLO: Strategy and Tactics*. London: Croom Helm, 1981.
Zogby, James J., ed. *Perspectives on Palestinian Arabs and Israeli Jews*. Wilmette, Ill.: Medina Press, 1977.
———. *Zionism and the Problem of Palestinian Human Rights*. Detroit: Association of Arab-American University Graduates, 1976.
Zurayq, Qustantin. *The Meaning of the Disaster*. Beirut: Khayyat Press, 1956.

ARTICLES

Abed, George T. "The Economic Viability of a Palestinian State." *Journal of Palestine Studies* 19, no. 2 (Winter 1990): 3–28.
Abu-Lughod, Ibrahim. "Flexible Militancy: Report on the Sixteenth National Council." *Journal of Palestine Studies* 12, no. 4 (Summer 1983): 25–40.
Adams, Michael. "Israel's Treatment of the Arabs in the Occupied Territories." *Journal of Palestine Studies* 6, 2 (Winter 1977): 19–40.
Aruri, Naseer. "Ittifakiyat Sina Kashakl min Ashkal Siyasat al-Ihtiwa' al-Amer-

ikiyah" (The Sinai Accord as a Form of the American Policy of Containment). *Shu'un Filastiniyah* 56 (April 1976): 75–89.

Avineri, Shlomo. "Beyond Camp David." *Foreign Policy* 46 (Spring 1982): 19–37.

Bader, Hamdan. "Ara' Harkabi wa-Mawkefuh min-al-Sha'ab al-Falastini wa-Kadiyatuh" (Harkabi's Views and His Stand on the Palestinian People and Their Problem). *Shu'un Filastiniyah* 48 (August 1975): 75–89.

Cobban, Helena. "The PLO in the Mid-1980s." *International Journal* 38, no. 4 (1983): 635–651.

Cooley, John K. "China and the Palestinians." *Journal of Palestine Studies* 1 (Winter 1972): 15–26.

———. "Iran, the Palestinians and the Gulf." *Foreign Affairs* 57, no. 3 (Summer 1979): 1017–1034.

Dor, Lea Ben. "Talking to the PLO." *Jerusalem Post*, 19 November 1976.

Eckstein, Harry. "On the Etiology of Internal Wars." *History and Theory* 4 (Spring 1965): 130–145.

Fallaci, Oriana. "A Leader of the Fedayeen: We Want War Like the Vietnam War." *Life* 48, no. 12 (22 June 1970): 18–20.

Goell, Josef. "A Different Breed." *Jerusalem Post*, 7 May 1976.

Galtung, Johan. "Conflict Theory and the Palestine Problem." *Journal of Palestine Studies* 2 (Autumn 1972): 32–49.

Hameed, Rashid. "Munazzamat al-Tahrir al-Filastiniyah fi 'Ashar Sanawat" (The Palestine Liberation Organization in Ten Years). *Shu'un Filastiniyah* 41/42 (January/February, 1975): 518–31.

———. "What Is the PLO?" *Journal of Palestine Studies* 4, no. 4 (Summer 1975): 103–17.

Hammami, Sa'id. "Al-Mu'tamarat al-Watiniyah al-Filastiniyah wal-Wihda al-Wataniyah" (Palestine National Council Meetings and National Unity). *Shu'un Filastiniyah* 18 (February 1973): 79–95.

Hamouri, Assad. "Al-Hilal al-Ahmar al-Filastini: Nathrah 'Ala Nashatateh" (The Palestine Red Crescent Society: A Look at Its Activities). *Shu'un Filastiniyah* 41/42 (January/February 1975): 539–545.

Harris, Lillian Craig. "China's Relations with the PLO." *Journal of Palestine Studies* 7, no. 1 (Autumn 1977): 123–154.

Jiryis, Sabri. "Recent Knesset Legislation and the Arabs in Israel." *Journal of Palestine Studies* 1, no. 1 (Autumn 1971): 38–57.

Khaled, Leila. "Hakatha Khataft Ta'erat al-Boeing" (This Is How I Hijacked the Boeing). *Shun'un Filastiniyah* 13 (September 1972): 2–19.

Khalidi, Rashid. "The Uprising and the Palestine Question." *World Policy Journal* 5, no. 3 (Summer 1988): 497–518.

———. "The 19th PNC Resolutions and American Policy." *Journal of Palestine Studies* 19, no. 2 (Winter 1990): 29–42.

Khalidi, Walid. "Thinking the Unthinkable: A Sovereign Palestinian State." *Foreign Affairs* 56, no. 3 (Summer 1978): 695–713.

Khalili, Ghazi. "Durus al-Intifadah" (Lessons of the Uprising). *Shu'un Filastiniyah* 57 (May 1976): 15–36.

Leibowitz, Yehoshiyahu. "Rights, Justice and Reality." *Ha'aretz*, 5 August 1977.

Lesch, Ann Mosely. "Israeli Settlements in the Occupied Territories, 1967–1977." *Journal of Palestine Studies* 7, no. 1 (Autumn 1977): 26–47.

Maksoud, Clovis. "Al-Abaad al-Amrikiyah al-Israeliyah Limashro' al-Malek Hussein Wa-Kayfiyat Ihbatoh" (Long-Term American-Israeli Objections to King Hussein's Plan and the Means to Its Defeat). *Shu'un Filastiniyah* 9 (May 1972): 3–22.

Meo, Leila. "Al-Filastiniyun Fil-Umam al-Mutahida" (Palestinians at the United Nations). *Al-Iktissad al-Arabi* (Arab Economics) 10 (April 1977): 29–33.

Mertz, Robert Anton. "Why George Habash Turned Marxist." *Mid East* 10 (August 1970): 28–37.

Miller, Aaron David. "The PLO: What Next?" *Washington Quarterly* 6, no. 1 (Winter 1983): 116–125.

Monroe, Elizabeth. "The West Bank: Palestinian or Israeli?" *Middle East Journal* 31, no. 4 (Autumn 1977): 403–22.

Muslih, M. Y. "Moderates and Rejectionists Within the PLO." *Middle East Journal* 30, no. 2 (Spring 1976), 127–140.

Nabulsi, Taiseer. "Intikhabat al-Difa al-Gharbiyah" (West Bank Elections). *Shu'un Filastiniyah* 11 (July 1972): 29–42.

Namel, Hussein Abu el-. "Uropa al-Gharbiyah wal-Arab wa-Israel" (Western Europe, the Arabs and Israel). *Shu'un Filastiniyah* 48 (August 1975): 131–167.

———. "Wathikat Koenig wal-Ma'azak al-Sahyuni" (The Koenig Document and the Zionist Problem). *Shu'un Filastiniyah* 61 (December 1976): 189–204.

Nashef, Taiseer. "Al-Nukhbah al-Siyasiyah fil-Mujtama' al-Arabi fi Filastin" (The Political Elites of the Arab Society in Palestine). *Shu'un Filastiniyah* 48 (August 1975): 131–167.

Omar, Mahjoub. "Sira' min ajl al-Wihda" (Struggle for Unity). *Shu'un Filastiniyah* 56 (April 1976): 18–30.

Perez, Shimon. "A Strategy of Peace in the Middle East." *Foreign Affairs* 58, no. 4 (Spring 1980): 887–901.

Perry, Glenn. "Security Council Resolution 242: The Withdrawal Clause." *The Middle East Journal* 31, no. 4 (Autumn 1977): 428–448.

Quandt, William B. "The Middle East Crisis." *Foreign Affairs* 58, nos. 3/5 (1979/1980): 540–563.

Rouleau, Eric. "The Future of the PLO." *Foreign Affairs* 62 no. 1 (Fall 1983): 138–156.

Saliba, Samir N. "Conflict Resolution: The Kissinger Approach to the Middle East Crisis." Paper presented at the annual meeting of the Southern Political Science Association, New Orleans, La. 7–9 November 1974.

Saunders, Harold. "An Israeli-Palestinian Peace." *Foreign Affairs* 61, no. 1 (Fall 1982): 100–121.

Sayegh, Anis. "Markaz al-Abhath: 'Ashar Sanawat min al-Tajriba" (The Research Center: Ten Years of Trial). *Shu'un Filastiniyah* 41/42 (January/February 1975): 176–198.

Seale, Patrick. "PLO Strategies: Algiers and After." *World Today* 39, no. 4 (April 1983): 137–143.

Segal, Jerome M. "Does the State of Palestine Exist?" *Journal of Palestine Studies* 19, no. 1 (Autumn 1989): 14–31.

Sharabi, Hisham. "Tahrir Filastin wal-Taharur al-Watani" (Palestinian Liberation and National Liberation). *Shu'un Filastiniyah* 3 (July 1971): 113–117.

———. "Development of PLO." *New Outlook* (November/December 1980): 16–19.
Sharif, Regina. "Latin America And The Arab-Israeli Conflict." *Journal of Palestine Studies* 7, no. 1 (Autumn 1977): 98–122.
Sharif, Walid. "Soviet Marxism and Zionism." *Journal of Palestine Studies* 6, no. 3 (Spring 1977): 77–97.
Tessler, Mark. "The Intifada and Political Discourse in Israel." *Journal of Palestine Studies* 19, no. 2 (Winter 1990): 43–61.
Yaari, Arieh. "The Lebanese War and the Diaspora." *New Outlook* 25, no. 7 (October 1982): 39–40, 49.
Zayyad, Tawfig. "The Fate of the Arabs in Israel." *Journal of Palestine Studies* 6, no. 1 (Autumn 1976): 92–103.

Index

Absentee Property Law, 181
Abu Iyad, 86, 133
Aflaq, Micel, 94
Afro-Asian People's Solidarity Organization, 41, 167, 169
Algeria, 83, 144, 145, 158, 213–214
Ali, Mehemed, 2–3
Amal, 138
Ansar Organization, 62
anti-Semitism, 7, 156, 157
apartheid, 184
Arab Higher Committee, 12, 13
Arab-Israeli wars: Arab-Israeli relations and, 63, 119–120; European-Arab relations and, 164; Fateh and, 81; National Council and, 59; 1948, 16; 1967, 53, 59, 81, 128, 139, 208; 1973, 63, 119; PLO infighting and, 53; popular mobilization units, 73–74; Soviet Union and, 159; Syria and, 139
Arab League, 18, 40–44, 122, 137
Arab Liberation Front (ALF), 64, 96, 144
Arab nationalism: Camp David Accords and, 122–123; Egyptian nationalism vs., 122; historical background, 1–4; in Palestine, 4–6, 9, 11; Palestinian refugees and, 18; support for PLO and, 32–33. *See also* Palestinian(s), as nationality group
Arab Nationalist Movement (ANM), 86–91, 93
Arab-Palestine Organization, 96, 97
Arab states, 115, 123–145; anti-Egyptian front, 127; establishment of PLO and, 19–20, 51, 208; financial assistance from, 119, 144; Israeli relations with, 63, 116–119; Palestinian media and, 69, 124, 125; Palestinian nationalism and, 21–22, 53, 104, 116; Palestinian state proposals and, 201–203; Palestinian unity and, 109; partition of Palestine and, 14; PLO failures and, 209; PLO viability and, 212; as reactionary, 87, 88; Soviet arms and, 158. *See also specific countries*
Arafat, Yasser, 21, 55, 61, 85–86; on Arab-Israeli negotiations, 200–201; China and, 165; Egypt and, 128; Jordan and, 130, 131, 132, 133; Palestinian state and, 67, 199, 200; Soviet Union and, 160; Syria and, 65, 66, 94, 95, 142; U.N. General As-

sembly and, 28, 42; U.S. contacts, 154; West Bank demonstrations and, 38
Argentina, 171
armed struggle: draft for, 58–59; guerrilla group philosophies of, 82–84, 88, 98; mass mobilization and, 56, 90; in National Covenant, 79; PLO policy of, 55; revolutionary violence, 98–103; strategic problems of, 103–106; urban warfare, 104–105. *See also* guerrilla groups
Assad, Hafez el-, 118

Balfour Declaration, 8, 217
Basel program, 7
Ba'th party, 19, 33, 94–96, 139
Battalions of Victory (*Kata'ib il Nasr*), 129
Begin, Menachem, 15–16, 43, 44, 185
Begin Plan, 190–191
Bitar, Salaheddin al-, 94
Black Moslems, 174
Black September, 96, 97–98
Bonaparte, Napoleon, 2
boycotts, 12
Brazil, 171
Brezhnev peace plan, 65
Britain: invasion of Egypt, 158–159; mandate in Palestine, 9–13, 27; pro-Palestinian groups, 175; Zionist movement and, 8, 10
bureaucratization, of PLO, 65
Bush administration, 156, 214

Camp David Accords, 64–65, 121–123, 142, 143
Carter administration, 27, 120–121, 154
Central America, 172
Central Committee of PLO, 56–57, 61–62
Central Council, 63, 67
Chatilla refugee camp, 138
Chile, 172
China, People's Republic of, 165–168
class, 87–88, 91–94
collective punishment, 187–188

colonialism: violence and, 100, 102; and world support for PLO, 151; Zionism as, 151, 180
Communist parties, 33, 67, 97, 173, 175, 193
Conference of Non-Aligned Countries, 168–169
constitution of PLO, 49–50
court system, of PLO, 61
Cuba, 171–172
curfews, 188
Czechoslovakia, 31

Dablan, Tahir, 129
Daoud, Mohammad, 130
Dayan, Moshe, 187
Declaration of Independence, 43, 67, 134, 195; text of, 223–226
Defense Regulations, 186
De Gaulle, Charles, 162, 163
Deir Yassin massacre, 15
democracy, in PLO, 74–76
Democratic Front for the Liberation of Palestine (DFLP), 91–93, 126
demonstrations, in Occupied Territories, 38–40
deportation, 187
discrimination, against Israeli Arabs, 181–183

Eastern Europe, 31
East Germany, 31, 41
economy, of Occupied Territories, 189–191
education, of Palestinians, 68–69, 70, 182–183
Egypt, 117–118; Arab front against, 127; Arab reconciliation with, 66; Arafat and, 128; Camp David Accords, 64–65, 121–123, 142, 143; inter-Arab rivalries, 19; Jordanian-PLO relations and, 129–130; nationalism in, 122; Palestinian population of, 121–122; Palestinian support of revolution in, 18; Palestinian workers in, 30; PLO relations with, 123–128; Saudi Arabia and, 143; Soviet Union and, 158,

160; Suez intervention, 158–159; Syria and, 140–41
elections, in West Bank, 36–38
European Economic Community, 162
Executive Committee, 51, 60, 63, 64, 65, 67; dissolved, 53; as Palestinian cabinet, 58
expulsion, from Occupied Territories, 187

Fateh (Palestine National Liberation Movement), 32, 59, 80–86, 211; Battle of Karameh and, 128; Black Panthers and, 174; China and, 166; commando disunity and, 66; ideology of, 209; intifada and, 193; military integration efforts, 55–58; National Covenant and, 60, 79; Saudi Arabia and, 144; Syria and, 142
Fedayeen. *See* guerrilla groups
Fez summit, 65, 85, 90, 94, 143
financial support, for PLO, 36, 75–76, 119, 144. *See also* Palestine National Fund
France, 158, 162, 163, 175
Freij, Elias, 35, 37, 40
Front for National Liberation, 86
Fundamental Law, of PLO, 49–50, 51, 58, 60

Galilee, Judaization of, 184
Gaza, 184–192; demonstrations in, 38; Fateh and, 80; Jewish settlements in, 185; Palestinian newspapers in, 34; Palestinian unity and, 35, 107. *See also* Occupied Territories
General Committee in Support of the Revolution, 59
general secretariat of PLO, 56–57
General Union for Palestine Workers, 30–31, 61
General Union of Palestinian Women, 59, 60, 61
Geneva Convention, 186, 187
Gharbiyyeh, Bahjat Abu, 98
Ghosheh, Samir, 98
Golan, 139, 184n., 185

government, PLO as, 43, 58, 208
guerrilla groups, 59, 79–111, 207–209; achievements of, 195–197; and Algerian insurrection compared, 213–214; Arab state loyalties, 104; armed struggle philosophies, 98; in British-administered Palestine, 11, 12; Central Committee for, 61; declining activity of, 197–198; dominance of PLO, 55, 59–60, 75, 208; draft for, 58–59; factionalism, 66, 105–106, 208–211; Higher Military Council, 63; integration problems, 55–58; intifada and, 106, 193; in Iraq, 144; Israeli countermeasures, 212; Jordan and, 128–134; Lebanon and, 134–138; Libya and, 145; national unity and, 106–111; 1967 Arab defeat and, 53–54; non-Palestinian groups and, 173–175; in Occupied Territories, 97; PLO opposition to, 53; PLO organization of, 68; PLO strategy, 79–80; political ideology, 79–80, 84–85, 87–88, 91–95, 209; sanctuaries for, 104, 211; support for PLO, 32; in Syria, 139; and Vietnam War compared, 213–214. *See also* Fateh; *other specific groups*
Guevara, Che, 82

Habash, George, 87, 89, 90–91, 150
Haddad, Wadi, 89–90, 175
Hamas, 106
Hammuda, Yahya, 61, 153
Hassan, Khaled, 86
Hawatmeh, Nayef, 91, 92, 93, 200
Heroes of the Return, 59, 93
Herzl, Theodor, 6, 7, 8, 102
Higher Military Council, 63
hijacking, 63, 88–89, 90, 130
Hittin division, 68
Hogarth message, 4
hospitals, 70–71
human rights, 150, 186–189
Hussaini, Hajj Amin al-, 12
Hussein, King of Jordan, 19, 42–43, 66, 128, 129, 130, 132, 145, 201
Hussein Ibn Ali, Sharif of Mecca, 3–4

Independence (*Istiqlal*) Party, 11–12
Information Department of PLO, 68–69
international relations, 40–44, 68, 209–210. *See also* Arab States; *specific countries*
intifada, 39–40, 99, 192–194, 210; commando groups and, 106, 193; Egypt and, 128; Jordan and, 134; mass mobilization and, 104; National Council and, 67; national unity and, 111; punitive measures, 187–188
Iran, 154
Iraq, 19, 30, 96, 119, 142, 144–145
Islam, and Arab nationalism, 1
Islamic countries, recognition of PLO, 41
Islamic Jihad, 193
Islamic Liberation Movement–Palestine, 106
Israel: Arab state accommodation with, 117–119; China and, 167; counter-guerrilla measures, 212; de facto peace with, 116; diaspora Palestinians and, 195; effects of armed resistance on, 195–198; establishment of, 15–16, 170; intifada and, 194; invasion of Lebanon, 65, 86, 123, 127–128, 134–138, 211, 212; Jewish support for PLO, 66, 67; Jordan-based commandos and, 129; Latin America and, 170; Palestinian perception of, 102; Palestinians of, 179–184; Palestinian state proposals and, 201, 202; Sadat and, 120–121, 124, 125–126; Soviet Union and, 159–160; support for PLO in, 34–35, 199–200; U.S. and, 120, 125, 151–152; Western Europe and, 162. *See also* Arab-Israeli wars
Israeli Nationality Law, 181
Italy, 175

Jackson, Jesse, 174
Jadid, Salad, 139
Japan, 172–173
Japanese Red Army, 175

Jerusalem, 14, 109, 185
Jewish Agency, 11, 43, 180
Jewish immigration, 181, 185–186, 196
Jibril, Ahmad, 93
Jiryis, Sabri, 179–180
Jordan, 19–20, 128–134; Camp David Accords and, 122; income from, 36; intifada and, 193; Israeli retaliations against, 129; Israeli trade with, 190; newspaper support for PLO, 34; normalization of PLO relations, 65; Palestinian guerrillas and, 56, 61–62, 124, 209; as Palestinian representative, 42–43; Palestinian state and, 85; Palestinian workers in, 30; Soviet Union and, 160–161; Syrian intervention in, 130, 140; U.S. and, 153; West Bank and, 109
Jordanian Communist Party, 33
Jordan River, Israeli diversion of, 19
Judaization, 57, 109, 184–185
judicial system, of PLO, 61

Karameh, Battle of, 55, 59, 81, 128, 208
Kawasme, Fahd, 38
Khalaf, Karim, 126
Khalaf, Salah, 85–86
Khaled, Leila, 88
Kissinger, Henry, 120, 125, 153
Koenig Report, 183–184
Kuwait, 30, 36, 85, 119, 142, 144–145

land, confiscation of, 181, 183, 190
Land Day strike, 183
Latin America, 169–172
Lebanon, 134–138; civil war, 125–126, 136–137; early Arab nationalism in, 3; Israeli aggression in, 65, 86, 123, 127–128, 134–138, 211, 212; Palestinian guerrilla groups in, 209; Palestinian workers in, 30; Soviet Union and, 161; Syrian intervention in, 95, 137, 141–142, 153, 161, 210–211; U.S. and, 153
Libya, 127, 144, 145

Majali, Habis al-, 130
Mao Zedong, 79, 81, 87, 165
Maronite Phalange Party, 135
martial law, in Occupied Territories, 182, 186
Marxism, 84, 87, 91, 93–94, 100, 173
Masri, Hikmat al-, 126
mass mobilization, 59; armed struggle and, 56, 82, 90; intifada and, 104; PLO department for, 69, 73–74
Matzpen, 183
Mazen, Abu, 199
media, Palestinian, 34, 68–69, 71; Arab suppression of, 124, 125, 127
Meir, Golda, 15, 54, 195
Mexico, 171
Milhem, Muhammad, 126–127
Military Department of PLO, 68. See also guerrilla groups
modernization, Palestinian violence and, 100
Moustafa, Abu Ali, 91
Movement of Revolutionary Young Palestinians, 59
Musa, Sa'id, 86

Naji, Talal, 94
Nasser, Gamal Abdel, 18, 19, 20, 91, 117, 122, 124, 159, 167
National Council. See Palestine National Council
National Covenant, 20–21, 49, 55, 58, 79–80, 198; Fateh in, 60, 79; text of, 219–222
National Front for the Liberation of Palestine, 64, 86
nationalism, violence and, 100, 102. See also Arab nationalism
nationality group, Palestinians as, 26–27
National Salvation Front, 94, 95
National Unity Committee, 62
Netherlands, 175
newspapers, 34, 68–69
Nicaragua, 172
Numeiry, Ja'afar, 131

Occupied Territories, 184–192; demonstrations in, 38–40; economic conditions, 189–191; Egypt-Israel accommodation and, 126–127; Geneva Convention and, 186, 187; human rights in, 186–189; intifada, 39–40, 99, 192–194, 210; Israeli punitive measures, 187–188; Judaization, 57, 109, 185–186; military rule of, 182; National Council representation, 62; Palestinian newspapers in, 34; Palestinian self-determination and, 29–30; PLO department for, 69–70; resistance groups in, 97; self-rule, 190–191; Soviet Union and, 159; support for PLO in, 35–40, 191; U.S. policy regarding, 155–156; Western Europe and, 163. See also Gaza; Palestinian state; West Bank
oil resources, 119, 150, 152, 167, 172
Omar, Abu, 115
Organization of African Unity (OAU), 41, 169
Organization of American States (OAS), 170
Ottoman Empire, 2–5

Palestine: Arab nationalism in, 9, 11; British mandate, 9–13, 27; early Arab nationalism in, 4–6; early Jewish settlements, 185; partition plan, 14–15; self-rule for, 11; United Nations and, 13–15. See also Occupied Territories
Palestine Armed Struggle Command (PASC), 56
Palestine Communist Party, 97
Palestine Liberation Army (PLA), 51, 59, 61, 68, 141
Palestine Liberation Front, 59, 86, 93
Palestine Liberation Movement, 59
Palestine Liberation Organization (PLO): Arab states and, 115–146; bureaucratization of, 65; democracy in, 74–76; establishment of, 19–21, 49, 58, 208; as government, 43, 58, 208; guerrilla control of, 55, 59–60, 75, 208; internal disunity, 53–58; international relations, 40–44, 107–

108, 149–175, 209–210; Israeli support for, 199–200; moderates in, 119; national unity and, 106–111; Occupied Territories support, 191; organizational structure, 49–76; Palestinian support for, 30–40; popular participation in, 73–74; problems of strategy, 103–106; self-determination of, 30; United Nations recognition, 149–150; viability of, 210–213
Palestine National Council (PNC), 31, 50–51, 58–67; first session of, 20–21, 49–50, 58; intifada and, 67; Occupied Territories representation, 62; as Palestinian parliament, 58
Palestine National Fund, 20, 36, 50, 62, 69
Palestine National Liberation Movement. *See* Fateh
Palestine News Agency, 69
Palestine Solidarity Committee, 174
Palestinian(s): classes of, 87–88; diaspora and, 194–203 (*see also* Palestinian refugees); expulsions, 109; in Israel, 179–184; as nationality group, 26–27; right to self-determination, 25–30; support for PLO, 30–40
Palestinian Communist Party, 33, 67
Palestinian Diary, 71
Palestinian Popular Liberation Front, 59
Palestinian refugees, 194–203; establishment of Israel and, 16–17; financial support from, 75–76; support for PLO, 35–40. *See also* refugee camps
Palestinian Revolutionaries Front, 59
Palestinian Salvation Front, 32
Palestinian state: Arab states and, 20, 118; Arafat and, 67, 199, 200; Galilee and, 184; Jordan and, 85, 132; Palestinian acceptance of, 63–64; recent PLO proposals, 198–200; resistance group programs, 92
Pasha, Nahhas, 122
Peel Commission, 12

Peru, 172
petit bourgeoisie, 88, 91–92
Political Department of PLO, 68
political ideology: of guerrilla groups, 79–80, 84–85, 87–88, 91–95, 209; of Israeli Arabs, 183; non-Palestinian revolutionary groups, 167, 173–175; Soviet foreign policy and, 157
political parties: Ba'th party, 19, 94–96, 139; in British-administered Palestine, 11–12; support for PLO, 32–33
Popular Democratic Front for the Liberation of Palestine (PDFLP), 61, 91–93, 132
Popular Front for the Liberation of Palestine (PFLP), 56, 59, 64, 84, 86–91, 93–94, 119, 132, 201, 212
Popular Liberation Forces, 68
Popular Mobilization, Department of, of PLO, 69, 73
Popular Mobilization Law, 59, 60, 73
Popular Palestinian Resistance Front (PPRF), 96
Popular Struggle Front (PSF), 96, 98
publications, of PLO, 68–69, 71
public relations, PLO information Department and, 68–69

Qaddafi, Muammar, 145
Qadisiyah division, 68
Qassam, Izz el-Din el-, 12, 54

Rabat Arab Summit, 107
racial attitudes, of Israelis, 183, 184
radio broadcast operations, 68–69, 124, 125, 127
Rakah, 183, 199
Reagan administration, 65, 85, 154–156, 214
Red Crescent Society, 70–71
refugee(s). *See* Palestinian refugees
refugee camps, 128–129, 136, 138
Research Center of PLO, 71
resistance. *See* guerrilla groups
revolutionary movements, non-Palestinian, 173–175
Rogers Plan, 124, 129–130

Sabra refugee camp, 138
Sadat, Anwar el-, 118, 120–121, 124, 125–127
Said, Nouri, 122
Sa'iqah (Vanguards of the Popular Liberation War), 59, 68, 94–96, 104, 141
Saiqa Brigade, 129
Saleh, Nimer, 86
Samed Institute, 72–73
Saudi Arabia, 119, 142–144
secularization, Palestinian violence and, 102
self-determination, 25–30, 64, 103, 155, 168
self-rule, in Occupied Territories, 190–191
settlement policies, in Occupied Territories, 185–186
Shawa, Rashad, 40
Shukairy, Ahmad al-, 19, 20, 49, 53, 59, 165, 208
Sinai Disengagement Agreement, 124, 140, 141, 154, 161, 210
Social Affairs Institute, 71–72
socialism, 90
South Africa, 102, 184
Soviet Union, 143, 152, 156–162, 202
Stalin, Josef, 158
strikes, 12, 38, 39, 183
students, Palestinian, 31, 61
Suez intervention, 158–159
Sweden, 30
Sykes-Picot Agreement, 4
Syria, 65, 67, 104, 138–142; Arafat vs., 65, 66; and inter-Arab rivalries, 19; intervention in Jordan, 130, 140; intervention in Lebanon, 95, 137, 141–142, 153, 161, 210–211; Israel and, 118; Mehemed Ali and, 2–3; Palestinian commandos and, 54, 94; Palestinian unity and, 109; Palestinian workers in, 30; partition of, 5; Soviet Union and, 161; U.S. and, 153
Syrian Arab Socialist Ba'th Party, 94–96

Tarazi, Zuhdi, 154
terrorism, 63, 88–89, 90, 97–98, 130, 150, 175. See also guerrilla groups
third world, 168–172
torture, 188
tourism, 190, 196
Truman, Harry S., 14

Unified Command, 56
Unified National Leadership of the Uprising (UNLU), 40, 193
unions, 30–31, 60, 61, 62, 74, 189
United Arab Kingdom, 132
United Nations: General Assembly resolutions, 155, 163, 184, 187; Latin American states in, 170; Palestinian refugees and, 17, 18; Palestinian self-determination and, 25–26, 27–28, 64; PLO recognition by, 41–42, 107–108, 149–150; post-British Palestine, 13–15; Security Council Resolution 242, 107, 124, 152, 155, 163–165, 200–202; Security Council Resolution 338, 63
United States: European influence on, 164; Israel and, 125, 151–152; Middle East policy, 120–121; Palestinian state proposals and, 202; partition of Palestine and, 14; PLO and, 67, 152–156; PLO-Egyptian relations and, 124–125; pro-Palestinian groups, 174–175
urban warfare, 104–105

Vanguards of Sacrifice Movement, 59
Vanguards of the Popular Liberation War. See Sa'iqah
Vengeance Youth, 59, 86. See also National Front for the Liberation of Palestine
Vietnam War, 213–214
violence, revolutionary causes of, 98–103
Voice of Palestine, 124, 125

WAFA (Palestine News Agency), 69
wages, in Occupied Territories, 189
wars. See Arab-Israeli wars

water resources, 19, 189–190
Wazir, Khalil, 85–86
Weitze, Joseph, 180
Weizmann, Chaim, 8, 10, 14, 44
West Bank, 184–192; demonstrations in, 38; economic conditions, 189–191; Jewish settlements in, 185–186; Jordan and, 19–20, 109, 132, 134; land confiscation, 190; municipal elections, 36–38; Palestinian newspapers in, 34; Palestinian unity and, 107; self-rule in, 190–191. *See also* Occupied Territories
Western Europe, 162–165, 174–175
West Germany, 30, 31, 162, 175

White Paper of 1939, 13, 27
women, PLO and, 31, 59, 60, 61
Working Committee for the Liberation of Palestine, 96, 97

Yabu, Yassir Abed, 93
Yamani, Ahmad, 91
Yemen, 19, 86
Young Turks, 3

Zionism, 6–9, 102; British and, 10–11; as racism, 184; settler-colonialism and, 151, 180; Soviets and, 157–158, 159; U.S. and, 14

ABOUT THE AUTHOR

JAMAL R. NASSAR is Professor of Political Science at Illinois State University, Normal. He has published extensively on the Palestinian-Israeli conflict and is coeditor of *Intifada: Palestine at the Crossroads* (Praeger, 1990). He has also taught political science at Bir Zeit University on the Israeli-occupied West Bank. Professor Nassar received his Ph.D. in political science from the University of Cincinnati, his M.A. from the University of South Florida, and his B.A. from Jacksonville University.

Augsburg College
George Sverdrup Library
Minneapolis, MN 55454